Rethinking Cari Differenc

CW00548867

CONTENTS

Feminist Review is published three times a year. It is edited by a Collective which is supported by a group of Corresponding Editors.

The Collective: Amal Treacher, Avtar Brah, Annie E. Coombes, Dot Griffiths, Helen Crowley, Lucy Bland, Lynne Thomas, Merl Storr, Pam Alldred, Sharon Morris, Vicki Bertram.

Guest Editor this issue: Patricia Mohammed
Editing assistance: Hilary Nicholson

Corresponding Editors: Ailbhe Smyth, Ann Curthoys, Hala Shukrallah, Kum-Kum Bhavnani, Jacqui Alexander, Lidia Curti, Meera Kosambi, Patricia Mohammed, Sue O'Sullivan, Zarina Maharaj.

Correspondence and advertising
Contributions, books for review and editorial correspondence should be sent to: Feminist Review, 52 Featherstone Street, London EC1Y 8RT.
For advertising please write to the publishers:
Journals Advertising, Routledge, 11 New Fetter Lane, London EC4P 4EE, UK.

Subscriptions
Please contact Routledge Subscriptions Department, Cheriton House, North Way, Andover, Hants SP10 5BE, UK. Tel: 44 (0)1264 343062; Fax 44 (0)1264 343005; for sample copy requests, e-mail sample.journals@routledge.co.uk; for subscription and general information, e-mail info.journals@routledge.co.uk A full listing of Routledge books and journals is available by accessing www.routledge.com

Notes for Contributors
Authors should submit four copies of their work to: *Feminist Review*, 52 Featherstone Street, London EC1Y 8RT. We assume that you will keep a copy of your work. Submission of work to *Feminist Review* will be taken to imply that it is original, unpublished work, which is not under consideration for publication elsewhere. All work is subject to a system of anonymous peer review. All work is refereed by at least two external (non-Collective) referees.

Please note that we cannot accept unsolicited book reviews.

Bookshop distribution in the USA
Routledge, 29 West 35th Street, New York, NY 10001, USA.

Typeset by Type Study, Scarborough
Printed in Great Britain by Bell & Bain Ltd, Glasgow

ISSN 0141-7789

Please send all correspondence to:
Feminist Review
52 Featherstone Street
London EC1Y 8RT

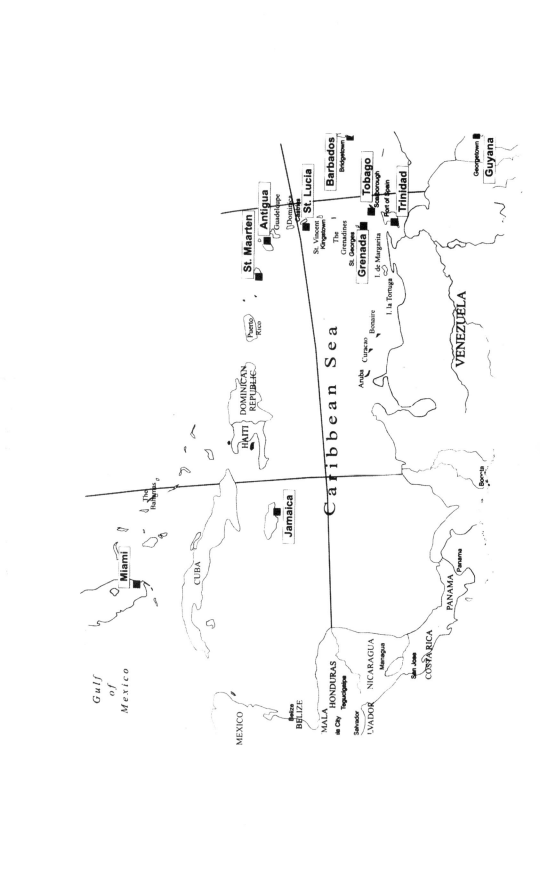

Editorial

Rethinking Caribbean Difference

The task of editing a special issue of *Feminist Review* on the Caribbean is a daunting one for several reasons. It forces a partiality on a region which spans at least four linguistic divisions. In this volume, by virtue of my place of birth and present residence and work (Trinidad and Jamaica respectively), there is a reflected dominance of the English-speaking Caribbean. Putting together a relatively small volume also forces a selectivity of the wealth of material which is being produced in gender and feminism at present in the region. This material has, over the last decade, become far more interdisciplinary, much broader than the largely academic discourse which is presented here. The final selection of essays and information, none the less, attempts to represent a cross section and overview of the wider experience of activism and scholarship in Caribbean feminism.

The idea of the 'Caribbean' is a historically persistent one, as are other geographical and political spaces. We are constantly exploring both differences and similarities within the region, explaining this to ourselves and to others outside of this space. The issue is entitled 'Rethinking Caribbean Difference' because of this and for another reason. Postmodernism, which preoccupies the debates in gender at present, certainly in the North, points us towards dispensing with universalized categories and dealing with the plurality of experiences of race, class, gender and sexuality (Alexander and Mohanty, 1997: xvii) . In other words it situates difference as central to analyses of social phenomenon. What I have attempted to do in this volume is to present the Caribbean as a space in which the shared colonial and the post-colonial experience has created an internal discourse which is specific to the region and to which all the writers in this volume speak. In the choice of papers differences are manifested in the approaches and positions taken by various writers. If the postmodern discourse invites us to accept difference and celebrate it, then these must also emerge. In this sense the volume has a further uniqueness in feminist circles as it includes two male colleagues who have been both prolific in, and supportive of, the

FEMINIST REVIEW NO 59, SUMMER 1998, PP. 1–4

scholarship we are engaged in, thus allowing feminism in the Caribbean to be a dialogue between men and women.

In the first paper in this volume I continue this trend of thought as I attempt to locate a standpoint from which to write indigenous feminist theory for the Caribbean. I argue that Caribbean feminism cannot be viewed as a linear narrative about women's struggles for gender equality, but a movement which has continually intersected with the politics of identity in the region. In the second paper Hilary McD. Beckles, a Barbados born historian in the region who has focused much of his attention on the recovery of women in Barbados slave history, analyses the category 'woman' as it was differentiated under the period of West Indian slavery. Beckles argues that the political fracturing of feminine identity during this time defined the distances in ethnic and class position between women of different groups, thus creating the hurdles to be crossed in the post-slavery rapprochement of the feminist project.

Rhoda Reddock has had a long history in both activism and the study of gender in the Caribbean. One of her major contributions has been recovering women in the nineteenth- and twentieth-century labour struggles in Trinidad, a pioneering body of work in the feminist scholarship of the region. In this paper, Rhoda explores the emergence of women's organizations and feminist consciousness in the twentieth-century Commonwealth Caribbean and, consistent with the first paper in this volume, illustrates the interlocked nature of women's struggles with the economic, political and social issues which affect the population at large.

A preoccupation with difference is also found in Rawwida Baksh-Soodeen's paper. Rawwida is a stalwart of the contemporary feminist movement and for many years worked as the Co-ordinator of the Caribbean Association for Feminist Research and Action. Baksh-Soodeen suggests that there are internal differences in the activism of the region and that there is need for a more integrated movement which reflects the experience of other ethnic groups, including that of Indo-Caribbean women. Sonia Cuales was born on the island of Curacao and has had a long and close association with the women who have been involved in the second wave feminist movement in the wider Caribbean since the late 1970s. Sonia's paper searches for some of the history of women and gender in the Netherland Antilles, and suggests that much of this knowledge still needs to be uncovered by future activists and scholars.

In a paper which explores the difference in one of the Spanish speaking societies in the Caribbean, Alice E. Colón-Warren and Idsa Alegría-Ortega examine the position of women and the challenges to gender relations and the feminist movement in Puerto Rico as a result of the policies of industrialization which were introduced into this society by its new colonizers in the twentieth century, the United States of America. Focusing on the French-speaking Caribbean territory of Haiti, Marie-Jose N'Zengou-Tayo, of Haitian descent, now resident in Jamaica, describes the journey of Haitian women from the nineteenth century to present day Haitian society, deploring the fact that the contribution of women to this society has neither been recognized nor sufficiently documented.

The uncovering of women's history and gender in the English-speaking Caribbean has been one of the key areas of scholarship and, directly or indirectly, crucial in the shaping of a feminist consciousness in the region. Bridget Brereton, a highly respected historian in the region, has been another pioneer in this field, constantly exploring new sources which are available, as well as demonstrating new methods of writing women into history. In this paper Bridget provides a glimpse of different women's lives in the Caribbean through the use of their diaries, autobiographies and letters. Linden Lewis, a Guyanese-born scholar now resident in the United States, retains a close connection with the lived realities in the region. His work on masculinity provides a sounding board of ideas and imagery, necessary for the dialectic of feminist scholarship. In a reading of a novel by Trinidadian author Earl Lovelace, Linden demonstrates the scope of the literary text as an insightful source for uncovering ideas of masculinity.

Eudine Baritteau examines the philosophical contradictions of liberal ideologies which English-speaking Caribbean states have inherited and draws on this experience to generate an analytical model of the political economy of gender systems which may be widely applicable both inside and out of the region. Jessica Byron and Diana Thorburn also examine the links between gender and political economy and society, approaching the subject through the relatively recent integration of feminist thinking in the discipline of International Relations. This is another pioneering approach to the study of gender in the region, challenging the theoretical foundations of this discipline still based on traditional male–female dichotomies, and suggesting a research agenda for ongoing feminist theorizing which integrates the dynamics of the global economy with the decisions taken by local states.

This volume includes reviews of some of the earliest books in contemporary gender scholarship produced in the English-speaking region by various Caribbean scholars, as well as short book notes by Hilary Nicholson on other more recent titles.

Several persons have assisted me during the various stages of putting together this volume. Althea Perkins and Ramona Lisa Mohammed were valuable in the earlier stages of its development. Shakira Maragh, a young

FEMINIST REVIEW NO 59, SUMMER 1998

research assistant attached to the Centre for Gender and Development Studies at Mona campus, Jamaica, where the volume has taken shape, has been warmly generous with her time and crucial in the realization of the finished product. My husband Rex Dixon provided both the artwork for the cover and the constant emotional support. I am most indebted to Hilary Nicholson for her sound editorial assistance and advice. Born in the United Kingdom, Hilary has lived in the Caribbean now for nearly three decades and is remarkable both for her zeal and her many talents. She is a real 'Sistren' in the feminist movement in the Caribbean.

Patricia Mohammed
Centre for Gender and Development Studies
University of the West Indies, Mona

Reference

ALEXANDER, M. Jacqui and MOHANTY, Chandra Talpade (1997) *Feminist Genealogies: Colonial Legacies, Democratic Futures*, New York: Routledge.

Rhoda Reddock

Bridget Brereton

Eudine Barriteau

Sonia Cuales and Patricia Mohammed

Left to right: Hilary Nicholson, June Castello, Althea Perkins, Michelle Rowley, Jessica Byron

Some of the contributors in this issue.

Towards Indigenous Feminist Theorizing in the Caribbean

Patricia Mohammed

FEMINIST REVIEW NO 59, SUMMER 1998, PP. 6–33

Abstract

This attempt to develop an indigenous reading of feminism as both activism and discourse in the Caribbean is informed by my own preoccupation with the limits of contemporary postmodern feminist theorizing in terms of its accessibility, as well as application to understanding the specificity of a region. I, for instance, cannot speak for or in the manner of a white middle-class academic in Britain, or a black North American feminist, as much as we share similarities which go beyond the society, and which are fuelled by our commitment to gender equality. At the same time, our conversations are intersecting as a greater clarity of thought emerges in relation and perhaps in reaction to the other. Ideas of difference and the epistemo-logical standpoint of 'Third World' women have been dealt with admirably by many feminist writers such as Chandra Mohanty, Avtah Brah and Uma Narayan. In this article I draw on the ideas emerging in contemporary western feminist debates pertaining to sexual difference and equality and continue my search for a Caribbean feminist voice which defines feminism and feminist theory in the region, not as a linear narrative but one which has continually intersected with the politics of identity in the region.

Keywords

identity; sexual difference; colonization; migration; Caribbean feminism; *creole*

Locating the Caribbean

In the last decades of the twentieth century, for those who live out of this stepping stone of islands and adjacent territories between the north and south Americas, the Caribbean represents a deep blue and verdant green, sheltered from the icy cold wet winters of the north and far south, rain fed by the prevailing winds across the Atlantic and continually bronzed by the tropical sun. This contemporary image was in the making for over 500 years. It was not these aspects which initially encouraged the Dutch sea-farers, the Spanish explorers, or the French and British planters and officials, to settle and colonize the landmasses. The region represented virgin territory to be used, developed, exploited and governed by the tres-passers. The indigenous Amerindian population had put up no gates or boundaries, no barbed wire fences, wore no armoured breastplates, to protect their underpopulated villages and settlements.

The narratives of misuses and abuses of colonization are tired old ones which will not be retired. The secrets and disguises of the past will be constantly rendered up for public scrutiny by each new generation of Caribbean peoples, descendants of the myriad group of migrants; enslaved, bonded, coerced or encouraged to work and settle in these lands. The historical past will be constantly interpreted by those who have adopted the region as their permanent or temporary home, untangled by those who physically live in the region, and debated by those who have migrated out of the region. Both consciously and unconsciously, the interrogation of the past with the present is the process of creating continuity and tradition. This continuity and tra-dition – of families, buildings, institutions, art, music, song, dance, cuisine, of political systems and political struggles, of language, and of cultural beliefs – all of these are markers of identity and difference. The different manifes-tations of these are the signature of the Caribbean on the world map – the way in which the circumstances of history, natural geography and resources of the region have evolved into something which is viewed by others and by ourselves as Caribbean, despite colonialism, and because of colonization.

To establish identity and difference is not simply to demarcate ownership or territorial rights, it is also an expression of the desire to belong (Moore, 1994: 2). Situating difference establishes the boundaries of belonging. In his Nobel acceptance speech of 1992 the poet Derek Walcott describes the region as 'The Antilles: Fragments of Epic Memory'; he writes (1992):

> Break a vase and the love that reassembles the fragments is stronger than that love which took its symmetry for granted when it was whole . . . it is such a love that re-assembles our African and Asiatic fragments, the cracked heirlooms whose restoration shows its white scars.

The project of defining identity is the most eloquent one now in the post-modern discourse. This preoccupation with ethnic identity did not begin in the academy but in the cultural assertions during colonialism, and during the post-colonial period, in the nationalist and independence struggles in the region. The scars which must be healed are not only those of physical brutality and privation. The deeper gashes are the deprivation of ethnic customs, and loss of ethnic pride and dignity. Undoubtedly, the scars of enslavement of African peoples are deepest. No other group, apart from the indigenous Amerindian population under colonization in the West Indies, suffered so much in terms of inhumanity, both physical as well as in the disruption and eradication of its cultural memory.

Ethnicity is a collective word which in its political appeal to the group, forgets sexual differences within a culture. Recognizing the different ways in which men and women within any cultural group experience enslavement, indentureship or migration is integral to understanding ethnic identity. The psychological scars of emasculation or defeminization caused by such uprooting are not skin deep and have residual effects on gender relations and gender struggles within a society far beyond the periods of disruption. Identity politics take the form not only of definitions against externalities, but are also about the internal and ongoing processes of constructing masculinity and femininity within the society. The dynamics of gender in each society or region operate not through grand revolutionary upheavals but through the ongoing negotiations between men and women both at the individual and collectively organized levels. Masculinity and femininity exist not simply in opposition but, I argue, equally in relation to each other (Mohammed, 1994: 32). In this process of reconstructing gender identities, the rhetoric – either nationalist or cultural – has generally been towards reinforcing an 'ethnic' ideal which predates the disruptions of colonization. Markers, such as dress or hairstyle, are good examples of how these appeals are made to women. In studying the colonized subject, the tendency has been to perceive the problem of reconfiguring gender identities as primarily that of the exploited group. It is, also, a problem which confronts the colonizers. Women whether born in Europe or creole born,[1] were themselves ill at ease with the situation. This is best illustrated by the author Jean Rhys whose novel *Wide Sargasso Sea* (1966) and subsequent writings describe, with more pathos than historical writings can achieve, the insecurity and fears which also underlie the perceived 'privileged' spaces. The construction of masculinity and femininity went on busily under colonization as it continues at present.[2] Within each society, the residual effects of eurocentricism and elitism of the white planter class on the dynamics of race and gender in each society still inform the ongoing construction of masculinities and femininities. Feminism within Caribbean society has therefore been involved in an unrelenting dialogue about what constitutes Caribbean manhood and masculinity and womanhood and femininity, as it has also been affected by the increasing consciousness of and struggles for gender equality which inform the global discourse.

In this paper I select three aspects of difference which, in my view, has led to the specific ways in which feminism in the Caribbean is both articulated in daily struggles and activism as well as debated within the academic discourse. The *first* 'moment'[3] of difference is situated around the question of political struggles in the region and the stances taken by women. Some of these appear to be antithetical to contemporary feminist goals *per se*. My overall argument is that feminism as an expression of sexual equality must itself be historically located, despite the global discourse which feeds its growth. The *second* moment contemplates the linguistic meanings of gender inside the region. I suggest here that the presentation and re-presentation of masculinity and femininity have internalized meanings within a culture, differentiated further still by class or ethnic groupings, but that this is key to the reproduction of gender identities within a society or region. The *third* moment, as it were, is closely linked to the idea of linguistic difference, but examines this in relation to the contemporary western feminist interrogation of 'sexual difference'. Here I am on more sandy ground as I am attempting to place these debates in the language of the English-speaking Caribbean. It seems to me that these issues of sexual difference versus equality also preoccupy our societies, but are not generally approached with the same theoretical stances. The concept of difference as it has been raised and deconstructed in feminist circles has generally focused on sexual difference between man and woman, and differences between women themselves; 'the feminist analysis of gender has undone one version of a presumably basic difference, thought to be rooted in nature, and come up with another, albeit more debatably basic than the previous one' (di Stefano, 1990: 64). If twentieth-century second wave feminism has problematized gender (Flax, 1990: 44), then the continuing goals of feminism, in my view, depend on the further deconstruction of 'difference' beyond the limits to which it has been already applied. I use the term to explore its overtones for understanding gender in the Caribbean.

In each of these sections I use illustrative examples to explain my points, but at the same time must outline here both my biases and assumptions. First, I am more familiar with the history, culture and struggles of the English-speaking Caribbean and therefore my theorization may have more relevance to these territories. Second, I am interested in feminism and the feminist movement as an historically progressive movement engaged in shifting human consciousness towards a greater acceptance of equality of the sexes, as well as a celebration of difference, both sexual and otherwise: not just lip service to equality and celebration of difference, but that which is realized in policies, programmes and in individual human relationships. The feminist movement has largely emphasized women's subordination and the ongoing need for a consciousness of gender equality to be built into the process of constructing gender identity. But female gender identities are not constructed in isolation from other components of identity such as race, class, nation and from masculinity. How identities are being affirmed or even constructed are based on real struggles which people and groups are engaged in and which they communicate to each other in coded messages within a culture, much the same way that lovers communicate with words, signals and body language, the meanings of which are not immediately apparent to the onlooker. This preoccupation with different components of identity and my particular interpretation of feminism, inform both my approach as well as the areas I select for interrogation.

Caribbean feminism and the politics of identity

Why is there this insistent desire to re-assemble the fragments of ethnic and gender identities and to belong to a space? Why has Caribbean society engaged in a continuous process of defining identity? In a contemporary sense, the Caribbean appears more as a political space rather than a geographical entity. 'When did the name Caribbean move from the sea to the imprecise geography of some or all the land masses surrounding it?' (Gaztambide-Geigel, 1996: 1). One Puerto Rican historian traces the legend of the word *Caribe* as rebellious and/or enslaved native, a title assigned by the Spanish. The region was named the West Indies by the Spanish in the sixteenth century. There is a confusion of the name of the region in a Dutch map of West America dating back to 1594. It was the English-speaking Europeans who named the islands the *Caribby* or *Caribbee* Islands 'thus transferring to the sea waters the name once given to the masters of the islands' and the French who underscored the direct heritage when they spoke of Mer des *Caraibes* or Sea of the Caribs. Gaztambide-Geigel, writes:

> Ironically when the Caribs, by then mixed with the Africans, had been reduced to 'reservations' in Martinique and Dominica, or had been exiled by the British to the Mosquito Coast and Honduras, they became immortalized when the sea they had mastered was baptized with their name.
>
> (Gaztambide-Geigel, 1996: 6–7)

Like a child, unsexed, named after the parents it has lost, the region and its peoples continue to examine the past. Edward Braithwaite also interprets the region similarly when he writes 'But we are really involved with two mothers (more as we grow younger)' (Braithwaite, 1985: 6). This process of becoming Caribbean continued past the abolition of slavery into the twentieth century with the addition of different ethnic groups. Each language group continues its association with its colonizer even while it constructs new destinies from within. The nationalist or independence struggles have differed for each society. In August 1791, two years after the French Revolution, the African slaves of the French West Indian colony of San Domingo revolted, a struggle which lasted for twelve years and led, in 1803, to the formation of the negro state of Haiti (James, 1963). Over 200 years later, in 1998, the islands of Martinique and Guadeloupe are still *departements* of France. The once Spanish colony of Puerto Rico exchanged hands and is now administratively linked to the United States of America but Spanish remains its mother tongue. The Spanish-speaking island of Cuba has forged its distinctive struggle for socialism, befriended and heralded in part by the region for its decisive political stance against the imperialism of the United States. By the twentieth century the English-speaking colonies, with the exception of the islands of Montserrat, Bermuda and the British Virgin Islands, are all independent states.

The region is imagined differently by the different groups who have settled into this space. The demographic distribution of races and ethnic groups brought together from east and west varies by territory and has led to different political tensions within each society founded on race or class/colour. In this demographic balance African descended peoples are the dominant group in most of the territories. This demographic dominance has largely posited the region as an African diaspora. Yet the writings of the second half of the twentieth century tell of other dispersions of peoples who feel the need to equally define their belonging within the region. Mary Noel Menezes records that 1985 marked the 150th anniversary of the arrival of the Portuguese in Guyana; *The Still Cry*, by Kumar Mahabir, and *Survivors of Another Crossing*, by Marianne Ramesar, record the histories of the Indians who, in 1995, celebrated 150 years in the island of Trinidad, as they did also in Jamaica. The story of Chinese migration to Trinidad was examined by Trevor Millett in Trinidad, and Sylvia Moodie-Kublalsingh adds the oral history of panyols or espanoles, Trinidadians of mixed Spanish, Amerindian and African descent, to a burgeoning list of fiction and non-fiction writers. All of these are expressions of the re-ordering of experience to continuously redefine identity. In the same breath, these are not primarily expressions of difference, but of different members of the same family. The Caribbean is not just one lost child, but the children of many parents, who have made similar but different passages across the ocean – a sentiment best expressed by the Mighty Stalin, a Trinidadian calypsonian in the song 'The Caribbean Man': 'we take the same trip in the same ship'.

History and experience moves on incessantly. In the twentieth-century development of capitalism, the Caribbean is no longer the site of plantations but the space from which labour can be reappropriated. The *Mer des Caraibes* is not, nor was it ever, a sea. It is a wide open-mouthed river with currents which run back and forth across the Atlantic, to Africa and Europe, far east to India and China, and now especially northwards to the United States and Canada. The currents which continue this flow, the legacies of colonization and the influences of present imperialism, make the Caribbean equally open to global discourses. In this definition of regional, national and ethnic identities, the Caribbean finds itself poised between sovereignty and openness – a small eddy in a large stream, but an eddy all the same. The Caribbean is the community, the society is the village, and the ethnic group represents the family at home and abroad with whom we establish a past, find solace in the present and seek assurance for a future.

Political struggles for identity which have taken place in the Caribbean must themselves be historicized and culturally investigated if they are to have meaning. In 1791, two years after the French Revolution in Europe, and one year before Mary Wollestoncraft published *A Vindication of the Rights of Women* and situated the base from which the liberal feminist struggle for women's equality began, the Caribbean was in the midst of the Haitian Revolution, described by C.L.R. James as the only successful slave revolt in history (James, 1963: ix). The class of women who would and could question the ideology of male dominance with the pen was limited. Lucille Mathurin Mair (1974), commenting on the period 1655 to 1770 in Jamaican history, writes that

> The dominant creole values of a society 'whose business was business' continued, during the classic slavery period of 1770 to 1834, to determine the condition and interrelationships of women. Racism and colonialism combined with sexism to shape their life patterns. Women's acceptance of prevailing norms confirms the orthodoxy of women as the silent, second sex, serving as a conservative if not reactionary social element.

At the same time, we should not conclude that women, black, white or brown, were indifferent or lacking in a consciousness of gender, however defined at that time in the Caribbean. Mathurin Mair concluded from her analysis of this period that 'Counter-evidence also suggests women's capacity for criticism, modification, rejection even, of these norms, in ways often peculiarly available to them, as women' (Mathurin, 1974: 1).

The peculiarity of women's situation is that they are at the same time inside and outside of politics. Mathurin Mair points to situation of white women in Jamaica during slavery. English law and custom dictated the status of the white woman in Jamaica. White women had no voice in the Parliament, could make no laws and the rule of primogeniture ensured that the eldest son inherited the estate of his father. A good marriage saved them from 'unnatural' spinsterhood, possibly from destitution; an unmarried daughter was a burden and shame to the family:

> Edward Long breathed a sigh of relief at his daughter's 'honourable alliance' to Mr. Howard in 1801 for he had 'dreaded leaving her at large in the world, either to be subject to the multitude of inconveniences which generally attend the situation of the single woman, or else to experience the mortifications of a state of dependence on someone of their relations'.

(Mathurin, 1974: 224)

None the less, men of substance took good care of their daughters and white women furthermore had the advantage of being part of the élite by virtue of their whiteness. The shortage of white females did not necessarily give a white woman advantage over black and brown women as concubinage with the two latter groups, was deeply entrenched in the creole way of life. Marriage itself also did not grant white women further independence since it placed them in 'coverture' restricting their capacity to act as free and rational beings. Yet, the white woman in Jamaica was in many ways the 'classic creole consumer of prestige' ensuring that the status symbols of the ruling class maintained its distance from the middle and lower classes (Mathurin, 1974: 248).

After slavery, in Trinidad and Guyana, the system of Indian indentured labour introduced another ethnic group into these societies, between 1845 and 1917. The majority of Indian women and men were wage labourers, some later becoming part of the land owning peasantry, the minority were professionals or owned businesses of their own. The status of most Indian women was that of household or field labourer. Few Indian women had the luxury to be educated and to be involved in a debate on questions of female liberation and equality. At the same time such questions were already being raised by progressive Indian women in India, women such as Dr Anandibai Joshi (1865–1887) and Pandita Ramabai (1858–1922) (Kosambi, 1994). This tradition of an anti-colonial female militancy in India was conveyed to Trinidad through the medium of the newspapers in a section entitled 'Indian News and Views' regularly featured in the Trinidad *Guardian* on Thursday and Sunday and produced by Indian journalist Seepersad Naipaul. One feature entitled 'Indian Women Hold Parley' drew attention to the All-India Women's Conference held in 1936 whose goals were to 'create a wider scope for the powers and responsibilities for Indian women, and to emphasize the value of women's work in every well ordered State' (*Sunday Guardian*, 5 July, 1936). Visitors to Trinidad, among them one Beatrice Grieg, drew local attention to the undeniably secondary status allocated to Indian womanhood in India and in Trinidad.[4] Both in India and in the West Indies, Indian women were inside and outside the political struggle. On the one hand, the allegiances to ethnicity were encouraged through the retention of a Brahminic ideal. Indian women were expected to mirror themselves after the image of Sita, the virtuous, long-suffering and faithful bride of Rama,[5] the latter epitomizing the male patriarch in control of his household – in order to counteract the 'westernizing' influences of the colonizer. Within the ethnic group, women as a group suffered as a result of this expectation of their roles and behaviour as women. It was unrealistic for women, who were themselves wage earners and homemakers, to confront their men and assert their autonomy and independence on occasion. Indian women in Trinidad were caught in the dilemma of also desiring the re-establishment of 'Indian' ethnicity as it was recalled from India and the reconstitution of community within Trinidad, therefore colluding at one level with the reconstruction of an Indian femininity and masculinity, and with renegotiating new ideas of Indian womanhood in Trinidad. With migration had come many opportunities to change some of the more gender oppressive features of caste and religion. New-found freedoms based on the demographic shortage of Indian women in the colony, as well as a greater capacity for wage earning on estates, allowed them to question and challenge the patriarchal expectations of Indian femininity.[6]

The questions which would be raised for women by the second wave of feminism became more complex, adding to the issues of class and religion/ethnicity, those of political nationhood, race, and sisterhood among women. What political alliances should they forge? What interests would compel them to act on behalf of other women, themselves, their families, or their ethnic groups? It is important to view the emergence of the women's movement as parallel to, and intersecting with, other struggles which are specific to each group and society. Another example serves to explain the multi-layered aspect of struggle.

In the Pan-African movement which had its origins in the Caribbean, there was no specific feminist rhetoric in a contemporary sense of the word. Marcus Garvey formed the Universal Negro Improvement Association (UNIA) in 1914, shortly after he returned from England. The first member of the association was Amy Ashwood, a young woman of 17 who would in due course become his wife. Of the original list of members, it was revealed that over half of them were women. From the earliest phases, there were allocations for women as secretaries in each division and presidents of various divisions. The social welfare tradition of the period found these women and those of the UNIA involved in activities such as concerts, fundraising for the poor, visiting hospitals, setting up an industrial school, trying to run a labour bureau and finding jobs for unemployed persons. At weekly meetings of the UNIA, in what was then largely a debating society, topics pertaining to women such as 'Is the intellect of woman as highly developed as that of man?' were also discussed. It is recorded that Garvey himself participated in this debate and argued in the affirmative. Another debate entitled 'Women or men: Whose influence is more felt in the world?' shows a concern for issues of women's equality without the rhetoric of contemporary feminism.

Subsequently, when the UNIA moved to New York, women continued to play decisive and leading roles in the organization, although here more black American women seemed to have been involved. What is clear, however, is that both in its name as well as focus, the issue was that of strengthening black nationalism. Garvey preached a doctrine of race first, self-reliance and nationhood, and linked the woman question to the race question in an intimate way. 'Race first meant that black folks would have to put their racial self-interest first' writes Martin (1988: 70).

> Garvey told black people, among other things, to take down the white 'pin ups' from their walls. He was opposed to the gross advertisements for skin lighteners . . . he encouraged through his organization a factory that made black dolls so that young black children would not have to deal with the question of beauty being seen through the eyes of white folk all the time.

In contrast to Garvey's progressiveness on the equal participation of women, Claudia Jones, a famous black woman of the Communist Party of the United States in the 1940s and 1950s, lamented the position of black women in the party. If women supported Garvey as a leader, then it was also because Garvey supported women. Tony Martin comments that the dignity of women was a crucial issue for Garvey and the UNIA (Martin, 1988: 68). Honor Ford-Smith suggests that there is a close connection between the anti-colonial and feminist movement in many societies who have similarly experienced colonization and that 'the Jamaican feminist movement of the 1930s and 1940s was nurtured within the Garvey movement'. Ford-Smith identifies the contradiction of this 'feminist' stance at the time. 'Strangely enough, the ideal image of womanhood upheld within the movement differed very little from the ideal image upheld by dominant colonial ideology in terms of the way it perceived women's position within the family, women's labour and sexuality' (Ford-Smith, 1988).

Parallel with the emergence of the UNIA in Jamaica and the United States was the preamble to the anti-colonial struggles which fed the later nationalist struggles in Trinidad. Jim Headley, who had worked for years in the Trade Union Movement in the United States, returned in 1934 to Trinidad to witness the eruption of hunger marches. Together with Dudley Mahon, of the Federated Workers Trade Union, and Elma Francois,[7] a former member of the Trinidad Labour Party, Headley founded the National Unemployment Movement. Within weeks of holding public meetings, pamphleteering and recruiting unemployeds to the organization, the NUM had on its list 1,200 members and became a political pressure group in the society. The NUM suffered a quick death as Headley himself, as one of the hungry unemployed who was additionally hassled by authorities, felt forced to leave the country. The other members of the group felt that the focus on unemployment was too limited as a basis for wider political mobilization and, later the same year, the Negro Welfare Association,

FEMINIST REVIEW NO 59, SUMMER 1998

founded by Elma Francois, Jim Barrat, Christina King, Payne and Rupert Gittens, came into being. The militancy of this period has been matched since then by other equally powerful messages such as the 'Black Power' riots of the 1970s in which women also fought as hill guerrillas alongside men. In the intervening period in Trinidad the co-optation of working-class and middle-class black women, by the nationalist demagogue who brought Trinidad to Independence, has come under close scrutiny in a rereading of the past with the still unfocused lens of the present.[8]

If women did not willingly support the national political struggles, sometimes any autonomous movement was defeated by dictatorship regimes. This was the case of the Dominican Republic under the Trujillo regime which lasted for more than thirty years. The regime adopted a patronizing patriarchal attitude, ostensibly supporting women's difference and at the same time quelling any revolutionary tendencies among women. There were, for instance, pensions for prolific mothers and 'demagogic concessions to "women's issues" such as women's suffrage and the enactment of a protective labour code'. Combined with the general repression experienced by the entire society, this was no climate for the development of any major women's movement before 1961. Despite this repression, three women, Minerva, Patria and Maria Teresa Mirabal, have emerged as icons for the contemporary women's movement in this society. The dictatorship had attempted to silence them through rape, and finally did silence them by assassination in 1960. Their deaths, however, accelerated the fall of Trujillo and his regime, although the succeeding regimes continued the manipulation of women and femininity for their own ends (Pineda, 1984: 132).

Despite their allegiances to nationalist and independence struggles, an unarticulated consciousness of gender equality must have run through the veins of each woman – black, white, Indian, Portuguese and Chinese, coloured, Spanish, French, Haitian, Barbadian – the same way the idea of racial equality had occurred to men and women long before the actual struggles for equality erupted in collectivities. To speak of a feminist movement in the Caribbean which predates the contemporary second wave movement is to bring alive on paper the individuals who would not be silent, those who spoke or wrote on behalf of others who felt similarly,[9] much as we do today. To speak of a feminist movement in the Caribbean is to identify the contradictions which women faced in the post-colonial struggles and the contradictions of the men who welcomed their comradeship. There were different battles to be fought on Caribbean soil when the suffragette movement in Britain at the turn of the nineteenth century began its pathbreaking and victorious fight which eventually benefited all women. By the middle of the twentieth century, when masses of post-war unemployed and professional women in the United States felt the anger of rejection, women in the Caribbean were each differently placed in their own societies. That first wave feminism in the region took on many strands of a liberal feminist discourse, indicated that women's rights were still being fought for in the context of the equal rights tradition which defined the anti-colonial and race struggles. That second wave feminism assumed other dimensions of thought – some radical, some marxist, some liberal – is consistent with the expansion of identity politics which began to perceive individuals as belonging to different classes and different races. That feminism in general and the feminist movement in the Caribbean appears to be eclectic is that it has responded at the same time to the issues of class, race/ethnicity, nationhood and to gender identity. Only the openness of the mid-twentieth century onwards has created both the global consciousness as well as the rapid spread of the ideas of gender equality, which were always part of these struggles.

Creole – the expression of Caribbean difference

The struggles for political identity are generally overt statements of difference. Not all aspects of identity politics are so explicit or given to manifest expressions. Within any culture the language and meanings shared by those who speak the same language, also provide another space in which identity is being shaped. Language itself is a crucial marker of identity, as it is also an indicator of continuity and tradition. In Trinidad, for instance, the French words *jour ouvert* (day break, or opening day) describe the traditional opening of the two day pre-lenten carnival celebrations. Early Monday morning, before the sun has risen, the people who have been partying the night before spill out onto the streets and dance/walk to the slow steady rhythm of the steelbands around the towns. The words *jour ouvert* to a Trinidadian describe a mood, a feeling, a moment, a desire to be in that space, which, unless it has been experienced by someone for many years, could have no such meaning. The words themselves tell a large part of the history of this society, the influence of the French on language/culture. In the same vein the term *creole* has become a metaphor for the Caribbean region, its people, language and culture. The genealogy of the word is interesting and the term itself has been 'creolized' in its Caribbean applications for it is by no means only applicable to, or uniquely used, in the context of the Caribbean.[10]

There is a continuing adaptation of the term, its use has varied over time in the Caribbean and has meant different things to different groups, sometimes simultaneously in the same society. Lady Nugent, wife of the English Governor of Jamaica from 1801 to 1805, described the white women born

Figure 1 All faces of the Caribbean: Market seller in Dominica.

Figure 2 All faces of the Caribbean: Mayan, Garifuna and Creole women of Belize.

Figure 3 All faces of the Caribbean: Indians in Trinidad

Figure 4 All faces of the Caribbean: Old men siesta in Baranquilla, Caribbean coast of Columbia.

in the island as creole to distinguish them from the white women who came from 'foreign', applying the word not only to describe their birth, but also to differentiate their behaviour, habits and customs which were different as a result of being born and raised in the island (Nugent, 1966). Locally evolved habits, customs, cuisine and popular culture increasingly began to be defined as *creole*. In essence *creole* customs and habits were viewed as departures from a norm established by the European colonizer and perceived as deficient in both form and content. None the less, the term clearly had resonance for the peoples in the different territories of the Caribbean.

In Trinidad, for example, in the nineteenth and early twentieth century, it was used to refer to the descendants of the French planter class born in the society, as well as to the local African population.[11]

Where language was key in the instrumentation of empire in the Caribbean, language has also been crucial in the definition of sovereignty. This battle was very early on appreciated by J.J. Thomas in his response to Anthony Froude's *The English in the West Indies: The Bow of Ulysses* published in 1887. Froude, a learned British scholar, travelled to the West Indies and was warmly welcomed by the local population. His book, officially commissioned by the British government, was a brutal and ig-nominious attack on the West Indians. Froude had been called upon by the West Indian colonists to block the efforts of the West Indian blacks, the first of the non-white colonial peoples who had become English speakers themselves, from functioning in their society according to the principles of parliamentary government. He argued that the black population was seeking a self-government which they did not have the capacity to exercise. J.J. Thomas, a largely self-taught scholar responded to his defamation with *Froudacity: West Indian Fables Explained* published in 1889, displaying in his turn equal erudition and command of a language which was not his first tongue. J.J. Thomas was a young black educated man of Trinidad. In one of his jobs as a village schoolmaster in rural Trinidad he developed a facility for languages in order to communicate with students who spoke a variety of different tongues. Without any formal training in languages, Thomas mastered French, began to learn Spanish and understood the significance of the living dialect which he could observe in its evolution. He recorded the Creole grammar of the French language, the dominant stream which emerged from the babel of different tongues at the time in Trinidad in a book entitled *The Theory and Practice of Creole Grammar*. Published in 1869, this book was said to have been better appreciated by philologists in England and Europe than at home at the time, unfortunately another aspect of creole culture.

Both of Thomas's contributions had immediate, and still has far-reaching, implications for the continued evolution of creole society.[12] More importantly, it appears to me that, in his systematic study of *creole*, Thomas signalled not just the internal integrity of the grammar, but also the idea of language expressing the meanings shared within a culture. This emergence of a shared language revealed another aspect of the society's evolution – that people of different tongues had begun to communicate in a common language of their own, a language which excluded others, not consciously or deliberately, but because the meanings of words and ideas were also derived from the lived experience of the territory. Though culled from the mixtures of languages which each of the different groups brought, the creole dialect in each region is predominantly influenced by the language of its chief colonizer. Within each society as well, the official language of the state and the élite continues to be the language of the main colonizing agent. In this relationship between two entities umbilically tied, we find the other dimension of creole society, the capacity to move back and forth between a language with its internal shared meanings, and the 'mother' tongue from which it was created. This skill for *double entendre* is nicely illustrated in J.J. Thomas's response to Froude in *Froudacity: West Indian Fables Explained*. He had the 'audacity' to confront the master 'using the master's tools'.[13] In Trinidad, the importance assigned to command of the language is evident in the early development of the calypso where the singer demolished his opponent with language by using either 'big words' or *double entendre* which could be variously interpreted by the listeners.

The derivation from other tongues as well as the ongoing communication with its local audience created of *creole* not a mimetic culture,[14] but a constantly evolving syncretization and hybridity. This is best explained through music[15] and dance. The Cuban *rumba* evolved partly through interaction of slaves of different African regions, with a European influence obvious in the use of the Spanish language. Where the *santeria* of Cuba is largely a transplanted Yoruba entity, the *rumba* is a distinctly creole or Cuban creation. The evolution and eventual acceptance of creole musics are closely interconnected with the internal and external political struggles for nationalism and élite recognition of Afro-Caribbean heritage (Manuel, 1995: 15).

The way in which all these aspects of national identity struggles, economic deprivation or empowerment, popular culture and desire come together is in the *creole expression* of the body in Caribbean society, the language of intimacy. The language of intimacy is not only that of sexual desire, it is the expression of familiarity, tenderness, of mutual understanding or their bedfellows – antagonism,[16] conflict and antipathy. All of these are inscribed in the language of the body, of masculinity and femininity, of man and woman, of gender and gender relations. There are subtle and indefinable ways in which a common language of the body and gender relations are shared within a culture, possibly even crossing race and class divides. These messages can be sought only in and through language as it is spoken and understood by people themselves. This element also explains the difficulty we have of understanding gender codes we encounter in a new society simply because we cannot immediately grasp the messages which are implicitly conveyed with and without words.[17]

What are such messages in the Caribbean?[18] A first message might be the ideas of womanhood or manhood. When does a child move from being a girl into an '*ooman*' or from boyhood into 'you tink you is *man*'. There are numerous indicators of manhood as the research from Brown and Chevannes illustrate from an ethnographic project on gender socialization which spanned the societies of Dominica, Guyana and Barbados (Brown and Chevannes, 1995). Starting with the inscribed religious doctrine

> From yu bawn yu is a man ... De Bible did say, 'Let's make man', and outa man dere cometh ooman, ... At all time yu mus' know seh yu is a man an' like yu is supreme. It go right back to religion y'know.

To biological criteria:

> From me bawn wid 'ood [hood or penis], me know seh me is a man.

To self-determined behaviour and roles:

> Him is man when him decide fe tek up responsibility. Like you start a relationship wid a girl. Suppose she get pregnant an she have a baby wid yu, yu start tek up dat responsibility. ... Yu can be a man from yu is a likkle bwoy. An yu can be a big ol' bwoy.

> When me really realized dat me turn a man was when me staat to work and hangle [handle] me own money, y'know. Buy my own clothes an t'ings like dat, me staat go out an' come in late, like look girlfrien' an t'ings like dat. Mi fadder used to tell me seh, me t'ink yu a man, yu come een dem hours ya a night.

Most importantly, male sexuality is a central definition of maleness, in relation to femininity,

> A wil' [wild] man always get a enormous amount a respec' ... a wil' man normally have money. An yu know that respect is based on money. If yu don' have money ... yu get no ratings from nobody

but perhaps more stridently in opposition to male homosexuality, the latter widely perceived as pure 'wutlessness' or learned behaviour on the part of homosexual men or women.

> Me love ooman bad, bad, bad, bad. Me hate gay wid a passion ... how me seet it is like de type a gay wha me hate is, him is man like me, or him bawn wid balls, but because of certain situations like all economics, like all money, an him waan look good an, him go tu'n gay ...
> (Brown and Chevannes, 1995: 116–18)

The girl must be beaten into a young lady, to be a young 'ooman' is unacceptable. Both the fiction of the region and other forms of popular culture are replete with these messages:

> All the same right is right and there is only one right way to bring up a [girl] child and that is by bus' ass pardon my french Miss Mary but hard things call

for hard words. That child should be getting blows from the day she born. The she wouldn't be so force-ripe now. . . . Little children have no right to have so many things in their brain. Guess what she ask me the other day nuh? – if me know how worms reproduce. . . . As Jesus is me judge. Me big woman she come and ask that.

(Senior, 1986: 69)

The allusion to 'force-ripe' – generally applied to prematurely ripened fruit – is a powerful metaphor for the construction of femininity. It situates the young girl in opposition to the 'big woman' who is mature and has the 'knowing' which the young girl should not possess before her time. The attainment of one's femininity is a process of grooming before attainment of sexual knowledge of the other sex.

While these processes of constructing masculinity and femininity take place in all societies, how they do so are both historically and culturally shaped and continue to be so, despite external influences. Like most culture, they are also passed on from one period to the next, and the terms and conditions are changed by the struggles between masculinity and femininity to define boundaries. For example the ideal of the 'browning' – the mixed light skinned woman – in Caribbean society is currently undergoing change, but these notions are the direct legacy of a colonial history of opposition between white and black sexualities. How does each culture agree on acceptable norms and practices of gender, for example, that in Trinidad 'a deputy is essential' or in Jamaica 'a man is entitled to his matie on the side'. The 'deputy' and 'matie' are the idiomatic references to the 'other woman', the 'bit on the side'. Is this a mutual agreement between men and women in society? Who determines the boundaries of what is permitted in sexual relations? How power and control mechanisms in gender relations are put in place in each society and how these are negotiated is also based on an internal dialogue which is constantly transpiring about sexual difference and equality.

Sexual difference and the Caribbean

The word 'feminism' has itself been part of the problem of feminism and writing on gender in the region. While such struggles and negotiations are and have been ongoing in the course of our history, as they are in most societies, the importation of a word brings with it the messages of gender in another culture. The image of the strident British suffragette has not been part of the history of Caribbean society, even while equally strident women have fought for nationhood and equality. The image of the 'bra-burning – sexually liberated' North American white woman in the 1960s has negative resonances in these parts. Where the word is used, as it must be, for a thing has to be named, it has to be constantly defined in context as 'I am not a feminist like those . . .' or 'I am a feminist but I am not one of those man-hating . . .'. This is an ongoing irritant in this area of work and struggle in the Caribbean and the issue will no doubt persist.

At the same time, a crucial debate in feminist theory is itself being discussed within the region, but perhaps with a different vocabulary. The post-colonial, national and ethnic contestations for identity have been forced to create a place for the interrogation of gender identity, leading one to agree with Irigaray that 'Sexual difference is one of the major philosophical issues, if not the issue, of our age' (Irigaray 1993: 5). The current debates in learned feminist circles are focused on the issues of equality and differ-ence. I think there is more or less agreement among scholars, north, south, east and west, that equality between the sexes can only be achieved if fem-ininity and masculinity are both valued for their difference. That the oppo-sition in sexual difference has proved to be a constraint now for further theorizing as well as activism (De Lauretis, 1987) has also become quite evident. Instead of reproducing these binary oppositions which we are simultaneously engaged in breaking down, feminist writing, I think, sup-ports the idea that difference or equality between the sexes can be approached pragmatically. There are instances in which sexual difference must be argued for rather than equality across the board, as in the case of maternity leave in employment. The difference-equality concepts and debate can be more usefully applied as a heuristic device to generate new questions about gender and new research issues (Hermsen and Van Lenning, 1991), thus leading to novel insights. Like the early feminist search for the 'origins of patriarchy' this debate cannot be resolved at this point. Whether we are naturally different as a species, or whether we have control over the construction of our identities and potentialities, remain part of the ongoing evolution of sex and gender. The question for each society becomes a process of understanding its own constructions of masculinity and femininity, to identify the legacies and issues which are recalled in the reconstruction of gender and intersected ethnic identities.

The language of this struggle is also culturally specific. For the rest of this paper I briefly situate ways in which this debate is carried out in the region. First, a large number of women, if not the majority, have always worked outside of the home and, if not fully, then certainly have been largely responsible for the support of their households. As central figures in pro-duction, women have also provided the continuity to household and family life. The question of class differences and privilege among women is a more recently acquired twentieth-century issue among the majority of black, indian and coloured peoples. The region has inherited a generalized stereotype of woman in society as *matrifocal* or mother centred, often confused for matriarchal and matrilineal both of which are not at all applicable. In this stereotyping women are not only assumed to possess extreme strength and resilience, but also to be responsible for the increasing *marginality* of the male. The paradox of both stereotypes rarely surface in popular discussions, although this has been debated to some degree at the level of scholarship (Smith, 1996; Barrow, 1996; Momsen, 1993). Matrifocality has not led to greater gender equality. Women's power in the home is equated with power in the society at large. Marginalization is rarely depicted as the relations between men and men, which is in fact the underlying subtext of two books by Errol Miller, *Marginalization of the Black Male* (1986), and *Men at Risk* (1991), both popular butts for feminist attacks in the region. Instead, marginalization is assumed to be the fault of female (over)achievers. Slavery was initially blamed for the emasculation of the male. The fact that women have emerged from the same system with their femininity and strength intact is often glossed over. Black men were shown little mercy or respect by the white élite and managerial class in matters pertaining to their personal lives. As shown in Thomas Thistlewood's Jamaican diary between 1750 and 1786,[19] at least one record exists about the extent to which black masculinity suffered at the hands of another male grouping. Emasculation was tendered by extreme humiliation and pain as, for instance, seen in the following entry:

> Friday, 30th July 1756: Punch catched at Salt River and brought home. Flogged him and Quacoo well, and then washed and rubbed in salt pickle, lime juice and bird pepper; also whipped Hector for losing his hoe, made New Negro Joe piss in his eyes & mouth &c.
>
> (Hall, 1992: 73)

It was equally nourished by the conditions under which intimacy between black men and women in the new setting was persistently invaded by the assumed rights over their body by the master.

> On the domestic scene, Mrs. Cope was brought to bed of a girl on the night of Saturday 26th; Mr. Cope was paying frequent nightly visits to Egypt where he would summon Little Mimber, for whom he had a passion until mid-April when he transferred his attentions to Sancho's wife, Cubbah.
>
> (Hall, 1992: 93)

This legacy, together with that of being commodified, sold and bartered as property and the host of other indignities, has continued in other ways, in the stereotyping of black masculinity in the Caribbean, also evident in the United States of America. The question of why, out of this legacy, blame has been conferred on to black women, and women in general, for a persistent emasculation of the male, needs to be investigated thoroughly. Certainly the stereotyped notions of contemporary Caribbean reality is of 'female headed households' in which women are both provider and nurturer, and are consistently themselves blamed for the 'spoiling' of their sons and husbands by inculcating irresponsible male behaviour as the norm. The feminist or women's attempt to achieve parity with men in various spheres is viewed, here as elsewhere, as an antagonistic measure to gain control over the other sex. The fact that women's struggles thus far in the region's political arena have been more than conciliatory, reconciling the need for ethnicity, nation and community and family with that of desire and intimacy, remains a persistently elusive part of the discussions which take place in the societies. None the less, there have always been supportive male colleagues or partners in this struggle for gender equality.

While this is the dominant discourse of the black diaspora, there is a continued interface with the gender systems of other groups who also live in the region, such that the idea of matrifocality and marginality, though still applicable in part, may take different forms in different societies. For instance, the presence of a large number of Indians in Trinidad and Guyana which has held firm to an ideology of patriarchal gender relations, creates differences in these apparently dominant ideas and perception of masculinity and femininity. Societies such as the Dominican Republic and Cuba, with large European Spanish populations, have other distinctions in gender systems as do societies influenced by the French, such as Haiti, Martinique and Guadeloupe. Belize is another uniquely developing situation, where, despite its similarity in the past to the English-speaking Caribbean islands, has had in the twentieth century a continuous influx of migrants from the neighbouring Spanish speaking central American populations, introducing into the society a Mayan group with an extremely patriarchal system of gender relations.[20] Much systematic research needs to be undertaken in these societies to establish a more comprehensive and accurate picture of the ongoing constructions of masculinity and femininity into the present.

If sexual difference in relation to economic survival and production is couched in largely antagonistic categories, the ideas of difference in sexualities between male and female is a firmly implanted one. In general men are allowed many partners, women are to be monogamous, although serial monogamy is acceptable as women are not expected to remain unmarried after the death of, or separation from, a husband or a partner. This different expectation of male and female sexuality is continually debated. Femininity is still defined in relation to virtue, motherhood and being a wife, while masculinity is at the same time bounded by expectations, as for instance that of being a provider, but allowed indefinite boundaries and privileges because 'he is man'. The debate on sexuality is by no means restricted to differences between men and women, but equally between women and women – all of which militates against a unified platform for gender consciousness. Much of this debate is contradictory. One dancehall lyricist appeals to a notion of working-class female sexuality as being free, exuberant and untamed and therefore the most desired. The downtown girl is presumed to be the most libidinous 'Gimme the girl wid the wickedess slam' (Beanie Man) in opposition to the 'browning' who represents the 'uptown' middle-class ideal woman of mixed race who is limited in her performance by the control and reserve which she is made to assume. In Trinidad the idiom of the 'red' woman has fairly similar applications although perhaps not so sharply contested as in the Jamaican context where class differences are more stark. The origin of this ideal from the 'mulatto' woman bred in slavery needs to be traced in so far as both sexuality and power over other men clearly were intersected in the historical construction of sexuality within the region.

The commitment to sexual difference in the English-speaking Caribbean, in terms of the opposition between masculinity and femininity, is very fertile ground for gender analysis. In societies where black masculinity constantly seeks to assert itself, where it is defined as power over other men and in relation to multiple relationships with the other sex, where monogamy and fidelity are perceived as signs of weakness or of being a 'soft man', masculinity is itself a very fragile thing. This fragility is evident in the antagonism and distance which must be maintained from male homosexuality and from homosexuality itself, the latter which is in general unacceptable as an alternative sexuality in these parts. My understanding of the non-English speaking territories, especially that of the Dominican Republic, suggests that the 'machismo' culture is very similar. Ironically,

Figure 5 Students of gender and development studies, at the University of the West Indies, Mona, Jamaica.

FEMINIST REVIEW NO 59, SUMMER 1998

again because of the shared legacies of colonization and continuing imperialism in which both masculinity and femininity have had to be defined in relation to the other, feminism has largely been, in my view, a nurturing one, a recognition of a shared condition, despite sexual difference and despite obvious inequalities. In the region, the construction of masculinity has emerged as an issue which is tackled by women and feminist scholars as it is now being treated seriously by some men.[21]

In the last decades of the twentieth century, for those who live in this stepping stone of islands and adjacent territories, between the north and south Americas, feminism provides a new lens to interrogate the past and renders new challenges and opportunities to establish boundaries of identity and difference. If the struggles for identity have also been about the desire to enrich the space and group to which we belong, then Caribbean feminism is itself an expression of the new conditions of that desire.

Notes

1 As will later be more fully explained, 'creole' born here refers to those born in the region itself.

2 This interpretation of the ongoing construction of gender identities under colonization is consistent with the ideas put forward in Teresa de Lauretis (1987) *Technologies of Gender*.

3 I use this term to signify this point of difference, and also as it resonates with the Marxist use of the word, building here on Ken Post's explanation in *Arise Ye Starvelings, the Jamaican Labour Rebellion of 1938 and its Aftermath* (1978, The Hague: Martinus Nijhoff). Post writes that 'each moment of antagonistic contradiction continually recreates the other and is the condition of its existence, but their relationship is such that both cannot develop equally' p. 28.

4 References to Beatrice Greig's visits and activism in Trinidad is found in Reddock (1994) and Mohammed (1994b).

5 These stories are evident in the Ramayana, and are told and retold by the pundits or Hindu priests in Trinidad to each generation of Hindu men and women. These ideas, though part of Hindu mythology, were pervasive among all Indians in Trinidad despite religion. I have examined the recurrence and pervasiveness of mythology in informing gender ideals and roles, despite migration, in an article entitled 'Ram and Sita: The Reconstitution of Gender Identities among Indians in Trinidad through Mythology', in *Gendered Ideologies*, Christine Barrow (ed.) (1998, Kingston: Ian Randle Publishers).

6 These ideas are more fully developed in Patricia Mohammed (forthcoming) *Gender Negotiations in Trinidad 1917–1947*.

7 Discussions on Elma Francois and other women involved in the early labour struggles in Trinidad are well developed in Reddock (1994). Reddock also draws attention to the existence of branches of the UNIA in Trinidad, indicating another aspect of struggle within the region which I have not sufficiently developed in the text – that is the way in which the ideas and activism in one territory often affected and influenced the others creating its own internal dynamic. The labour struggles of the 1930s is a good example of how this takes place, as is the Grenada Revolution in the late 1970s early 1980s which affected the Caribbean in ways still being revisited by political scientists such as Brian Meeks.

8 There have been different interpretations of women's roles in the People's National Movement led by Eric Williams to the extent to which they brought and helped to sustain his power for near three decades, from 1956 to 1981. My own analysis of history leads me to a partial leniency with the 'consciousness' of gender in the past. While leaders and politicians have no doubt been aware of women's importance or crucial roles in various platforms, the consciousness of the time did not lead women themselves to demand equal treatment or recognition as the unspoken ideology of patriarchy affected both men and women.

9 In the Caribbean there is an extensive literature which is growing on the women of the past who have been active in many different ways in these struggles for gender equality. See, for instance, Linnette Vassal's *Voices of Jamaican Women 1898–1939* (1993, Kingston Jamaica: Department of History, University of the West Indies).

10 Richard Allsop discusses its etymology in the region. It was first used with pride by European colonists, especially the French, to refer to themselves as born and bred in the 'New World'. It later came to distinguish local breeds of livestock from imported, and by extension, in a system where slaves were viewed as property as well, to refer to locally born slaves to differentiate them from the original Africans brought under the system. Allsop notes that the status of the word then took a nose dive among the white population, but rose among the local population, thus creating two further distinctions. It was a label applied to a class of non-white persons of 'breeding' or an excluded class of 'ill-bred blacks'. In the latter sense, while unfairly applied, the word appeared to have returned to its original source. Two Spanish etymologists Corominas and Pascual, who have traced its origins to Portuguese also indicated that the word may have originally been of African origin used among the Negroes (*sic*) 'born in the Indies' to distinguish those 'born in Guinea from those born in America because they consider themselves more honourable and of better status than their children because they are born in the fatherland, while their children are born at home' (Allsop, 1996: 176–7).

11 When I was growing up as a child in the late 1950s in a village of Lengua in South Trinidad, a village primarily inhabited by Indians, the few persons of African descent who lived in this village were referred to as Creoles by all the Indians. For Indians it had possibly become synonymous with Africans. To my

FEMINIST REVIEW NO 59, SUMMER 1998

knowledge its use was not pejorative, but rather to define difference of race, as everyone was accustomed to doing in this society to distinguish the many different groups which co-existed.

12 While this analysis focuses on the etymology of the term and its meaning for English-speaking societies in the region, I am aware that the mutation of language is similar for all societies. In Haiti, a French creole patois is the *langue parole*, in the Dominican Republic and Cuba as well as Puerto Rico, the Spanish varies from that spoken in Europe although the common base still exists. An Argentinian colleague once commented to another Dominican colleague in my hearing that he thought that the Dominicanas spoke a 'bad Spanish', in the very same way that the various dialects of English spoken by those of us in the English-speaking Caribbean were thought to be 'bad English'. Near the end of writing this paper I have just come across a book entitled *Caribbean Creolization: Reflections on the Cultural Dynamics of Language, Literature and Identity* edited by Kathleen M. Balutansky and Marie-Agnes Sourieau (1998, Jamaica: The Press, UWI). The collection of essays in this book bears out some of my suggestions in this section on a definition of the Caribbean as *creole*.

13 The allusion here to black US feminist Audre Lorde's famous statement of using the master's tools to demolish the master's house is deliberate and relevant for feminism in the Caribbean.

14 Yet there is mimicry inherent in its evolution. Many of the words we used in an Indian household in Trinidad to describe kitchen implements were derived from Bhojpuri Hindi, the dialect which was shared by the largest groups which came and therefore became the dominant one. For example, we 'balayed' the roti, meaning to roll out the dough. None of these have any meaning for a Hindi speaking Indian from India as it is the creation of a verb from a noun through the rules of English grammar and not those of Hindi. Yet this and other such terms are still widely used today in many Indian households. The emergence in Trinidad of the genre of music referred to as chutney/soca is itself a blend of the Indian with the soul music which emerged out of the United States and the calypso of Trinidad.

15 The work of Carolyn Cooper, *Noises in the Blood* (1993 London: Macmillan) is useful and more highly developed on these themes. From my reading, Cooper's work largely supports the points I am making. She looks at the emergence of the dancehall artist in Jamaica, examining the African resonances of this genre and arguing in this and subsequent writings that this popular culture form is an oral expression of nationalism from a hitherto silenced group.

16 By antagonism here I acknowledge that gender relations are also extremely ridden with conflicts and antagonism between men and women, women and women and men and men. My particular approach in this essay has been admittedly a bit one-sided, dwelling on the mutually negotiated aspects of gender relations as compared to the confrontations caused by its opposition. This was pointed out to me by Yaba Badoe, who also made many other very insightful comments on a draft of this paper, for which I am very grateful. I attempt to

deal with the antagonism which results from women's challenges to male patri-archy through the matrifocal/marginality debate in the region.

17 I lived for several years in the Netherlands. Before that I had also lived in the UK for some time. While in Britain, because I shared a language and past history, the messages of gender were clearer and more accessible. For the entire period of my stay in the Netherlands, because I had no real knowledge of the language, it was impossible for me to understand either the business of inti-macy between men and women, or the subtle aspects of racism which were no doubt part of the black migrant's lived existence in this society.

18 I realize that from this point onwards, much of my analysis speaks directly to the English-speaking Caribbean. None the less, from my understanding of the other territories, as well as close association with persons from the different societies, I argue that many of these ideas of masculinity and femininity and the body are applicable across the region. For instance Huguette Dagenais in her paper 'Women of Guadeloupe: The Paradoxes of Reality' (in Momsen, 1993) comes to the same conclusion about the paradoxical status of the Guadelou-pean woman as studies in the English-speaking territories do.

19 Douglas Hall selected and published extracts from Thomas Thistlewood's diary in a book entitled *In Miserable Slavery: Thomas Thistlewood in Jamaica, 1750–86* (1992, Macmillan, UK). Thistlewood lived in western Jamaican as a small landowner for 36 years. He was an inveterate diarist and he chronicled during this time, almost daily, the activities of himself and those around him, thus leaving a legacy which, despite its obvious limitations or personal biases, etc., also provide us with information which was otherwise not recorded in his-torical documents of the time.

20 While I have not studied this systematically, recently I worked in Belize with community-based workers involved in a project on Sexual and Reproductive Health sponsored by the International Planned Parenthood Federation, New York. Some of the problems and issues which confront women in the society are those expressed by the rural Mayan women of a very patriarchal control over their sexuality and lives.

21 See, for instance, articles in the First Symposium on Masculinity in the Caribbean hosted by the Centre for Gender and Development Studies at St Augustine, Trinidad in January 1996.

References

ALEXANDER, M. Jacqui and MOHANTY, Chandra Talpade (1997) *Feminist Genealogies: Colonial Legacies, Democratic Futures*, New York: Routledge.
ALLSOP, Richard (1996) *A Dictionary of Caribbean Usage*, Oxford and New York: Oxford University Press.
BARROW, Christine (1996) *Family in the Caribbean: Themes and Perspectives*, Kingston and Oxford: Ian Randle and James Currey.

BRAH, Avtar (1996) *Cartographies of Diaspora: Contesting Identities*, London and New York: Routledge.

BRAITHWAITE, Edward (1985) *Contradictory Omens: Cultural Diversity and Integration in the Caribbean*, Kingston, Jamaica: Savacou Publications.

BROWN, Janet and **CHEVANNES, Barry** (1995) *Report to Unicef on the Gender Socialization Project of the University of the West Indies*, Jamaica: UWI.

DE LAURETIS, Teresa (1987) *Technologies of Gender: Essays on Theory, Film and Fiction*, United States of America: Indiana University Press.

DI STEFANO, Christine (1990) 'Dilemmas of difference: feminism, modernity, and postmodernism' in **NICHOLSON** (1990).

FLAX, Jane (1990) 'Postmodernism and gender relations in feminist theory' in **NICHOLSON** (1990).

FORD-SMITH, Honor (1988) 'Women in the Garvey movement in Jamaica' in **LEWIS** and **BRYAN** (1988).

FROUDE, Anthony (1887) *The English in the West Indies*, London.

GAZTAMBIDE-GEIGEL, Antonio (1996) 'The invention of the Caribbean in the twentieth century' paper presented to the 28th Annual Conference of the Association of Caribbean Historians, Barbados.

HALL, Douglas (1992) *In Miserable Slavery: Thomas Thistlewood in Jamaica, 1750–86*, London and Basingstoke: Macmillan Caribbean.

HERMSEN, Joke J. and **VAN LENNING, Alkeline** (1991) *Sharing the Difference: Feminist Debates in Holland*, London and New York: Routledge.

IRIGARAY, Luce (1993) *An Ethics of Sexual Difference*, New York: Cornell University Press.

JAMES, C.L.R. (1963) *The Black Jacobins: Toussaint L'Ouverture and the San Domingo Revolution*, New York: Vintage Books.

—— (1969) 'The West Indian intellectual' Introduction in **THOMAS** [1889] (1969).

KOSAMBI, Meera (1994) 'The Meeting of the Twain: The Cultural Confrontation of Three Women in Nineteenth Century Maharashtra' *Indian Journal of Gender Studies*, Vol 1, No. 1. New Delhi/Thousand Oaks/London: Sage Publications.

LANGUAGE (1982) *Caribbean Quarterly*, Vol. 28 No. 4, December, Jamaica: University of the West Indies, Department of Extra-Mural Studies.

LEWIS, Rupert and **BRYAN, Patrick** (1988) editors, *Garvey, His Work and Impact*, Kingston, Jamaica: Institute of Social and Economic Research, University of the West Indies.

MAHABIR, Noor Kumar (1985) *The Still Cry: Personal Accounts of East Indians in Trinidad and Tobago during Indentureship*, Trinidad: Calaloux Publications.

MANUEL, Peter (1995) *Caribbean Currents: Caribbean Music from Rumba to Reggae*, Philadelphia: Temple University Press.

MARTIN, Tony (1988) 'Women in the Garvey movement' in **LEWIS** and **BRYAN** (1988).

MATHURIN, Lucille (1974) 'A historical study of women in Jamaica from 1655 to 1844' PhD dissertation, University of the West Indies, Mona, Kingston, Jamaica.

MENEZES, Mary Noel (1992) *The Portuguese of Guyana: A Study in Culture and Conflict*, Gujarat, India: Anand Press.

MILLER, Errol (1986) *Marginalization of the Black Male*, Mona, Jamaica: University of the West Indies.

—— (1991) *Men at Risk*, Kingston: Jamaica Publishing House.

MILLETT, Trevor (1993) *The Chinese in Trinidad*, Trinidad: Imprint Caribbean.

MOHAMMED, Patricia (1994a) 'Gender as a primary signifier in the construction of community and state among Indians in Trinidad' *Caribbean Quarterly*, Vol. 40, Nos. 3 & 4.

—— (1994b) 'Nuancing the feminist discourse in the Caribbean' *Social and Economic Studies*, special issue edited by Brian Meeks, Jamaica: Institute of Social and Economic Research.

MOMSEN, Janet (1993) editor, *Women and Change in the Caribbean*, London, Kingston, and Bloomington: James Currey, Ian Randle, and Indiana University Press.

MOODIE-KUBLASINGH, Sylvia (1994) *The Cocoa Panyols of Trinidad: an oral record*, British Academic Press.

MOORE, Henrietta (1994) *A Passion for Difference*, Cambridge: Polity Press.

NICHOLSON, Linda J. (1990) editor, *Feminism/Postmodernism*, New York and London: Routledge.

NUGENT, Maria (1966) *Lady Nugent's Journal of Her Residence in Jamaica from 1801 to 1805*, edited by P. Wright, Kingston: Institute of Jamaica.

PINEDA, Magdalena (1984) 'The Spanish-speaking Caribbean: we women aren't sheep' in Robin MORGAN (1984) editor, *Sisterhood is Global*, New York: Anchor Books.

RAMESAR, Esmond (1974) editor, *Language and Society* Caribbean issues, a Journal of Caribbean affairs), Trinidad: Extra Mural Studies Unit, University of the West Indies.

RAMESAR, Marianne Soares (1994) *Survivors of Another Crossing*, Trinidad: University of the West Indies.

REDDOCK, Rhoda (1994) *Women Labour and Politics in Trinidad and Tobago: A History*, Trinidad: New Beginning Movement.

RENNIE, Bukka (1973) *History of the Working Class in the Twentieth Century*, Trinidad: New Beginning Movement.

RHYS, Jean (1966) *Wide Sargasso Sea*, Great Britain: Richard Clay.

SENIOR, Olive (1986) *Summer Lightning and Other Stories*, Harlow: Longman.

—— (1991) *Working Miracles: Women's Lives in the English Speaking Caribbean*, Barbados: Institute of Social and Economic Research.

SMITH, R.T. (1996) *The Matrifocal Family: Power, Pluralism and Politics*, New York and London: Routledge.

THOMAS, J.J. [1889](1969) *Froudacity: West Indian Fables*, London: New Beacon Books.

VASSELL, Linnette (1993) *Voices of Women in Jamaica*, Kingston, Jamaica: Department of History, University of the West Indies.

WALCOTT, Derek (1992) 'The Antilles: fragments of epic memory' Nobel acceptance speech, *Trinidad and Tobago Review*, Jan.–Feb., 1993: 23–6

WEEKS, Jeffrey (1986) *Sexuality*, London: Ellis Horwood.

WOLLESTONSCRAFT, Mary [1792] (1975) *A Vindication of the Rights of Women*, editor, Carol Poston, New York: W.H. Norton.

Historicizing Slavery in West Indian Feminisms

Hilary McD. Beckles

FEMINIST REVIEW NO 59, SUMMER 1998, PP. 34–56

Abstract

This paper traces the evolution of a coherent feminist genre in written historical texts during and after slavery, and in relation to contemporary feminist writing in the West Indies. The paper problematizes the category 'woman' during slavery, arguing that femininity was itself deeply differentiated by class and race, thus leading to historical disunity in the notion of feminine identity during slavery. This gender neutrality has not been sufficiently appreciated in contemporary feminist thought leading to liberal feminist politics in the region. This has proved counter productive in the attempts of Caribbean feminist theorizing to provide alternative understandings of the construction of the nation-state as it emerged out of slavery and the role of women themselves in the shaping of modern Caribbean society.

Keywords

slavery, history, feminism, freedom, post-colonial, nation-state

Historians of the Caribbean have had little difficulty discerning traditions, dating back to the beginning of European colonialism, of women's public activity. An examination of these traditions allows for the isolation and assessment of women's ideas and perspectives about the changing nature of their identities and interests. Collectively, their public expressions constitute the emergence within colonialism of the infrastructure of a feminist sensibility. While women of all races and classes did not retreat from publicly voicing their experiences, there was no politicization of their gender identity within discourses of Enlightenment democratization (e.g. civil equality and social justice). It remains difficult, therefore, to map the evolution within written texts of a coherent feminist genre. The overall result, then, is a historiographical textual representation of women as victims, in diverse ways and to varying degrees, of the masculinist enterprise of colonialism (Beckles, 1995: 125–40; Moitt, 1995: 155–76; Hodges, 1992: 101–7).

Women were socially differentiated within the gender discourses of slave-based societies. Indeed, the very notion of 'woman' was consistently challenged by women within the highly politicized gender order of colonialism, and for them it was a deeply problematic category. Women were principal participants in the contests over the definitions and characteristics of womanhood and femininity. The denial by some women of the 'woman-ness' of other women became the basis of a conflict that internally exploded the potential of coherent representations of feminine identities and weakened the analytical value of the concept of 'woman'. As a consequence, historians of slavery can now speak discursively about the internal chaos of the concept as it relates to gender and race.

The diversity of women's experiences in West Indian slave societies undermines formal claims to order in the knowledges conceived by the politically challenged term 'woman', as well as feminism as an advanced, radical conceptual device. Encounters with the historical contexts and meanings of these categories have been divisive to say the least. Responses by female scholars especially have ranged from eclectic extractions for the construction of political projects of mythic glorification (such as the invention of heroism and the propagation of super-survivalist narratives that illuminate women's persistent civil rights struggles for social justices) to the outright denial of the value of 'history' in the organization and promotion of relevant feminist knowledges (Silvestrini, 1989; Reddock, 1985: 63–80; Gautier, 1983: 409–35).

Recent histories of women in slave societies have promoted perceptions of their diverse mentalities and confirmed the extreme historical disunity in notions of feminine identity. Reflecting on this state of affairs, contemporary women activists recognize that future integrative, trans-feminist strategies for solidarity are likely to generate further fragmentations and contests. Histories, as organized knowledge, then, have produced for women's movements and feminist theorists something of a mixed bag. For some, these works constitute an enormous reservoir waiting to burst forth and destroy all unifying representations of women placed in its path; for others, they represent 'another country' whose inhabitants are long dead, buried, and therefore silenced. Either way, histories of the slavery experience are viewed with considerable ambivalence and scepticism (Morrissey, 1986: 339–69; Brereton, 1995: 63–93).

It has not helped matters that dominant textual constructs of the slavery regime, the longer part of the colonial period, represent it as the social experience on which rest contemporary ideologies of race, class and gender relations. Slavery is conceived also as the master mould from which are cast the persistent conflicts among women over definitions and ideological ownership of womanhood and femininity. The contested politics of womanhood, furthermore, has been accounted for in terms of women's formally differentiated exposure to slaveowning colonial masculinities and institutionalized hegemonic patriarchy. These politics have also been explained in relation to the changing gender orders promoted by slavery and expressed culturally through civic institutions and productive arrangements. An important consequence of this internal political fracture in feminine identity was hardened ethnic and class positions between women that made problematic all projects of post-slavery rapprochement.

Elite white females in slave society sought to exclude, on the basis of race, black and brown females from membership of the ideological institutions of womanhood and femininity – and, by extension, access to socially empowering designations such as 'lady' and 'miss'. The attack upon non-white female identity promoted a gender culture of exclusion that was rationalized and maintained as new gender representations surfaced in distinct ideological and material situations. Texts written by white women with a social familiarity of slavery yield ready evidence of these developments. Mrs Carmichael, for example, an Englishwoman who lived in St Vincent and Trinidad during the 1820s, described black women in her published travelogue as 'masculine', brutish, and lacking feminine sensitivities. Maria Nugent, wife of Governor Nugent of Jamaica, shared these opinions twenty years earlier. She tells us, furthermore, in her published diary, that the children of black women in her household were far from cute and cuddly, as was her own Jamaican born child, but resembled 'little monkeys'.

Mrs Carmichael's reference to black women as masculine was consistent with white men's view about the labouring capacity of female slaves. For her, black women were outside the pale of feminine identity – hence her conclusion that 'to overwork a negro slave [of any sex] is impossible'. Such texts served to consolidate and propagate the general opinions formulated by white male overseers and managers about black women. Plantation records prepared by white men, for example, speak of black women's apparent ease at 'dropping children', capacity for arduous physical labour, and general 'amazonian cast of character'. Collectively, these accounts, written by white women and white men, indicate the varying ways and intensity with which the ideological project of defeminizing the black woman was carried out (Bush, 1991: 245–62; Gregg, 1993; Nugent, 1966: 45; Carmichael, 1969: 12, 96; Williams, 1990: 198).

The Caribbean experience is consistent with the findings of Elizabeth Fox-Genovese on US southern slavery. Fox-Genovese has argued that rather than exerting a gender politic that softened the 'evil and harshness' of black women's enslavement, élite white women lived, and knew they lived, as privileged members of a ruling class, and were fundamentally racist in outlook. The worlds of white and black women, as a result, despite dramatic experiences of intimacy, were filled with mutual antagonism, cruelty and violence. Slave women did not reasonably expect protection and support from white women, and had no line of defence against sexual assault. Patricia Morton asserts that, as a consequence of the damage done by slavery to gender identities, black women confronted the master's power in 'ultimate loneliness' and that in this circumstance 'gender counted for little' (Fox-Genovese, 1988: 33, 47–8, 326–7, 333; Morton, 1996: 9).

The power relations of race, class and sex, as the constituent elements of an economic accumulationist strategy, are significant in understanding why women adopted divisive ideological positions. But the politics of gender denial had much to do with white women's perceptions of self-interest in slave societies that virtually guaranteed the social insecurity of property-less persons, and celebrated the cultural crudity resulting from moral deregulation at the frontier. Freedom was scarce, unfree life was cheap, and any social representation that offered privileges was aggressively pursued as a matter of life and death. White women used their caste and class power to support the patriarchal pro-slavery argument that black females were not 'women' in the sense that they were, and certainly not feminine in the way that they wished to be. For the black woman the scars of centuries of denial went deep; with the onset of free society the raw wounds remained, sending tensions down the spine of all recuperative socio-political strategies.

The centering of 'woman' within slavery provided the context within which definitions of womanhood and femininity were contested. The black woman was situated at the (re)productive core of the slave system with a unique legal status. The white woman was locked into constitutional mechanisms that ensured her progeny's alienation from slavery and her association with the reproduction of freedom. Slavery and freedom, as an Enlightenment paradigm in action, situated black and white women in bi-polar relations that promoted the interests of patriarchy, and, more importantly, produced among women contradictory perceptions of identity and self-interests. The importance to the black woman of the fact that neither the white woman, nor her progeny, could be enslaved should not be minimized. Across imperial lines and through time the slave woman was legally constructed in one consistent way; she was the principal barrier to freedom since all children at birth took the status of mothers and not fathers. The very small minority of mixed-race children with white mothers were born free; their enslaved or free black fathers more often than not paid dearly, mostly with their lives. These provisions were established in slave codes that organized race and gender relations in all colonial jurisdictions (Morrissey, 1989; Bush, 1990).

Free black women were not targeted in this way by colonial legislatures. White society merely assumed that all black and mixed race women were slaves, imposing on them the onus to prove otherwise. Their freedom, then, was compromised by its vulnerability to constant scrutiny and violation. Since the concept of a free black woman seemed contradictory, most free black women found themselves constantly challenging attempts to reinslave them; many were unable to prove and enforce their freedom, oftentimes because they were kidnapped and removed to unfamiliar jurisdictions. Their offspring, none the less, were entitled to freedom at birth, irrespective of the status of fathers, which in theory placed them on an equal footing before the law with white women. As members of the community of free women, however, their lives were shaped by fundamentally different experiences, the result of their race and gender locations with the slave system (Sio, 1987: 166–82; Heuman, 1981; Campbell, 1976).

The first radical opposition and movement of Caribbean women, however, emerged within the politics of the bloody wars the autochthons launched against colonialism and slavery. Kalinago (Carib), Taino (Arawak) and Ciboney women, in the Lesser and Greater Antilles, are referred to in texts written by European conquistadors as militant and generally hostile to the imperial enterprise. Though there are no detailed accounts of women who emerged as heroic leaders in these battles, scattered references document aspects of their daily social and military offensive against Europeans. The memoirs of Michel de Cunes, for instance, in which details of Columbus' second voyage are outlined, tell us about the armed resistance of native women to the Spanish landing at St Croix and Guadeloupe. He described them as 'armed to the teeth' with bows and arrows, and even when subdued and captured resisted demands upon their labour and sexuality. He tells us, furthermore, about Columbus' refusal to adopt a less sanguine response to these women warriors. They were fired upon by his soldiers in the normal manner of war – captured and taken prisoners (Cohen, 1988: 139, 196; Kerns, 1983).

It was the norm in most parts of the Caribbean to enslave indigenous women taken as prisoners. As such, they did not expect to live in ways dissimilar to enslaved African women. They certainly worked on the plantations and in the mines of Spanish hacendados alongside African women. In the English and French colonies, however, it was not uncommon to find some of them treated in ways more 'free' than 'slave'. Many were also recruited on the mainland and indentured in the islands as domestics and artisans. Reference to their cultural resistance under circumstances of domestic slavery also require careful examination. Tragically, their political voice within anti-colonial and anti-slavery discourses has not been invoked by feminist historians in ways that offer historical depth, ideological tone and texture, to the radical tradition.

The stereotyped perception of free, mixed race women as 'divided to the vein' in terms of their political and ideological positions within the race and gender orders of slave society has proven useful in critical analysis of social history. It should be emphasized that, as far as the sugar colonies are concerned, the majority of mixed race women remained enslaved, worked in field-gangs and were not differentiated from African women in terms of life experiences. Few escaped slavery, and most remained consigned to labour gangs alongside their black mothers. They lived in the plantation villages created by their African family and shared their experiences. That some African women were also 'brown' in complexion complicated the idea that miscegenation assured social privilege. As a result, it was common for most mixed race women to be socially absorbed into the dominant African mainstream, thereby negating the impact of the colour coding system that characterized the hierarchical order of colonial society. Miscegenation, however, did open doors for a few black women and the rush to enter liberated spaces was a feature of everyday life.

Mixed race women who attained legal freedom established in conjunction with their male counterparts a distinct socio-political identity. Some, however, were forced by circumstances of birth to retain social connections with their enslaved kith and kin. For sure they did not wish to return to slavery, but sought to enhance the civil rights options of their offspring by adopting strategic political positions. One such strategy was to opt for pro-creation with propertied white men. Another was to enter intimate social friendships with élite white women whose need for friendship and companionship reflected the considerable restrictions placed on their lives within the patriarchal system. Examples of the success of these strategies are well known. Lady Nugent, for example, encouraged into her inner circle a cadre of 'coloured ladies' whose support she counted on, and who were set apart from the creole white women she could hardly tolerate. Nugent's coloured 'ladies' represented her chamber in waiting, and were considered by her more suited to this role than the 'uneducated' white creole women she encountered (1966: 66).

The black females of the Governor's household were also excluded from the inner circle. These women Lady Nugent described as her 'blackies', and in her opinion were childlike, lazy, dirty, and morally undeveloped. While she held considerable class antipathy for Jamaican creole white women,

FEMINIST REVIEW NO 59, SUMMER 1998

and racist attitudes to black women, the coloured ladies of property she found to be of a high civic quality, though victims of what she considered the disgraceful sexual adventurism of undisciplined élite white males. She supported her husband's colonial enterprise in much the same way that the coloured ladies supported hers. As 'in-betweeners', Lady Nugent and her coloured ladies formed a social alliance. She offered these co-opted women a considerable measure of social respectability and psychological comfort, though these benefits carried little prospect for expanded civil rights (Nugent, 1966: 47, 76, 125).

At the same moment in Barbadian society Elizabeth Newton, owner of Newton and Seawell plantations, had cultivated a special friendship with Doll, her housekeeper. Doll subsequently claimed that she was assured freedom for herself and three daughters on her mistress's return to England. Elizabeth did return to England, but made no arrangements for their manumission. Doll and her daughter continued to work on the estate as housekeepers under successive managers and pressed their claims for treatment as privileged, if not free, persons. The success of their mission was striking, but most impressive were the multiple levels on which the strategy was carried out. Doll's daughters were skilful advocates of their own interests; Jenny had a child with a white man; Betsy 'ran away' to England and became free; and Doll lived as the 'wife' of the white manager. Over time a section of the family 'whitened' through miscegenation, acquired artisan skills, literacy, freedom, and considerable property – including slaves (Beckles, 1989: 65–8, 127–8, 159–62).

It is instructive to note, however, that while Doll and her daughters initially benefited from the special relationship with a white woman, most mixed race women were linked to white males and acquired their advancement as part of a negotiated package that included sexual arrangements. It was the common charge during the eighteenth century, by persons opposed to this avenue to freedom, that the overwhelming majority of manumitted coloured and black women were mistresses and prostitutes to white men of property. It was also generally asserted that these women bore the scorn and endured the envy of the sexually repressed white wives of such men. The image that emerges from these records is of intense sexual contest between white, and coloured and black women for the loyalty and favours of élite males who considered the matter settled by the offer of marriage and title to the former and sex and freedom to the latter. Beyond this point of reference, images of the mixed race free woman disintegrate into archival fragments awaiting social reconstruction.

The fact should not be ignored that while slaves were constitutionally prohibited from owning property they were allowed by custom to possess and 'freely' use properties, including other slaves. What set apart Doll's family on Newton's estate was not only their 'semi-free' status, derived from a special relationship with their owner, but also quasi-ownership of slaves acquired through family links with a white male. Mary Ann, Doll's half-sister and a free mulatto, owned slaves who were placed at the disposal of her enslaved black sister and nieces. Slave owning and usage protected Doll's daughters from various forms of hard labour and enabled them to develop attitudes towards manual work that corresponded with those held by white women (Beckles, 1996b: 169–88).

All free women, then, were socialized culturally within the colonial project to function in ways supportive of the slaveowning system of accumulation. It is also in their roles as rural slaveowners and estate managers that white women are seen clearly, and in larger numbers, as autonomous participants. Lady Nugent, for example, spoke very highly of Lady Temple, owner/manager of Hope sugar plantation in Jamaica. Her skills as an entrepreneur and slave manager are described in a manner that indicated her enormous success in a 'man's' world. Mrs Simpson, owner/manager of Money Musk plantation, also received commendation from Lady Nugent for her shrewd estate management, as well as her determined effort to resist male suitors in pursuit of her property and subsequent reduction to 'wife' and housekeeper (Nugent, 1966: 28, 58–9). Mary Butler's analysis of planter women, furthermore, shows the extent to which they were important players in the capital markets of Jamaica and Barbados. While Butler does not suggest their centrality in terms of shaping colonial policy or wielding political power, she does indicate that no section of society saw them in these roles as unusual or unacceptable. It was normal, for example, to see a white woman as rational business agent examining the genitals of male slaves on the auction block before making purchases, or to see them in solicitors' offices negotiating the purchase, sale or mortgage of significant urban and rural properties. Such images reflected the commonplace nature of business activity within white households (Butler, 1995: 92–109).

Slave holding records for towns in most English colonies show that urban white women generally owned more female than male slaves. 'Female on female slavery', then, was the principal model of urban slavery. White women were 50 per cent of the owners of slaves in Bridgetown in 1817 on properties stocked with less than ten slaves. Overall, 58 per cent of the slaveowners in the capital were female – inclusive of a small number of free black and free coloured women. Over 60 per cent of the slaves these women owned were female. The interpretation of these data has influenced the writing of both woman's history and gender history, and has enabled historians to propose complex theoretical readings of slavery traditions. The analytical methodologies they have used present social radicalism as endemic to slave relations, and suggest that it resulted from the ways in which anti-slavery consciousness and politics developed around modernist ideals such as individual liberty and social justice.

Blacks, it seems, had taken responsibility for the popularization of the idea that as colonial subjects they had a stake in the Enlightenment project of human progress. Slave society, then, could produce only one kind of organized radicalism that is recognizable within modern political thought – anti-slavery struggle. Slaveowners' anti-colonial activities, tied largely to issues such as imperial taxation and constitutional autonomy, would not qualify since the politics of these ideas were not part of the anti-slavery movement. Resisting imperial hegemony was not radical from a subaltern perspective in so far that it lacked liberationist values in terms of the race, class and gender order of colonial society (Beckles, 1993; Burnard, 1992).

White female slaveholders did not publicly adopt an anti-slavery stance. Rather, despite their own marginalized social position within dominant patriarchy, with its repressive socio-sexual culture, they were known for their private and public support of the pro-slavery enterprise. While their pro-establishment politics can be understood, the privileged positions they occupied place them admirably, perhaps, to have presented colonial society with an alternative social vision. Their pro-slavery positions stand in stark contrast to those of their ethnic sisters in the US slave colonies and metropolitan Europe, whose struggles in the vanguard of anti-slavery movements may have won the day for abolitionists by winning the popular support for legislation on emancipation.

White women, then, offered the faint heart-beat of a feminist opposition to supportive 'texts' during the long slavery period, though it may be suggested by way of mitigation that their private miscegenation with black men, and their occasional private grumbles about the 'horrid nature' of slavery, should be taken into account as part of a discreet, subjective oppositional politics. Lady Nugent's decision to dance with a black man during a ball at the Governor's residence sent an enormous shock through the sensitivities of upper-class female Jamaican society. It was understood, and stated, that only a Governor's wife could possibly have survived the disdain and derision that followed. The aggression shown by the same female élite society towards Elizabeth Manning who, as a prominent member, was accused by her husband of extensive sexual relations with enslaved black men on the estate, helps to discredit the claim that there was perhaps a silent, submerged anti-slavery conscience among sections of white female upper-class society (Brathwaite, 1984; Nugent, 1966: 156).

The suggestion that manumission rates are the crucial element in understanding slavery in particular jurisdictions constitutes an interesting test of the extent to which different categories of slaveowners sought to promote freedom for their own slaves. The evidence available to us indicates two important trends; one, that freed non-whites were more likely to free their slaves than whites; second, that white women figured very low in their responses to slave freedom through this mechanism. Higman has shown, for example, that though white women constituted the majority social category of urban slaveholders in Bridgetown, they were the least significant in terms of manumitting slaves. The period 1817–20, for which reliable figures are available, shows that some 10.4 per cent of the slaves owned by free black men were manumitted, followed by those belonging to free coloured men (3.0 per cent), free black women (2.7 per cent) free mulatto women (1.6 per cent), and white women (1.5 per cent). White men, whose slaveowning was concentrated largely in the rural economy accounted for 0.6 per cent. White women, then, compared to free black or coloured women, were less willing to free their mostly female slaves (Higman, 1984: 385–86; Handler and Pohlmann, 1984: 390–408).

Women's groups such as the 'Ladies Society for the Promotion and Encouragement of Arts and Manufactures', which was established in Barbados in 1781 as the woman's wing of a planter élite organization by the same name, was concerned with the alienation of white males and female labourers and artisans within the plantation economy. They lamented the way in which slavery had undermined the chances of social advancement for white workers by enabling blacks to monopolize skilled occupations. As an organization it was dedicated to promoting the welfare of propertyless whites and functioned as a pressure group within the context of pro-slavery political economy. At no stage did its members oppose the logic and specific natures of slavery as oppressive relations of race, class, sex and gender. It constituted more of a precursor for subsequent public alms institutions than an oppositional force within the slave system (Handler, 1974: 124).

Considering the view that free coloured women experienced contradictory relations to slave society, it should not be surprising to find that some of them publicly opposed slavery and appeared in the vanguard of the anti-slavery movement. For such women the need to protect their black kin, and make sense of their own experiences, informed the public postures that constituted their anti-slavery politics. Some of them, in addition, developed sophisticated philosophical critiques of the slave system as representing a moral contradiction of humanist and Christian values. Sarah Ann Gill of Barbados, for example, comes forcefully to mind. Described in the 1820s as a 'Christian heroine of Barbados', Gill used her platform in the Methodist Church to campaign in a way that no one else did on the principle that slavery and Christian morality were incompatible, and that a good Christian could not be a slaveholder.

By urging Christian whites to free their slaves and take a general anti-slavery posture, Gill incurred the public political wrath of Barbadian slave-owning white society. Following the infamous destruction of the Methodist chapel in Barbados in 1823 by a mob of irate Anglican whites, Gill used her home as the meeting place for her political campaign. In 1824, whites who wished to commemorate the anniversary of the destruction of the chapel threatened to destroy her home. Her tenacity and persistence won the admiration of slaves in Barbados as well as the support of metropolitan leaders in the Methodist ministry – including abolitionist advocates such as Thomas Buxton who secured a debate in the House of Commons of the circumstances surrounding the destruction of the chapel. No free woman in the West Indies positioned herself in the deep end of public anti-slavery politics in the way that Gill did. When the Methodist Church removed her from the Barbados context and assigned her to South Africa, she continued her work in the anti-slavery campaign, and established a reputation on both sides of the Atlantic within the movement (Handler, 1974: 157–8).

Less effective, but more intellectually radical, were the Hart sisters of Antigua whose contributions to Caribbean anti-slavery politics and letters mark them as formidable figures of their time. Anne and Elizabeth Hart were free coloureds who came to prominence as young poets, pamphleteers and polemicists. Like Gill, they were associated with radical Methodists within the religious opposition to slavery. Their critique and rejection of slavery in Antigua during the era of amelioration was highly provocative and their literary work rated among the best in the region. The Hart sisters were pioneers within the ranks of free Caribbean women of their time in terms of their ideas about women's rights, gender issues, and the wider question of social justice.

Elizabeth, in particular, was publicly abused by slaveowners during the 1820s on account of her radical demands for public education for slaves, and the protection of slave women from the sexual tyranny of white males. She maintained, however, a reputation as an aggressive anti-slavery thinker and writer until her death in 1833. The focus of her politics was the impact of slavery on the black family, the moral erosion of community life by slavery, and the call for the educational tutoring of all women and children. She spoke about the devastation of slavery on the intellectual capabilities of black children, as well as its assault upon the feminine identity of black women. Her multi-layered critique of slavery shattered the coherence of pro-slavery arguments in Antigua. Moira Fergusson has suggested that the work of both sisters constitutes a reply 'to all those who cast aspersions on the intellect of African Caribbeans'. They drew to public attention the oppressiveness of the gender order of slave society by speaking and writing about the sexual vulnerability of young black women, and described sexually exploitative white males as 'predators' who subjugate enslaved women for perverse pleasure.

The Harts' campaign for the protection of young slave women from sexual abuse was linked to their aggressive literary polemic against female prostitution in the colony. On these issues they were also organizational activists. Their role in the establishment of a support network within Methodist evangelicalism for young black women can be seen in the extensive fundraising efforts carried out during the 1820s on behalf of the 'Ladies Negro Education Society'. They were not only literary advocates of women's self-help strategies, but committed organizers and institution builders. For them, then, feminist radicalism entailed two levels of public engagement: first, a vocal intellectual opposition to the gender and racial order, and second, an activism within organizations that brought them into close contact with the pro-slavery forces of society (Ferguson, 1993).

Enslaved black women, however, presented slave society with its principal feminist opposition. Oppressed by the gender orders of black and white communities, and with little room to manoeuver to acquire the respectability necessary to secure a platform for public advocacy, slave women were undoubtedly the most exploited group. The inescapable tyranny of white and black masculinity created several levels on which gender oppression was experienced and resisted. Their problematization of everyday life was a response to their core function as the conduit through which slavery was naturally reproduced, and their vulnerability to legally sanctioned sexual exploitation. They developed integrated systems of thought and actions that countered efforts to morally and politically legitimize their enslavement. Resistance began in West Africa and continued during the middle passage. Anti-slavery mentalities, therefore, preceded the plantation. It connected African women to their creole progeny delivered on the plantations by enchained wombs; collectively, these women set their hearts and minds against slavery (Beckles, 1989).

In an assessment of the 'organs of discontent' on West Indian slave plantations, Dirks argued that when conflict arose it was usually the 'female gang members who complained the loudest because everyone knew that they were less likely to be flogged than men'. It earned women the reputation, he noted, for being the instruments of instability and the more unmanageable element of the work force. The evidence, furthermore, comes down in favour of slave women's equality under the whip, and indicates their prominence in the creation of social turmoil and the articulation of protests. Jacob Belgrave, for example, the free coloured owner of a large

Barbados sugar plantation, told the authorities that, shortly before the April 1816 slave revolt, he was verbally abused by a gang of slave women who alleged that he was one of the fellows opposed to England's abolition of slavery. During the revolt his estate was singled out for special treatment. He claimed property destruction of £6,720, the third highest in the island from a total of 184 damaged estates (Beckles, 1989: 171; Dirks, 1987: 160–1).

In this regard, Bush's work has done much to extend the conceptual parameters of the analysis. In a series of essays, the themes of which constitute the empirical core of a subsequent monograph on enslaved women in the Caribbean, she demonstrated the fluidity and range in forms of women's struggles, and the diversity of their anti-slavery actions and attitudes. Enslaved women, she showed, promoted a culture of intransigence in relation to work; they ran away from owners, terrorized white households with chemical concoctions, refused to procreate at levels expected by their owners, insisted upon participation in the market economy as independent hucksters, slept with white men as part of a strategy to better their material and social condition, and did whatever else was necessary in order to minimize the degree of their unfreedom. Through such 'channels', Bush states, 'women helped to generate and sustain the general spirit of resistance'. The Black women's anti-slavery continuum, then, acted as a political infrastructure that destabilized the terms of everyday life within the race, gender, and class order (Bush, 1985: 239).

The tale of the two Nannys is particularly instructive of the way in which historians of the Caribbean have constructed an heroic feminism within the radical tradition. The reference here is to Nanny of the Maroons, Jamaica's sole official national heroine, and Nanny Grigg who is described in the literature of the 1816 Barbados slave rebellion as a revolutionary ideologue. Both Nannys are described as militant women who led, physically and conceptually, their menfolk into violent confrontation with slave-owners and the imperial troops who defended them. Nanny of the Maroons was a guerrilla commander whose successes against pro-slavery forces in Jamaica are now legendary. The Barbados Assembly's official report into the 1816 rebellion describes Nanny Grigg as a literate, knowledgeable woman who believed and propagated the view that in order to secure freedom it was possible to replicate the Haitian Revolution. The report stated that she held considerable political authority among her male peers, and swayed them in favour of the armed solution to the slavery question (Mair, 1975a; Beckles, 1985).

Slave women like Mary Prince, on the other hand, who wrote memoirs, did not lead troops into battle, nor mobilize any community for such action, but her contribution to the radical tradition was considerable. As a freed woman in England she presented an effective critique of pro-slavery ideology and interest. Her 'voice' in metropolitan anti-slavery circles constituted an important 'literary' force from the West Indian women's anti-slavery vanguard. Prince left no room for an ambivalent interpretation of slavery; black women wanted freedom from slavery, she argued, and did all that was possible to this end. In her acclaimed narrated autobiography, Prince speaks of the 'sweetness' of personal freedom, and the collective desire for liberty that kept the black community in endemic opposition to the colonial order. She 'wrote back' in ways similar to the Hart sisters, and echoed the voices of all black women who could not be heard.

The details of Prince's life story illuminate the experiences of black women within the gender order of slavery. With respect to Mrs Wood, her mistress, she was particularly consistent. Prince brands Mrs Wood as a racist, a sadist, and lacking in feminine sensitivity. Prince recalls cases of brutality she and other women suffered at Mrs Wood's hands. She documents Mrs Wood's contempt for the marriages of slavewomen, and the malice directed towards their husbands. Critically, she tells of Mrs Wood's description of her as a 'black devil', and the punishments she received for 'thinking' and speaking about freedom. Prince's expression of compassion for suffering slave women linked her in solidarity to the politics of the Hart sisters; like them she held the belief that black women suffered to a more degrading degree the inhumanity of slavery (Ferguson, 1987).

Texts produced by enslaved women constitute the most reliable site from which feminist scholars can depart in the development of a critique of plantation culture, particularly its masculinist social ideology and practice. The reading of these texts as presentations of knowledges in the radical tradition, however, has contributed to two discernible ideological positions within feminist thinking, the first of which ironically has militated against its development and maturity. The first position concerns the manner in which the stereotyped armed and deadly 'rebel woman' was singled out and promoted as a heroine within the struggle against slavery and patriarchy. The process of selection for this status resulted in the exclusion of other types of less well-documented rebellious women whose oppositional politics remains textually suppressed. The deification of the militant 'rebel woman' demanded in turn the promotion of mythic narratives that represented them as persons larger than life, and alienated them from the 'common' woman who laboured in the trenches of everyday resistance. The second position has to do with the less developed concept of the 'natural rebel' as a discursive instrument. It has been argued that the adoption of this concept would revolutionize the theory of anti-slavery by moving it away from the limited parameters of armed struggle to embrace popular culture, religion, and economics – indeed the areas of social encounter where oppositional social consciousness was expressed and registered.

Reading the theoretical significance of this conceptual diversity is important in developing explanations for the strategic positions adopted by feminists in recent times. The reason why institutional political projects, such as independence, took hegemonic precedence over women's liberation has not been rigorously debated by theoreticians of the women's movement. The continued political containment of women's resistance to patriarchy became an important sub-project of postcolonial discourse. Feminist radicalism that could not be accommodated within the official parameters of the emergent nation-states was deemed subversive, anti-social and unpatriotic. Feminists, then, had a difficult time locating and practising a nationalism that did not betray the core tendencies of their radical traditions. The effective 'nationalization' of the radical women's movement, and in turn the ascendancy of liberal feminists, can therefore be read, in part, as a history of ideological acquiescence. The state offered many benefits, and these were attractive and considerable. Some women fell in line, and radical feminism was put aside as articulations of extremists within the 'lunatic fringe'.

The construction of the nation-state as the final victory for anti-colonial forces carried within its very conception and design several layers of enforced agreement that quickly emerged as the new and revised oppressive hegemony. Emphasis upon national unity as the ultimate social condition meant that political contests over inequitable ownership and control of productive resources, women's objection to masculinist domination of public institutions, resistance to racism against people of African descent in everyday life, and the critique of socio-cultural privileges attained by representatives of white supremacy ideologies, were oftentimes presented as hostile to the national interest. Newly politically empowered men, described as 'founding fathers' of nation-states, who in fact were essentially leaders of political parties and corporate institutions, defined and declared what was the national interest and how it should be protected. They alone finally determined who were the supporters and enemies of the nation, and which discourses were nation-building and which were subversive.

There was no autonomous, privileged place for feminist movements within the hegemonized masculinist politics of nation-building. Tokenism and paternalism, however, ran rampant within the formative years of postcolonialism. Radical feminists were prominent occupants of a discredited community that included Rastafarians, religious fundamentalists, communists, black power chanters, and other advocates of allegedly 'untenable' causes. Black men especially considered themselves politically enfranchised, if not liberated, by their social 'ownership' and management of state power. They possessed the public institutions of governance, stamped their personalities on them, and cultivated political cultures that were patently hostile to female participation.

Nation-states, as hegemonic civic enterprises, functioned essentially as 'boys only clubs' – the odd woman was admitted but on terms set out by her brethren. It became fashionable to have one woman in each high office – the cabinet, judiciary, diplomatic corps, permanent secretariat, and so on. In cases where women's radical tradition was strong, as in Jamaica, it was strategically contained by calling upon women to form their own wing within the political party. These fora in turn became places where radical feminists were isolated and critiqued, and despite the enormous display of intellectual and organizational energy on the part of many, official leadership tended to fall into the lap of their liberal pro-establishment sisters.

The set-back to radical feminism, therefore, took place at two levels; one, conceptual self-subjugation to an invented notion of nationhood as a cul-de-sac of the historic struggles against imperialism and male domination; two, acceptance of the nationalist paradigm in which development discourse fixed 'Independence' as a seminal moment for women within the evolution of feminist identity. A political effect of these strategic positions was that women, formerly enslaved and colonized, but now 'free' and empowered with citizenship, scaled down and subordinated their struggle against male political power and economic domination; conceptually it meant the acceptance by some women that their histories and identities would in future be decisively determined by forces opposed to their conflict with patriarchy.

The break with Empire, it seemed, became a critical movement in women's liberation, and the beginning of a reformulation of political identity. The accepted idea that colonialism was a principal driving force in shaping women's experiences and consciousness allowed nationalism to function for them as a splintering ideology. While it was recognized, by socialist theoreticians especially, that the constitutional design and ideological make-up of the nationalist state was politically reactionary, feminists did not politicize the implication of this argument for women's movements. While they may have been distracted by the popular realization that socialists themselves did not break with liberal democrats on issues of sex and gender, questions about their greater responsibility for the objectives of women's movements remain unanswered.

There were many lessons that West Indian feminists could have learnt from

FEMINIST REVIEW NO 59, SUMMER 1998

studies of the rise of the Haitian nation-state between 1804 and 1826. Despite the abundance of evidence which shows the active involvement of women in the revolutionary process the independent nation of Haiti was constructed, in both its constitutional and administrative scaffolds, as an expression and representation of masculinist authority that systematically sidelined and repressed women into second-class citizenship. Indeed, successive constitutions within the first two decades of independence denied women rights that men took for granted as expressions of their citizenship. Restrictions on employment access to public office, the setting of terms on the exercise of the franchise, alienation from land ownership rights, and control over marital relations, were imposed throughout regional jurisdictions. In order to ensure that 'foreign' [white] men could not own land in Haiti, women who married such men were deprived of citizenship in order to prevent white inheritance by marriage. The same penalties did not apply to Haitian men who married white women.

Haitian women, then, the first females in the Caribbean to achieve citizenship within a modernizing nation, were constitutionally reduced to inferior status through a virulent masculinist ideological praxis that designed and promoted the state as an instrument of the military élite whose socioeconomic status was rooted in landownership. President Dessalines' Independence Constitution of 1805 provided in article 9 that 'no one is worthy of being a Haitian if he is not a good father, a good son, a good husband, and above all, a good soldier'. Lands appropriated by the state following the defeat of the slaveocracy were distributed among soldiers according to rank, and to male public servants in lieu of wages. Women received no land under either policy. With respect to adult suffrage, says Leyburn, President Petion's constitution of 1816 targeted women punitively when the right to vote was denied 'women, criminals, idiots, and menials' (Sheller, 1996; Leyburn, 1980: 243). Since women were alienated from landownership and denied access to the military, their powerlessness and honourlessness within the emergent nation was assured. Freedom from slavery and the destruction of colonialism were objectives for which women had fought and died, and nationalism did not secure them an equal return.

The refusal of feminists to draw upon and theorize such historical encounters within their radical tradition has to do with the selective, eclectic approaches adopted with respect to reading history. The Haitian Revolution occupied a central place in the knowledges organized by recent feminist leaders and writers. The pantheons of national heroes established in most West Indian post-colonial societies connect directly to an understanding of history in which Haitian revolutionaries are idealized. Toussaint L'Ouverture emerges as the 'Abraham' – the father of fathers –

in the redemption of the black race. He was not associated, however, with statements and policies supportive of the political empowerment of females who fought in the war of liberation. Neither did Jean-Jacques Dessalines, the first President, target women for equal recognition.

Feminists selected aspects of this revolutionary process that strengthened their analysis and agendas, but ignored those features that spoke more concretely to their gendered condition as women. The same can be said of their readings of maroon history and societies. While maroon societies represented movements of heroic resistance, careful and balanced research should show also how enslaved women on the estates were kidnapped by maroon men, pressed into oppressive social relations, and otherwise kept in bondage.

Recently, Eudine Barriteau-Foster, Caribbean feminist social scientist, lamented the fact that the considerable research done under the auspices of the 'Women in the Caribbean Project' (WICP), academically administered and conceived by 'liberal feminists', furthered the crisis of radical feminism and problematized the advance of postmodern feminist theory-building. The limitations of the liberal feminist research agendas, she asserts, resided in its deliberate submission to Enlightenment political discourses that could not subvert or destabilize the hegemonic gendered power relations of patriarchy. The social and ideological effect of this academic politics, she concludes, was that liberal feminists continued into post-colonialism to 'emphasize the homogeneity of women and call for their integration into public life, which they saw as gender neutral and therefore potentially benefiting to women'. Recognizing, however, that West Indian women were excluded from the centre spaces of modernizing nation-building projects, WICP leaders resisted the critique of 'epistemologies and methodologies that maintained that exclusion in the first place'. As a consequence, Barriteau-Foster calls for historical research that would promote the task of producing a locally grounded postmodern feminist theory (Barriteau-Foster, 1996: 142–59).

What is not clear, however, is how a postmodern approach will perform both tasks; explain the historical circumstances that produced systems of knowledge and social organization that disaggregated and excluded women, and at the same time provide them with liberationist epistemologies and a working agenda for collective strategic action. The idea that postmodernism generates intellectual positions rather than political strategies that de-energise the subaltern by emphasizing the endless incoherence of social action and the imprisonment of social agency within language and texts would require a systematic response from Barriteau-Foster. Her ultimate challenge, then, would be to redefine and relocate Caribbean women's movements within the ideological space provided by postmodern feminism in order to create and promote social activism that reflects a coherent feminist opposition and vanguard.

Postcolonial social relations, framed as national society, continue to express and promote enormous diversity in the mentalities and experiences of women. To account for these gendered interactions in terms of encounters with, and reactions to, representations of masculinity, and its patriarchal structures, is to deny, in great measure, that there is a historically created feminine cosmology that cannot be conceptually domesticated in this way. Patriarchy does not define and texture all spaces of lived experiences, particularly those that are newly excavated or created specifically by women in action. Practices such as the 'higglerization' (of women's lives and national society) constitute a case in point. Working-class women, the evidence suggests, have historically popularized, before the colonial encounter, the economic institution of commodity trading. During slavery and after they protected this economic culture in many ways, but used it strategically in circumstances of economic decline and material crisis. Everywhere, black women were found buying and selling (confronting the licencing authority of the state) a range of goods and services – some procured from distant countries – and creating in the process what formal economists now call the informal sector.

Postcolonialism, then, cannot claim credit for the intense social activism found among women. National society did offer an environment more conducive to its proliferation in so far as it facilitated and offered liberating forms of personal freedom in areas such as professionalism and petty entrepreneurship. Working-class women have struggled to find survivalist activities which, within the context of national economies dominated by men, are always considered stabilizing and subversive. Such activities, however, offer areas of analysis that speak of social empowerment, contestations with hegemonic economic spheres, and political recognition for women as autonomous accumulators. Middle-class and professional women have found space within the proliferating NGO movement that sought to perform development services on behalf of communities considered not capable of helping themselves.

Higglerization and NGOization, therefore, stand as a dichotomy within the struggle of a radicalized and conceptually fragmented West Indian women's movement challenging the issue of scarce resources and its relation to poverty and women's liberation. These mentalities and experiences are considered oftentimes as poles apart in terms of development discourse. Encounters by the women reveal that they do not always see each other as working towards the same end. Indeed, there is considerable mutual suspicion and empathy. Postmodern feminist theorizations should ideally recognize and accept these radically different strategic approaches by women to decision making, and reflect the extent to which specific searches for autonomy and empowerment transcend the notion of an all embracing woman's identity (Leo-Rhynie, 1997).

In conclusion, then, it seems that it will not be possible to generate – from the extreme diversity of women's experiences with slavery and colonialism and postcolonialism – a viable or attractive theory of women's oppression and liberation in the Caribbean. What existing theory has done, particularly with regard to slavery's legacies in postcolonialism, is to reveal the poverty and dangers of theory in general, and calls into question the very project of feminist theorizing. Attempts to deal with contemporary social relations in terms of cohesive sex and gender categories will certainly open more analytical doors than any one house can possibly have, hence the futility of seeking to conceptualize a unified structure that can account for a flow of traffic from all directions. Conceptual openness, methodological plurality, vigorous social history, and less historical eclecticism, may better serve the task of understanding and changing the oppressive power systems of the gender order. A major task of conceptual deconstruction is therefore required.

Historical paradigms derived from slave society, such as 'white women consumed, black women laboured and coloured women served', need to be destabilized by sound detailed historical research that views these diverse experiences of women in terms of multiple encounters with complex systems of wealth and status accumulation rather than as direct expressions of hegemonic patriarchy. The visibility of those many white, coloured, and black women who traded in slaves in West Africa and the New World, for instance, and who owned plantations and urban properties and subscribed to the principles of colonial accumulation within the Atlantic, should be carefully researched as a way of understanding the importance of gender to colonial discourse. Likewise, ongoing projects of nation-state building that promote allegedly gender free notions of nationalist cohesion should be contested and unmasked as skilful projections of modernizing masculine political power.

References

BARRITEAU-FOSTER, Eudine (1996) 'Postmodernist feminist theorising and development policy and practice in the Anglophone Caribbean: the case of Barbados' in Marianne H. MARCHAND and Jane L. PARPART (1995) editors, *Feminism/Postmodernism/Development*, London: Routledge, pp. 142–59.

BECKLES, Hilary McD. (1985) *Black Rebellion in Barbados: The Struggle Against Slavery*, Bridgetown: Antilles Publications.

—— (1989) *Natural Rebels: A Social History of Enslaved Black Women in Barbados*, New Brunswick: Rutgers University Press.

—— (1993) 'White women and slavery in the Caribbean', *History Workshop Journal*, No. 36.

—— (1995) 'Sex and gender in the historiography of Caribbean slavery' in **SHEPHERD** *et al.* (1995) editors, pp. 125–40.

—— (1996a) editor, *Inside Slavery: Process and Legacy in the Caribbean Experience: Elsa Goveia Memorial Lectures*, Kingston: Canoe Press.

—— (1996b) 'Property rights in pleasure: the marketing of slave women's sexuality in the West Indies' in **Roderick McDONALD** (1996) editor, *West Indies Accounts: Essays on the History of the British Caribbean and the Atlantic Economy*, Kingston: University of the West Indies Press.

BRATHWAITE, Kamau (1984) 'Caribbean women during the period of slavery' Elsa Goveia Memorial Lecture, Cave Hill Campus, University of the West Indies, Barbados.

BRERETON, Bridget (1995) 'Text, testimony and gender: an examination of some texts by women on the English speaking Caribbean, 1770s to 1920s' in **SHEPHERD** *et al.* (1995) editors, pp. 63–93.

BURNARD, Trevor (1992) 'Family continuity and female independence in Jamaica, 1665–1734' *Continuity and Change*, No. 2.

BUSH, Barbara (1985) 'Towards emancipation: slave women and resistance to coercive labour regimes in the British West Indian colonies, 1790–1838' in **David RICHARDSON** (1985) editor, *Abolition and its Aftermath: The Historical Context, 1790–1916*, London: Frank Cass.

—— (1990) *Slave Women in Caribbean Society, 1650–1838*, Bloomington: Indiana University Press.

—— (1991) 'White "ladies", coloured "favourites" and black "wenches": some considerations on sex, race and class factors in social relations in white creole society in the British Caribbean' *Slavery and Abolition*, 2: 245–62.

BUTLER, Kathleen Mary (1995) *The Economics of Emancipation: Jamaica and Barbados, 1923–1843,* Chapel Hill: University of North Carolina Press.

CAMPBELL, Mavis C. (1976) *The Dynamics of Change in a Slave Society*, Rutherford, NJ.: Fairley Dickenson University Press.

CARMICHAEL, Mrs (1969) [1833] *Domestic Manners and Social Condition of the White, Coloured and Negro Population of the West Indies* 2 vols, New York: Greenwood.

COHEN, J.M. (1988) editor, *The Four Voyages of Christopher Columbus*, London: Century Hutchinson.

DIRKS, Robert (1987) *Black Saturnalia: Conflict and its Ritual Expressions on British West Indian Slave Plantations*, Gainesville: University Presses of Florida.

FERGUSON, Moira (1987) editor, *The History of Mary Prince: A West Indian Slave, Related by herself, 1831*, London: Pandora.

—— (1993) editor, *The Hart Sisters: Early African Caribbean Writers, Evangelicals, and Radicals*, London: University of Nebraska Press.

FOX-GENOVESE, Elizabeth (1988) *Within the Plantation Household: Black and White Women of the Old South*, Chapel Hill: University of North Carolina Press.

GAUTIER, Arlette (1983) 'Les esclaves femme aux Antilles francaises, 1635–1848' *Reflexions Historiques*, Vol. 10, No. 3: 409–35.

GREGG, Veronica (1993) 'The Caribbean (as a certain kind of) woman' paper presented at the Engendering History conference.

HANDLER, Jerome (1974) *The Unappropriated People: Freedmen in the Slave Society of Barbados,* Baltimore: Johns Hopkins University Press.

HANDLER, Jerome and POHLMANN, John T. (1984) 'Slave manumissions and freedmen in 17th century Barbados' *William and Mary Quarterly*, Vol. XLI: 390–408.

HEUMAN, Gad (1981) *Between Black and White: Race, Politics and the Free-Coloured in Jamaica, 1792–1865*, Westport, Conn.: Greenwood Press.

HIGMAN, B.W. (1984) *Slave Populations of the British Caribbean 1807–1834,* Baltimore: Johns Hopkins University Press.

HODGES, Graham (1992) 'Restructuring black women's history in the Caribbean: review essay' *Journal of American Ethnic History*, Fall: 101–7.

KERNS, Virginia (1983) *Women and their Ancestors: Black Carib Kinship and Ritual*, Chicago: University of Illinois Press.

LEO-RHYNIE, Elsa, BAILEY, Barbara and BARROW, Christine (1997) editors, *Gender: A Caribbean Multi-disciplinary Perspective*, Kingston: Ian Randle.

LEYBURN, James (1980) *The Haitian People*, New Haven: Yale University Press.

MAIR, Lucille (1975a) *The Rebel Woman in the British West Indies During Slavery*, Kingston: Institute of Jamaica.

—— (1975b) 'The arrival of black woman' *Jamaica Journal*, Vol. 9, Nos. 2–3.

MOITT, Bernard (1995) 'Women, work, and resistance in the French Caribbean during slavery, 1700–1848' in SHEPHERD *et al*. (1995) editors, pp.155–76.

MORRISSEY, Marietta (1986) 'Women's work, family formation and reproduction among Caribbean slaves' *Review*, 9.

—— (1989) *Slave Women in the New World: Gender Stratification in the Caribbean*, Lawrence: University of Kansas Press.

MORTON, Patricia (1996) editor, *Discovering the Woman in Slavery: Emancipating Perspectives on the American Past*, Athens, GA: University of Georgia Press.

NUGENT, Maria (1966) *Lady Nugent's Journal of Her Residence in Jamaica from 1801 to 1805*, edited by **P. Wright**, Kingston: Institute of Jamaica.

REDDOCK, Rhoda (1985) 'Women and slavery in the Caribbean: a feminist perspective' *Latin American Perspectives*, 40: 63–80.

SHELLER, Mimi (1996) 'Engendering citizenship: nationhood, brotherhood, and manhood in the Republic of Haiti in the nineteenth century', paper presented at the Caribbean Studies Association Conference, North London University, July.

SHEPHERD, Verene, BRERETON, Bridget and BAILEY, Barbara (1995) editors, *Engendering History: Caribbean Women in Historical Perspective*, Kingston: Ian Randle.

SILVESTRINI, Blanca (1989) *Women and Resistance: Herstory in Contemporary Caribbean History,* University of the West Indies, Jamaica: Department of History.

SIO, Arnold (1987) 'Marginality and free coloured identity in Caribbean slave society' *Slavery and Abolition*, Vol. 8, No. 2: 166–82.

FEMINIST REVIEW NO 59, SUMMER 1998

SOLOW, Barbara and ENGERMAN, Stanley (1987) *British Capitalism and Caribbean Slavery: The Legacy of Eric Williams*, New York: Cambridge University Press.
WILLIAMS, Eric (1990) editor, *Capitalism and Slavery*, London: Andre Deutsch.
WORCESTER, Kent (1996) *C.L.R. James: A Political Biography*, New York: State University of New York.

Women's Organizations and Movements in the Commonwealth Caribbean:

The Response to Global Economic Crisis in the 1980s*

Rhoda Reddock

Abstract

In this paper I explore the emergence of women's organizations and feminist consciousness in the twentieth century in the English-speaking (Commonwealth) Caribbean. The global ideas concerning women's equality from the 1960s onwards clearly informed the initiatives taken by both women and states of the Caribbean. None the less, the paper illustrates, by use of examples, the interlocked nature of women's struggles with the economic, social and political issues which preoccupy the region's population. I examine in greater detail two case studies of women's activism and mobilization around the impact of structural adjustment policies in the two territories of Jamaica and Trinidad and Tobago. By tracing the connections between and among the organizations and initiatives of women in the region, the paper situates the feminist movement in the English-speaking Caribbean as a continuously evolving one, fusing episodic struggles in different territories, engaging women of different classes and groups, and continuously building on past experience.

Keywords

feminism; women's organizations; politicization; activism; structural adjustment; trade unions

Dating back to the nineteenth century we can locate women of the English-speaking Caribbean in women's organizations. In the main these have been religious-based women's organizations, primarily in the various denominations of the Christian Church. The organization of women was particularly important in this region as in the late nineteenth and early twentieth century it was the main mechanism for transferring and inculcating Western European values of women's place in society, for determining the post-emancipation sexual division of labour, and for ordering social and domestic organization of communities.

Not surprisingly, therefore, some of the earliest recorded organizations of women were charity organizations. An example of one such is the Daily

FEMINIST REVIEW NO 59, SUMMER 1998, PP. 57–73

Meal Association of Trinidad, a committee of Anglican ladies who, in 1938, distributed '100 substantial meals to poor persons and a Christmas meal of roast beef and plum pudding' (Franklin's Yearbook, 1939). Others could be classed as domesticating or 'housewifizing' (Mies, 1986) organizations, among these the Anglican Mother's Unions, Mother's meetings of the Baptist Church, Ladies Missionary Aid Sewing Classes of the Presbyterian Church and the Guild of the Holy Family of the Roman Catholic Church. These organizations all sought, with varying degrees of success, to inculcate 'respectable' standards for Christian families which, in many instances, ran counter to the practised reality and remembered traditions of the majority of the African descendants and, to a lesser extent, Asian populations in the region. In addition to the denominationally based organizations, the umbrella organization the YWCA (Young Women's Christian Association) also had a long history in this region.[1]

The large-scale organization of women continues to take place within religious bodies. On the one hand, religion represents a legitimate space in which women can freely participate outside of the home, without the question or need for justification to spouse or family. On the other, it provides spiritual solace and community in a world in which hard work, social, economic, physical and /or emotional violence are the order of the day. Not surprisingly, religious groupings of women, many dating from this era, still survive today, but there is a need to examine the extent to which they have remained the same or have been undergoing transformation.

Large-scale mobilization and organization of women has also occurred within the labour movement and political organizations. The early labour movement, from which many political parties emerged, was a more amorphous grouping than present-day trade unions. A broad concept of 'worker' was used to facilitate the inclusion of persons involved in a wide range of economic activities. The Jamaica Federation of Labour, for example, led by Bain Alves in 1919, included unions of predominantly female banana carriers, coal carriers, hotel workers and barmaids (French and Fordsmith, 1984: 269). This tendency which facilitated the mobilization of women workers spilled over into the early trade unions of the 1930s. For example, Daisy Crick, a housewife, rose to the position of trustee of the Oilfield Workers Trade Union (OWTU) of Trinidad and Tobago.

By the early 1940s, however, the introduction of 'responsible' trade unionism in the aftermath of the labour disturbances of the 1930s put an end to this trend. The new trade unions were now designed to include only 'real workers', that is waged employees, and unions were to be divided along industry lines. These developments proved a major deterrent to female labour organization especially after the Second World War when increasing numbers of women were being excluded from wage labour (Reddock, 1988).

In the 1950s the emerging nationalist, socialist and Marxist parties often recruited members from the middle-strata women's movement. Such women included Amy Bailey of the Jamaica Women's Liberal Club, Ada Date-Camps of the Trinidad and Tobago League of Women Voters who joined the People's National Movement (PNM), and Janet Jagan of the Women's Political and Economic Organization (WPEO) a leading member of the Women's Progressive Organization (WPO) and People's Progressive Party of Guyana.[2]

Today, women continue to be active in unions, especially those which represent occupations dominated by women. Nevertheless, even in these unions, few attain or accept leadership positions. Despite a significant female membership, the trade union movement continues to be male-dominated in terms of leadership, its agenda and style of operations.

The new women's movement

The re-emergence of the women's movement internationally in the late 1960s and early 1970s ushered in a new era in Caribbean women's struggle. Unlike the earlier movement, the impact of this new movement has been broader and touched many more aspects of personal and political life. Interestingly, many of the first women to be influenced were the stalwarts of the traditional women's organizations from the era of the 1950s. It could be said that the new consciousness seeping into the region reminded these older women activists of the marginal position they still held within the political organizations of which they were members and in the governments which their parties formed.

Two developments are significant in this regard. In 1970, Viola Burnham, of the People's National Congress of Guyana, called together her colleagues from other parts of the region to form CARIWA – The Caribbean Women's Association – with headquarters in Guyana. This organization attempted to link the various national-level councils or co-ordinating councils of women to which most of the traditional women's organizations were affiliated.

In the early 1970s, both the Women's Revolutionary Socialist Movement (WRSM) of the PNC in Guyana and the Women's Auxiliary of the People's National Party (PNP) in Jamaica worked vigorously within their parties for the establishment of national machinery on women's affairs. In 1973 the Council on the Affairs and Status of Women in Guyana (CASWIG) was instituted. In that same year Jamaica became one of the first countries in the world to establish a Women's Bureau, an achievement which resulted largely from the action by feminist-oriented women in the party such as Lucille Mathurin-Mair and Mavis Gilmour. They had presented a paper to the party leader in 1972 entitled 'Women and Social Change', which argued for the establishment of a co-ordinating agency 'empowered to initiate, promote and review through the relevant Ministries those urgent needs of girls and women' (quoted in Henry, 1986 :12). This document embodied the women's policy platform of the 1970s, and led to the formation of a Women's Bureau based in the Prime Minister's office (Henry, 1986: 12–13). Its future development was far from smooth.

In 1977, the PNP Women's Auxiliary in Jamaica was transformed into the PNP Women's Movement and on 8 March 1978 joined with the Committee of Women for Progress[3] in the first recorded observation of International Women's Day in Jamaica. Today many earlier political activists are still at the forefront of the regional women's movement, but the impetus for the radicalizing of the movement came eventually from the smaller feminist-oriented groupings.

Through the efforts of these party-affiliated women's organizations and other activists, a number of regional structures were established. In June 1977, on the initiatives of Peggy Antrobus, former director of the Jamaica Women's Bureau, the members of CARIWA and the non-governmental organizations the Caribbean Conference of Churches (CCC), a meeting was called in Jamaica to develop a regional position on the United Nations Decade of Women. Participants at this meeting included representatives of twelve Caribbean governments,[4] the University of the West Indies (UWI), CARIWA, regional and international development agencies and other Jamaican government and non-government organizations.

Out of this meeting a Regional Plan of Action emerged. Among other things, this Plan called for the establishment of national women's machinery, a women's desk within the CARICOM Secretariat, and a programme of activities within the Extra-Mural Department of the UWI. Their recommendations were quickly adopted and, by 1978, the Women and Development Unit (WAND) of the UWI Extra-Mural Department was instituted in Barbados, followed, in 1980, by the Women's Desk of the Caricom Secretariat in Guyana, and in 1979/80 the Women and Development Programme of the United Nations Economic Commission for Latin America and the Caribbean (UN/ECLAC) based in Trinidad and Tobago.

These regional institutions have collaborated with national government machineries as well as with non-governmental organizations. WAND focused specifically on the OECS[5] countries, developing the use of participatory methodologies initially with communities, then with community development organizations, and with women's activist organizations.

In the late 1960s and early 1970s small groups of women had also begun to meet and discuss their situation, many influenced by the ideas emanating from the radical black power, anti-war, new left and women's liberation movements of North America and Europe. The contradictions among the various strands of new politics were felt most by the women of these movements especially those organized into 'women's arms' or 'auxiliaries'. One writer recalls the launching of the women's section of the National Joint Action Committee in 1971 in Trinidad at the suggestion of the 'brothers'. The encouragement to launch a woman's section she noted had the 'cautioning clause that this auxiliary, supportive arm was to have nothing to do with what they labelled "white women's liberation" in North America and Europe' (Henderson, 1988: 364).

Many of the smaller groups such as the Jamaica Association for the Repeal of Abortion Laws (JARA), the Committee for the Defense of the Rights of Women in Trinidad, or Women Against Terrorism in Guyana, comprised middle-strata women, some of whom were affiliated to small left-wing political parties. It is interesting that, whether at the regional, state or small group levels, the Caribbean women's movement has been partially activated and propelled by women schooled in male-oriented political culture.

In spite of this strong radical thrust in Trinidad and Tobago, one of the earliest 'second wave' women's groups to be formed was the Housewives Association of Trinidad and Tobago (HATT). Launched in 1975, its objectives included 'the task of encouraging the exchange of information and ideas for the promotion of joint action among women in the national interest' (Henderson, 1988: 365). In its short active life this group was able to mobilize a national membership which extended to the sister island of Tobago. Although it concentrated on consumer issues its major contribution was a published survey on the work conditions of domestic servants.

In 1977 the Sistren Theatre Collective was formed in Jamaica, one of the first in a line of feminist-oriented autonomous women's groups to emerge from this period onwards in the Caribbean. Unlike many others, it had a predominantly working-class membership and used drama as a tool for consciousness-raising and entertainment.

By the 1980s small radical or feminist-oriented women's groups mushroomed throughout the region. Belize Organization for Women and Development (BOWAND) in Belize was born out of a WAND Workshop. By 1981 Trinidad and Tobago had spurned Concerned Women for Progress (CWP) which later splintered into two other organizations – the

Group by 1983, and Workingwomen (Women Working for Social Progress) by 1985, the latter still in existence.

Other organizations followed; these included the Committee for the Development of Women in St Vincent and the Grenadines (CDW) (1984), the Belize Rural Women's Association (1985), Sisi No Dada of St Kitts/Nevis (1985), Red Thread of Guyana (1987) and the Women's Forum of Barbados (1988). The activities of these organizations, many of which have quite a small membership, concentrated on consciousness-raising through popular education, income generating projects, skill-training in both traditional and non-traditional areas, media monitoring and development of alternative media – radio programmes, videos, theatre, newsletters, exhibitions and slide-tape shows.

Although small and voluntary, the impact of these groups has usually far surpassed their size. This influence was achieved usually through campaigns on topical issues which were able to draw in a wide cross-section of women, including those from the more traditional women's organizations. Among the more successful of these campaigns has been the Maternity Leave Law Campaign in Jamaica in 1978–9; the Campaign against Violence to Women in St Vincent and the Grenadines in 1985–6 and the campaign over the Sexual Offences Bill in Trinidad and Tobago during the same period. The issue of sexual violence in its many forms has been a key factor in mobilizing women throughout the region, uniting women of all classes, races and ethnic groups. The regional struggle has brought to women some understanding of body politics and its relationship to the wider socio-political and economic system. As noted by Patricia Mohammed, the impact of this new consciousness was felt in the sphere of popular music where the lyrics of calypsoes, one of the indigenous musical genres of the region, began to reflect women's resistance to male violence towards women (Mohammed, 1989).

These developments served to radicalize the traditional women's organizations and force them to shift their focus from charitable works back to their original concern, the emancipation of women. Changes could be discerned, for example, in the activities of the YWCA which at a regional level began to concern itself more with issues such as women's health, and world peace. Among women in church groups, for example, was the Barbados Anglican Mothers' Union which took up the issues of sexual violence and the ordination of female priests. In Barbados and Trinidad and Tobago, the Business and Professional Women's Clubs established institutions to assist battered women, while the Soroptimists concentrated their efforts on women and work.

Among the non-Christian religions the influence has also been felt. In

Jamaica, women within Rastafari have begun to assert their identity and, while one representative of the organization Mada Wadada (Mother Love) found it impossible to conceive of a group *of* women and *for* women, others noted that 'More and more internationally, brethren come to acknowledge the positives of their sisters and adopt new strategies to achieve economic independence and consequently independence of their children' (Mada Wadada, 1988).

Similarly, in Trinidad and Tobago, the Hindu Women's Organization, formed in 1987, sought to mobilize the Hindu woman, and 'deal specifically with matters affecting the Hindu woman and her relationship with the wider society' (Gopeesingh, 1988).

The women's movement has had less influence on the labour movement. Women's committees have been established in some unions to replace women's auxiliaries but, in spite of an ILO/DANIDA regional programme for women trade unionists, real change has been minimal. Individual women and groups of trade union women have been active, but they have not really been able to crack the male-dominant core of the labour movement.[6]

In April 1985, the Caribbean Association for Feminist Research and Action (CAFRA) was formed. It filled a long-felt need for a progressive feminist-oriented network of Caribbean feminists and feminist organizations. The significance of CAFRA lay in its decision to challenge head-on the prejudice and negative assumptions traditionally associated with the concept of 'feminism'. In so doing it sought to define a Caribbean feminism which links women's subordination with other systems of subordination – race, class and nation – and sought to go beyond traditional boundaries of language and culture. CAFRA membership includes the Dutch, English, French, Spanish and American-speaking Caribbean as well as women elsewhere who constitute the Caribbean diaspora.

Programme activities include support to women's groups or organizations in the region in research and action on women in agriculture, women's history and creative writing, communication, information and collaboration across linguistic barriers, and the establishment of a documentation base for use by individuals and organizations.

Around 1987 another regional network, Women for Caribbean Liberation (WCL) was launched. Headquartered in Antigua, this group initially emerged as a network of women associated with socialist-oriented political organizations who had met in Antigua in 1984 for the First Caribbean Women's Encounter. Their activities initially were focused on women's work and on the popularization of information on developments in Haiti. This network no longer exists.

While these initiatives impress on one that there is a well-developed and effective women's movement within the region, developments have been uneven, both within countries and within the region. Women's activities daily come to terms with the fact that achievements so far have only scratched the surface, and the lives of the majority of women are yet to be touched. The impact of the present world economic crisis in these countries did not make the task of female mobilization any easier.

The women's movement and the challenges of the crisis

References to 'the crisis' do not always make clear what phenomena or period is referred to. For some it was the events set in motion by the increase in oil prices in the 1970s, while for others it was the problem faced by Third World countries in paying their accumulated debt, and the threat which this posed to the international capitalist economy.

A comprehensive way of analysing 'the crisis' is put forward by Claudia von Welhof (1982), when she conceptualizes it as a new phase in capitalist development: one of those periods in world economic history when the international capitalist system seeks to restructure itself, in order to counter the built-in tendency for the rate of profit to fall.

This new phase, according to von Werlhof, is characterized by the introduction of monetarist policies in Western industrialized countries à la Thatcher and Reagan. This 'bitter medicine' included large-scale divestment and privatization of state enterprises and a general lowering of the costs of production. The main mechanisms to achieve this were the 'rationalization' of firms through redundancies or the removal of the rights and protections gained by workers over the last two centuries (von Werlhof, 1982: 2–3).

Caribbean countries, like other parts of the Third World, were also forced to 'structurally adjust' themselves to the changes in the capitalist world economy. Attempts at the national level to challenge the traditional trade order and to implement policies of social and economic redistribution were put to an end. This occurred in Jamaica in the 1970s and Grenada in 1983.

In addition, the tradition of exploiting unprotected female agricultural workers and petty-traders facilitated the transfer of labour-intensive industries to Third World countries under conditions reminiscent of the early period of the European Industrial Revolution (von Werlhof, 1982: 3). Not surprisingly the exploitation of female labour – whether unpaid domestic labour or waged labour in the Free Trade Zones or Informal Sector – is a central component (if not the motor) of present structural adjustment policies. These policies have revoked workers' rights and curtailed benefits. The main mechanism for policy implementation is the International Monetary Fund.

This structural economic change has been accompanied by ideological and political crises. In addition, increased rates of exploitation have been understandably accompanied by a reduction in human rights, and challenges to workers, minorities and women's rights. The road to development, either through state-directed modernization or socialist transformation, was no longer clear. The crisis reflected the cumulative impact of years of colonial exploitation and structural inequalities. This was manifested through widespread famine in a world of plenty (one aspect of the ecological crisis), increased militarism, as people fought to maintain reasonable standards of living, and increased tensions among ethnic groups and nationalities in a situation of scarce resources (Sen and Crown, 1987: 28–31).

The focus on the politics and economics of 'development' of the Third World women's movement from the late 1960s to the 1980s is not accidental. Women from the economically deprived groups have had to bear the brunt of the costs of these policies and they have not accepted it without a fight.

The developments described above did not take place uniformly throughout the Caribbean region. Jamaica, for example, felt the sharp impact of the 'Oil Crisis' by the early 1970s. Some would argue that the United States' antagonism to the 'democratic socialist' policies of Jamaica's PNP government contributed greatly to the economic destabilization which hastened this country's fall into the arms of the IMF.

In contrast, in Trinidad and Tobago, an oil producing country, the 'oil boom' which lasted from 1973 to 1980 rescued the country from the economic decline of the late 1960s and early 1970s, creating an artificial veneer of prosperity. The basic problem of diversifying the economy from petroleum dependence was, however, not tackled. By the mid-1980s with the decline in oil prices, these problems resurfaced. The IMF now saw this as their opportunity to 'discipline' Trinidad and Tobago for its disregard of monetarist advice during the 'Boom Years'. In 1986 a centre-right government came into power and guided the country along the path of structural adjustment à la IMF.

FEMINIST REVIEW NO 59, SUMMER 1998

Beyond survival: women against structural adjustment policies

Jamaica – the IMF struggle

The struggle of Jamaican women against the policies of the IMF in the 1970s is particularly interesting. The democratic socialist programme of the PNP government, which came into power in 1972, had sought to respond to the demands of the women within the party: as noted, national machinery for women's affairs was instituted long before most other countries in the world. In the words of Maxine Henry, the early years 1973–5 'saw a plethora of legislature (*sic*) and social programmes which benefitted women directly or which improved the quality of their life through providing legislative or material assistance to their children' (Henry, 1986: 15). These initiatives included the Special Employment (or Crash) Programme which provided jobs for the urban unemployed most of whom were women. Between 1974 and 1975 a backyard day-care centre programme provided child-care facilities at community level. In addition, free education, school meals and school uniforms enabled women to become more economically independent (Henry, 1986: 16).

These social programmes were supported by new legislation on equal pay, a minimum wage, and the status of children which removed the principle of illegitimacy. These policy changes coincided with developments within the party itself to strengthen the women's body and improve the position of individual women within the party.

By 1977 the economic and social situation had worsened. The country faced growing external pressure over its political direction, while escalating crime threatened the social security of its people. This process was worsened by the rejection of the popular self-reliant Emergency Production Plan to which women had contributed (Antrobus, 1987: 12). Jamaica entered into negotiations with IMF.

By late 1977, after the IMF agreement, the spate of shortages, lay-offs and cut-backs on social programmes made the mobilization of women across social classes by the PNP much more difficult (Henry, 1986: 25–6). The beginnings of the women's struggle against the IMF dates from this point. The PNP Women's Movement (PNPWM), together with the Marxist-oriented Committee of Women for Progress (CWP), collaborated to form the Joint Committee for Women's Rights (JCWR). From this period, the JCWR in collaboration with other organizations began campaigning for viable alternatives to the IMF aimed at eventually forcing the government to reconsider its agreement.

One of the first campaigns emerged around a Maternity Leave Law. According to an interview with Joan French, this issue had emerged when the National Union of Democratic Teachers (NUDT) called a meeting, in 1978, of members of the PNPWM, the CWP and grassroots women members of the JLP to discuss improvements to the maternity leave clause in its contract. In the existing clause teachers and civil servants had limited provisions, and unmarried mothers, who were among the majority in Jamaica, were discriminated against (Kaufman, 1985: 175).

Amidst grave opposition from various employer groupings (Henry, 1986: 27), the Maternity Leave Law Campaign received a boost when, at a rally of 600 women on 8 March 1979, the Prime Minister, Michael Manley, announced proposed legislation for three months maternity leave (Kaufman, 1985: 175). In her address, PNPWM president Beverley Manley 'put pressure on the government to enact this legislation quickly. She said in effect, that women had voted for the PNP and now did not expect the PNP to sit on its backside in implementing the maternity law' (Kaufman, 1985: 175).

The Maternity Leave Law campaign gained momentum: it included demonstrations, public forums, letter writing and a petition which collected 9,000 signatures (Vassel, 1988b: 1; Henry, 1986: 27). At the end of 1979 the law was passed. The new law gave all working women over 18 eight weeks paid maternity leave and another fourteen weeks without pay. No woman could lose her job as a result of pregnancy. Employers of domestic workers were required to make National Insurance contributions and to entitle them to leave payments from that fund (Kaufman, 1985: 175–6). Support among women for this legislation was by no means unanimous, and it further alienated some middle-strata and professional women from the PNP. Nevertheless, this success was a major gain for women's collective action in Jamaica.

The campaigns of this era were not limited to the provision of Maternity Leave. A major consumer campaign took place in 1980 which Henry described as 'a rear guard action . . . to maintain a "holding position"' (1986: 28). At the 7th Annual Conference of the PNPWM, a ten-point programme was put forward to address the increasing prices of food items. As a result, by mid-1980, a programme of Voluntary Price Inspectors was instituted and cases of hoarding were exposed (Kaufman, 1985: 177–8) and on one occasion CWP members prosecuted a supermarket in court for bad trade practices (Vassel, 1988b: 2).

By this time, however, widespread disillusionment had set in as a result of the social deprivation and escalating crime. In October 1980 the Jamaica Labour Party (JLP) won the election ushering in a new phase in Jamaican economy and polity.

Trinidad and Tobago – women against free trade zones

As noted earlier, structural adjustment policies were introduced in Trinidad and Tobago later than in other parts of the region. As a result, the debate on the introduction of export processing, or free trade zones (EPZs/FTZs), began only in 1988. However, the earlier Jamaican experience with the IMF and structural adjustment policies in general, and with EPZs in particular, was instructive for the region's women's organizations.

In 1988 the group, Women Working for Social Progress (known as Workingwomen), marked International Women's Day with a two-part Women's Consultation on the Economy. The consultation sought to examine the consequences on women of the prevailing economic policies in Trinidad and Tobago and to discuss some alternative strategies for development. The opening address by Linette Vassel, Chairperson of the CWP of Jamaica during the turbulent 1970s, focused on the policy developments of the structural adjustment process in Jamaica – a process which the audience found amazingly familiar.

Participants at this consultation called for a seminar on Export Processing Zones so that women could gain a better understanding of the phenomenon. On 27 May 1988, therefore, a public forum was held entitled 'Employment for Women: The Free Zone Experience'. The event was attended by representatives of a range of women's organizations including the two main political parties, the ruling National Alliance for Reconstruction (NAR) and the Peoples National Movement (PNM), the trade unions, the Rape Crisis Society and others.

The most significant outcome of this forum was the formation of a working group called Women against Free Trade Zones: Work with Dignity. This Working Group[7] lobbied energetically throughout 1988. They participated in television programmes, wrote articles and letters to newspapers, spoke in communities and organized showings of the film *The Global Assembly Line* throughout the country.

This attack on such a crucial component of government economic policy did not go unnoticed. From very early the National Organization of Women (NOW), the women's arm of the ruling NAR, disassociated itself from any criticism of FTZ policy. In the weeks which followed Working Group members were under constant attack in the press. The height of the campaign was reached in September 1988 when a Korean/American woman anthropologist, Seung-Kyung Kim, visited Trinidad and Tobago at the invitation of the Working Group. Kim had worked in an electronics factory in South Korea between 1986 and 1988 and was able to share first-hand experience of an FTZ and of the 'Korean miracle' with the Trinidad and Tobago public. On the final night of her visit she was barred from speaking; immigration officials had finally located a loophole through which to silence her. Although attacks on the Working Group continued, Kim's visit made a lasting impression on women.

In July 1988, legislation enabling the establishment of export-processing zones was tabled in the two houses of Parliament. Members of the Working Group, as well as other women, attended the sessions. Once more these women were attacked by male and female parliamentarians. The Working Group were called 'self-righteous prophetesses', 'women who have never suffered the indignity of being unemployed, underemployed or sexually exploited in the quest to provide a semi-decent existence in one of the lowly but important types of domestic jobs' (*Daily Express*, 12–7–88: 1). A female government minister, whose portfolio included that of the status of women, suggested that the Working Group members were themselves comfortably employed and were no doubt guilty of exploiting their household help (Jones, 1988: 16). One reality was that at least three of the nine group members were unemployed.

The struggle was a particularly difficult one: understandably job creation for poor women was an extremely strong argument. In the end, with more balanced argument in the Senate, the Bill was passed.

The campaign did serve, however, to squarely place on the table the experi-ence of export-processing zones in other countries and to open the issue to a debate which included those of economic alternatives. There were two main gains from this struggle. The first was the general education of the public on this issue. Secondly, and usually forgotten, were the public state-ments wrought from government officials on the implementation of the EPZ policy. Statements for example made during the parliamentary debate that 'All the normal laws of the country would apply in the EPZs, protecting the rights of citizens working there and maintaining the country's sovereignty' (Beau Tewarie, Minister without Portfolio, *Express*, 12–7–88); or that 'Government is making it clear to potential investors in the free trade zones that trade unionism is a fact of life in the country and employees in the zones would be free to join unions of their choice' (Ken Gordon, Minister of Industry, Enterprise and Tourism, *Trinidad Guardian*, 29–6–88: 1).

Although these provisions were not included in the Bill passed, their existence on record can be a basis for action in the future. In the end as concluded by Workingwomen member Marylin Jones,

> the issues was broader than whether or not to establish FTZs. 'We have to look at a multi-faceted agenda that comes with development and growth.' . . . The

national policy had to reflect a willingness to close the gap between rich and poor.

(Express, 29–6–88: 2)

Conclusion

The cases of Jamaica and Trinidad and Tobago discussed above represent two of the largest collective responses of women to the impact of structural adjustment policies in this region. It is interesting to note that the consciousness and experiences of the new women's movement has provided the organizational and philosophical base for such action. On a smaller scale, in other territories, actions have taken place and in 1985, at the WAND/ECLAC Caribbean Celebration to mark the end of the UN Decade for Women, a joint declaration on this issue was made (see Appendix I). The impact of these early struggles and policies reverberate throughout the region and continue to influence the new strategies, approaches and alternatives as the Caribbean Women's Movement itself grows in stature.

Appendix I

Preamble:-

Recognising the efforts made by governments of the region towards the achievement of the goals of the United Nations Decade for Women, this forum makes the following statement:

STATEMENT OF CARIBBEAN WOMEN
BRIDGETOWN, BARBADOS
March 31, 1985

We Caribbean women, based on our day-to-day living experiences, affirm that conventional growth-oriented models of development currently being pursued by some governments of the region cannot lead to the achievement of the goals of the United Nations Decade of 'Equality, Development, and Peace'. These models have led to increasing unemployment and inequalities in our societies. The women of the Caribbean are therefore concerned by the emphasis of spending being directed from the improvement of the quality of life to expenditure on armaments and consumer luxuries.

These developmental models have led to increased social tensions, dislocations and economic disparities which have erupted in violence at domestic, societal, national, regional and international levels. The present world economic crisis has particular effects on women economically, socially, culturally, and politically. As a consequence of the present economic crisis, women are again being expected to take on more of their governments' responsibility for the health, education, and social well-being of the society.

As tensions within the region increase, as unemployment rises, and as more attention is being paid to building military establishments, we call on all governments in the region to seriously reassess their goals and strategies.

The goals of the Decade of 'Equality, Development, and Peace' are inextricably linked. The achievement of any one depends on the achievement of all. In a similar way, the situation of women is a reflection of the forces and circumstances affecting the entire society. These goals in the light of the above, take on added significance.

We believe that women's full and equal participation in all aspects of social, political, and economic power can point a clear path towards people-oriented 'Development Alternatives with Women for a New Era' within the entire region.

The women of the Caribbean, therefore, call on all governments, women's organisations, public and private sector organisations and regional organisations, to incorporate the Plan of Action of this forum into their organisational manifestos, and national and regional development plans.

'CARIBBEAN CELEBRATION'
March 29–31 1985
Marine House
Bridgetown, BARBADOS

Notes

* **Editor's Note:** This paper was originally titled 'Women's Organizations and Movements in the Commonwealth Caribbean in the Context of the World Economic Crisis of the 1980s' and was prepared from the Research Group 'Women's Movements and Visions of the Future' – Development Alternatives with Women for a New Era (DAWN) in June 1989.

1 In 1989 the Grenada branch celebrated its centenary (Rainford, 1988).

2 Janet Jagan, became the President of Guyana in 1997.

3 Formed in 1976 and aligned to the communist Worker's Party of Jamaica.

4 Antigua, Bahamas, Barbados, Jamaica, Guyana, St Kitts/Nevis, St Lucia, Belize, Dominica, Grenada, St Vincent and Cuba.

5 Organizations of Eastern Caribbean States, non-campus territories of the UWI system include: Barbados, Bahamas, Dominica, Grenada, St Lucia/Nevis, St Vincent and the Grenadines.

6 In 1997, one union, the bank and General Workers Union, organised a series of gender workshops for its membership.

7 Throughout the campaign members of the working group represented Workingwomen, Democratic Women's Association, Bank and General Workers

Union, Trinidad and Tobago women's NGO Network and The Caribbean Association for Feminist Research and Action.

References

ANTROBUS, Peggy (1987) 'Gender implications of the debt crisis in the Commonwealth Caribbean: the case of Jamaica' paper presented at the Conference of Caribbean Economists, Kingston, Jamaica, 2–6 July.

BELL, Jeanette (1988) 'The Women and Development Unit (WAND) 1978–1988' paper presented to the WAND 10th Anniversary Consultation, Barbados, 7–11 November.

FRANKLIN, C.B. (1939) *Franklin's Trinidad and Tobago Yearbook, 1939*, Port of Spain: Franklin's Electric Printery.

FRENCH, Joan and FORDSMITH, Honor (1984) 'Women, work and organization in Jamaica, 1900–1944' unpublished manuscript, Institute of Social Studies, The Hague/DGIS Research Project.

GOPEESINGH, Brenda (1988) 'Hindu Women's Organization, Trinidad and Tobago' paper presented to the WAND 10th Anniversary Consultation, Barbados, 7–11 November.

HENDERSON, Thelma (1988) 'The contemporary women's movement in Trinidad and Tobago' in P. MOHAMMED and C. SHEPHERD (1988) editors, *Gender in Caribbean Development*, Women and Development Studies Project, UWI, Mona, Cave Hill and St Augustine.

HENRY, Maxine (1986) 'Women's participation in the social and political process in Jamaica in the 1970s' (mimeo), Department of Government, UWI, Mona, June.

JONES, Marylin (1988) 'Trinidad and Tobago: women against free trade zones' *Cafra News*, Vol. 2, No. 3.

KAUFMAN, Michael (1985) *Jamaica under Manley: Dilemmas of Socialism and Democracy*, London: Zed Books.

MADA WADADA (1988) Presentation to WAND's 10th Anniversary Consultation, Barbados, November.

MIES, Maria (1986) *Patriarchy and Accumulation on a World Scale*, London: Zed Books.

MOHAMMED, Patricia (1989) 'Women's responses in the 70s and 80s in Trinidad: a country report' *Caribbean Quarterly*, Vol. 35, Nos 1&2, March/June.

RAINFORD, Elaine (1988) 'Regional YWCA' paper presented to the WAND 10th Anniversary Consultation, Barbados, 7–11 November.

REDDOCK, Rhoda (1984) 'Women labour and struggle in 20th century Trinidad and Tobago', doctoral dissertation, University of Amsterdam.

—— (1988) 'Caribbean women and the new emancipation of the 1930s: a pyrrhic victory' paper presented to UNESCO/UWI Seminar on *Slavery, Emancipation and the Shaping of Caribbean Society*, UWI, St Augustine, December.

SEN, Gita and CROWN, Caren (1987) *Development, Crisis and Alternative Visions*, New York: Monthly Review Press.

VASSEL, Linnette (1988) 'Organisation of Women for Progress (OWP)' presentation to Wand 10th Anniversary Consultation, Barbados, November.

VON WERLHOF, Claudia (1982) 'The proletarian is dead: long live the house-wife' paper presented at a Joint Seminar on Households and the World Economy, University of Bielefeld, Bielefeld.

Issues of Difference in Contemporary Caribbean Feminism*

Rawwida Baksh-Soodeen

FEMINIST REVIEW NO 59, SUMMER 1998, PP. 74–85

Abstract

This paper interrogates Caribbean feminist theory and activism in relation to the Euro-American experience and to challenges emerging from the Third World discourse. The author argues from the standpoint position that second wave Caribbean feminism has been largely Afro-centric and simultaneously interlocked with processes of independence and national identity struggles. She suggests that there is a need for the movement to reflect the experiences of women of other ethnic groups in the region. In this regard, in Trinidad and Tobago the Indo-Caribbean voice has been emerging and broadening the feminist base. In more recent years also the divisions between feminist and non-feminist groups are subsiding, strengthening the ultimate capacity of this movement for change in the region.

Keywords

Caribbean feminism; race; class standpoint; identity; networking

This paper carries out two main tasks. First, where applicable, it links the issues of difference in Caribbean feminist politics to the Euro-American experience, and in particular those related to race and class. Second, it argues that in the discussion of race and class differences within Caribbean feminism, there is the need to distinguish: (i) the different (objective) reality from the Euro-American experience; (ii) the link between feminism, nationalism, and anti-imperialist struggles in the Caribbean. The latter is similar to the struggles of Third World women internationally (including those located in the First World); and (iii) the ultimately embracing rather than divisive nature of Caribbean feminism. I begin by examining the concept and experience of international feminism in the contemporary period. Then I turn to the Caribbean experience of feminist organizing from the late 1970s to the present, and discuss the movement, its attempts to transform, change and transcend internal differences.

The universal and the particular

The 'second wave' of the feminist movement which began in the USA and Britain in the late 1960s took for granted that 'there was a potentially uni-ficatory point of view on women's issues which would accommodate divergences and not be submerged by them' (Delmar, 1986: 10). Underlying this was the assumption of the universality of women's subordination and its corollary, the possibility of a global sisterhood which could challenge patriarchal power and dominance. The buzz-word 'sisterhood' and its related slogan 'sisterhood is global', actively felt and used in this early period of euphoria, characterized the prevailing consciousness.

In addition Delmar noted that:

> in spite of the success of women's liberation in bringing to the fore and rein-forcing feelings of sympathy and identity between women, political unity (another of the meanings of 'sisterhood') cannot be said to have been achieved. Unity based on identity has turned out to be a very fragile thing.
>
> (Delmar, 1986: 11)

Differences within the Euro-American movement in the 1970s were based on different explanations of women's subordination, and hence different proposed strategies for change. The f(r)actions resulting from this split were liberal feminism, marxist feminism, radical feminism, and socialist femin-ism (Jagger and Rothenberg, 1984, cited in Ollenburger and Moore, 1992: 17). These schools of feminist thought and action emerged at different his-torical points, but, by the 1970s–80s, they co-occurred as different strands of the movement. They also provided the ideological frameworks for analysing the causes of women's oppression within the Euro-American feminist movement. Apart from these four frameworks, race/ethnicity became the key platform for exposing differences in women's lived experi-ences of subordination, resulting in feminists defining themselves as 'black', 'native American', 'Asian', 'women of colour' and so on. It is, however, important to establish that the latter groups were themselves not monolithic in their ideological position on the causes of gender inequality. In her paper, 'Cartographies of Struggle: Third World Women and the Politics of Femin-ism', Chandra Mohanty states that in a collection of writings by black and Third World women in Britain entitled *Charting the Journey* (Grewal *et al.*, 1988), the editors 'are careful to focus on the contradictions, conflicts, and differences among black women, while simultaneously emphasizing that the starting point for all contributors has been "the historical link between us of colonialism and imperialism"' (Mohanty, 1991a: 8).

In *Charting the Journey*, the editors' state:

> This book is about an idea. An idea of 'Blackness' in contemporary Britain. An idea as yet unmatured and inadequately defined, but proceeding along its path

in both 'real' social life and in the collective awareness of many of its subjects. Both as an idea and a process it is, inevitably, contradictory. Contradictory in its conceptualization because its linguistic expression is defined in terms of color, yet it is an idea transcendent of color. Contradictory in its material movements because the unity of action, conscious or otherwise, of Asians, Latin Americans and Arabs, Caribbean and Africans, gives political expression to a common 'color', even as the State-created fissures of ethnicity threaten to engulf and over-whelm us in islands of cultural exclusivity.

(Grewal *et al.*, 1988: 1)

Mohanty links the feminism in the advanced industrialized countries based on race/ethnicity to the emergent Third World feminism. In fact, she geo-graphically re-orients the discussion of Third World feminism to include immigrants and subjected peoples of colour in the North. In summarizing the construction of Third World feminism in the discourse, she arrives at four main commonalities:

1 The idea of the simultaneity of oppression as fundamental to the experi-ence of social and political marginality and the grounding of feminist politics in the histories of racism and imperialism;
2 The crucial role of a hegemonic state in circumscribing Third World women's daily lives and struggle;
3 The significance of memory and writing in the creation of oppositional agency; and,
4 The differences, conflicts, and contradictions internal to Third World women's organizations and communities (1991: 10).

In 'Concepts in Feminist Theory: Consensus and Controversy', a paper presented initially in Trinidad and Tobago at the inaugural seminar in Women's Studies of the University of the West Indies, Amrita Chhachhi (1988: 76–9) attempts to answer the question of whether feminist *theory* is 'white' or 'black'. She argues that feminist theories, like all other social theories, are expressions of two factors: the social, economic, and politi-cal context in which they emerged; and a synthesis of past intellectual tra-ditions. From Chhachhi's point of view, the rejection of all feminist theory as 'western', 'Eurocentric', or 'ethnocentric', results from a failure to dis-tinguish between the application of feminist theories to the historical, political, and socio-cultural specifities of black/Third World women, and the notion of all theory as 'white'. Chhachhi argues that at the level of basic conceptual analytical tools, there is little disagreement among black and white feminists. She suggests:

most often the limitations of Euro-American feminist studies lie at the second and third levels of analysis in that abstract concepts are imposed mechanically and ahistorically and hence become a substitute for an historically specific analysis which takes into account the complexities of social reality.

(Chhachhi, 1988: 79)

The current postmodernism stream within philosophy has had a profound impact on the social sciences, humanities, and feminist theory. Two key concepts developed by the Frankfurt School are 'critical theory' and 'standpoint epistemology', both of which have influenced feminist politics. Critical theory challenged the use of the scientific method for social enquiry, rejecting the idea that there can be 'objective' knowledge altogether. Standpoint epistemology is the concept that less powerful members (individuals and groups) are potentially capable of a more complete view of social reality than the privileged, precisely because of their disadvantaged position(s). In order to survive, they have a 'double vision', a knowledge or awareness of and sensitivity to both the dominant world view and their own minority perspective (e.g., female, black, and poor) (Nielsen, 1990: 10). Feminist standpoint epistemology(ies) focus on the specificity of women's oppression, linking this to women being able to see the viewpoints of both women, and men (the dominant group), and hence having an understanding that is potentially more complete, deeper, and sensitive than men's (Nielsen, 1990: 24–5).

Critical theory and standpoint epistemologies speak to the notion that there is no single truth, that the location of individuals and groups in the social structure determines their construction/interpretation of truth or reality, and that the oppressed have a more powerful claim to a complete understanding than dominant groups. These concepts have contributed to providing the theoretical space for the challenge to white feminists posed by Third World feminists (whether geographically located in the North or South). And further, they help to explain the present movement of Third World feminism's standpoints of race, class, and nation from the periphery to the centre, the so-called cutting edge of the discourse.

Considerations on race and class

The Caribbean has arguably been the site of the greatest colonial penetration internationally since Europe began its mercantilist expansion in the fifteenth century. In no other region were entire peoples wiped out and artificially replaced by hundreds of thousands of people from other continents for the sole purpose of serving European economic interests. In the contemporary period, European colonialism has been replaced by US imperialism, most starkly seen in Puerto Rico and the US Virgin Islands which are American colonies. But the rest of the Caribbean territories are perceived by the US as its satellites, and are hence the target of aid and trade arrangements. The Caribbean has also been the focus of US military aggression through a protracted war against Cuba, and against Grenada during its period of revolutionary government in 1979–83. It further controls, puppeteers, and destabilizes Caribbean governments to serve its capitalist and geo-political interests. In the most recent period, the Caribbean has also been a willing market for US goods and services, including satellite TV, and television evangelism.

The history of the Caribbean territories as colonies of European imperial powers has been one overshadowed by African slavery. Resulting from this is the present-day demographic landscape in which Africans predominate, except in the Spanish Caribbean and in Trinidad and Tobago, Guyana, and Suriname. The post-colonial discourse, which has emerged since the Independence movement of the late 1960s and 1970s,[1] has attempted to grapple with the experience of colonialism from an anti-imperialist framework, which included the perspectives of race and class. If, in the pre-Independence period, the major impetus was the struggle for nationalism, in the post-Independence period, the key issues have been structured race and class inequalities, their alleviation by state intervention, and the continuing existence of colonial economic and political forces which perpetuate these social structures. In the Caribbean, the post-Independence discourse has been one of reclaiming identity. The reclaimed identity has been predominantly African. Images of 'shipwreck' and 'exile' are common to the literary work of post-Independence writers such as Derek Walcott, Vidia Naipaul, George Lamming, Wilson Harris, and Samuel Selvon. Naipaul has been the only well-known literary voice speaking to the Indo-Caribbean experience of indentureship and exile.

The issue of race

The 'second wave' of the feminist movement in the Caribbean in the 1970s intersected with this post-Independence discourse in interesting ways. Issues of race and class were almost exclusively about the experiences of the 'creole'[2] or black/white/coloured populations of the societies. There was no multicultural framework (despite a sociological theory of 'cultural pluralism' developed by M.G. Smith in the 1960s) within which the specific experiences and interests of non-African women could be viewed or contextualized. In fact, this has only begun happening (specifically in Trinidad and Tobago) since the mid-1980s, and interestingly, it has its roots in the assertion by the Indian population of their distinct racial and cultural identity. I would hence define the dominant discourse within Caribbean feminist politics (theory and practice) as Afro-centric, as opposed to either a Euro-centric or multicultural paradigm.

Caribbean feminist historiography inherited from the post-colonial studies on African slavery such sociological concepts in relation to the African slave woman as 'matrifocality', 'male marginality', 'female-headed household' and so on. In the Caribbean, there is a well-established view of the

African woman as a slave, as a symbol of strength and power holding the family together under slavery. Edith Clarke wrote *My Mother Who Fathered Me*; Lucille Mathurin wrote *Rebel Woman in the British West Indies During Slavery*; Sistren Theatre Collective of Jamaica wrote about Nanny, the Maroon slave who led her people to rebellion against the white planter class. Rhoda Reddock's PhD thesis, 'Women, Labour and Struggle in 20th Century Trinidad and Tobago', presents the African slave woman as worker compared to the European bourgeois ideal of the woman as housewife. The notion of the woman as worker was also true for the Indian woman under the system of indentureship. Hence, the bourgeois house-wife ideal was only practised among the white planter/merchant class during the colonial period, and was adopted by the African and Indian middle classes (although not entirely) in the post-colonial period. Since the dominant discourse within Caribbean feminism is Afro-centric, what this means is that feminist analyses of Caribbean society have tended to focus on the black and coloured populations and 'creole' culture. Hence the lower-class family is always discussed in terms of the female-headed house-hold despite the fact that among Indians (in societies with significant Indian populations), the lower-class family shows forms ranging from the joint Indian family, the three-generation extended family, the nuclear family, to the female-headed household.

Further, feminist organizing has also been largely viewed as the domain of African women, rather than as a space in which women of different racial/cultural identities and experiences interact. Women who have been 'left out' in this process include the remaining indigenous inhabitants, Indian, Chinese, and other groups such as the Indonesians. The experience of the white woman has also been left out, deliberately I think, because the discourse has emerged from the standpoint of people who have been bru-tally enslaved by Europeans. The white woman is hence perceived as belonging to the oppressor race, class, and culture, despite the fact that a few white women have also been part of the feminist movement in Caribbean. Indian women, like myself, who are actively involved in the movement have ourselves come to an analysis of colonialism largely through the Afro-centred discourse developed at the University of the West Indies. It is only during the 1990s that I have personally begun to grapple with the specificity of Indo-Caribbean women's experience. Evidence of this is, however, beginning to emerge, both in the discourse[3] and organi-zationally. In the latter, the Hindu Women's Organization (HWO) was formed in Trinidad and Tobago in the mid-1980s.

The issue of racial difference within the Caribbean feminist movement is, however, distinct from that experienced in the USA and Europe. In the first place, it may be said that the post-colonial Caribbean has a majority

African population who are politically, if not economically, in control. Thus the bitterness of the Afro-American/European feminist struggle is not evident in the Caribbean. Since colonialism both past and present is a major force at work in the Caribbean, Afro-Caribbean women have (in reaction to the sexism of the left political groupings to which they belonged) asserted an autonomous space for struggle, but continue to collaborate with Caribbean men in left political parties, and the labour and NGO movements, particularly on political and economic issues. I think that the possibility of a multi-cultural feminist platform exists because, while African and Indian women, on the one hand, have distinct cultural identities and experiences of oppression, on the other, they share a common experience of plantation slavery and indentureship. In Trinidad and Tobago, for instance, it would be difficult for an Afro-Caribbean feminist to argue that her oppression has been greater than mine, when slavery was abolished in 1838, but indentureship almost a century later in 1917. My father was among the last children to have been brought from India as an indentured labourer in 1912.

The issue of class

There are three main aspects of the 'class issue' within Caribbean feminism, which may be broadly related to its emergence and subsequent development in the 1970s to the present.

The first few women to define themselves as feminists in the 1970s came to their analysis largely through their involvement in nationalist struggles, left political groupings, trade unions, the black power movement, and so on. Although their self-definition as feminist was in reaction to the sexism of the men in these movements, their feminism did not assume the radical form of white feminists in the US and Britain in a similar situation. This can only be explained by the fact that they saw themselves first and foremost as black women living in societies which were in early transition from colonial rule, where race and class were still inextricably linked to the political/economic/social hierarchies, and where black men obviously also belonged to the oppressed group. It needs to be pointed out, however, that these women often belonged to an emerging black (including Indian) educated middle class. They could be defined as 'black socialist feminists', who would have empathized with the writings of Angela Davis, for example, and with the general struggle by black women of the Euro-American feminist movement.

The second aspect of class is apparent in the subsequent development of the movement. Feminist debates in the media, public fora, demonstrations, coincided with the UN Decade for Women and a raised consciousness internationally on 'the issue of women', which led to a new group of women joining the movement. Differences, related to the class status of individual women, became apparent. In Trinidad and Tobago, for example, differing class interests led to the split in 1984 of The Group, a small consciousness-raising group which had included women from the 1970s. On the issue of violence against women, there was general agreement. However, whenever national issues relating to class inequalities arose, there was a decided withdrawal on the part of the new 'middle-class' feminists, who could perhaps be characterized as having a radical feminist approach.

Thirdly, the Caribbean feminist movement is argued (by its detractors) to be comprised mainly of articulate, well-educated, middle-class, urban women. This suggests, among other things, a static European concept of class as a status ascribed at birth, and hence which governs and makes possible (or not possible) certain opportunities and experiences. This notion of class does not speak to the often very rapid social mobility which was typical of some Caribbean societies in the post-Independence period. In a single generation, it has been possible for many women to move out of their class of birth through education. Marriage has not been as important an agent of social mobility for women in a post-colonial context where the majority of the population belonged to the working classes, or where, among the African working-class population, the female-headed household model predominates. If I may use my own experience as a concrete example, I have moved from the indentureship of my father to post-doctoral education in a single generation. So while it may be argued that my current status is middle class, this says nothing of my personal history of poverty, of being defined and defining myself as a lower-class woman and, further, it says nothing of the contradictions I faced both in the (objective) opposing polarities of the different classes which I encountered (in the education system for example), but also of my own contradictions and ambivalence. Finally, in relation to my experiences, it says nothing of the political, social, and cultural choices I have made and continue to make.

There are varying dynamics regarding class within the Caribbean feminist movement. Cecilia Babb, a Rastafari woman from Dominica who lives in Barbados, whose class position would be very hard to define and who also defines herself as a lower-class woman, said at a CAFRA meeting in 1990 that for 'grass roots' women, the issue is survival, that of putting food on the table for their children, often in situations where they are the sole breadwinners. And that, 'until this survival is managed it is very difficult for grass roots women to engage in theoretical debate, mobilization, lobbying and group demonstrations, on issues which impact on the very survival we are trying so hard to ensure' (1991: 9).

I conclude this section by pointing out two more factors which account for the specificity of Caribbean feminist politics.

The first is the issue of scale. Caribbean countries are usually small island states (except for Belize, Guyana, Suriname, and French Guiana), with relatively small populations ranging from a couple of hundred thousand to a few million. At its peak, the Caribbean feminist movement has never included more than a few hundred self-defined feminists. The impact of small groups of women in these societies has to be understood in the context of the size of the societies; the groups' outreach through the media and public fora; their coincidence with the international feminist movement and the UN Decade for Women; and the presence of organizations and institutions with regional outreach such as the Women and Development Unit (WAND) in Barbados, and the Caribbean Association for Feminist Research and Action (CAFRA).

The second factor is related to the transition which is observable within Caribbean feminist organizations from the early period of the 1970s and mid-1980s to the late 1980s–1990s. In the 1970s to mid-1980s, the self-defined feminists tended to see themselves as distinct from institutionalized women's organizations, which they perceived as traditional, as serving to maintain the status quo regarding women's place in the society through welfare-oriented outreach. These organizations included the Business and Professional Women's Clubs, the Soroptomists, the Lionesses and the Mothers' Unions of churches. The current period of the 1980s–1990s has, however, seen the active building of bridges across this divide and also linking with the Gender and Development Studies Centres at the university campuses, and women's machineries in the various governments of the region, and inter-governmental institutions such as the Caribbean Community (CARICOM), UNIFEM and UN/ECLAC. This networking is related, on the one hand, to the increased awareness of feminist concerns by the traditional women's organizations and, on the other hand, to a general shift away from ideological dogmatism on the part of self-avowed feminists.

Conclusion

It is possible to identify a number of unique features based on the Caribbean's experience of feminist organizing. First, Caribbean feminist politics may be located at the intersection between two separate discourses. The one is the post-Independence discourse which has been grappling with the past and present experiences of colonialism and neo-colonialism, from an anti-imperialist framework which includes the perspectives of race and class; and the other is the feminist discourse(s) which originate(d) internationally. The dominant stream within Caribbean feminism may be said to make the connection between race, class, and nation in its theorizing, its vision for change, and its practice. Second, however, is the fact that the Caribbean post-Independence and feminist discourses gave pre-eminence to the historical experiences and present-day situation of African-Caribbean people, leading to an Afro-centric rather than a multicultural paradigm. I contend that this is an area requiring discussion and action in the future. Third is the tendency towards networking and coalition-building, between (i) feminist, 'traditional' women's organizations, women's machineries in the various governments of the region, women's studies groups/programmes in the universities, and inter-governmental organisations; and (ii) the feminist movement and the left political parties, the labour movement, and the NGO movement.

This latter aspect of Caribbean feminism is ultimately embracing rather than divisive. It is, in my view, a product of factors such as Caribbean peoples' collective resistance to colonial forces past and present, the creation of a culture of sharing/caring in the face of scarce resources and deprivation evident in Caribbean family/household forms; economic institutions such as the 'su-su', the 'gayap';[4] strategies for childcare and care of the sick and elderly in societies when most women have always been workers inside and outside of the home.

Notes

* The views expressed in this essay are my personal perspectives and analysis and not necessarily those of the Commonwealth Secretariat, the organization in which I am now employed.

1 I include here the academic disciplines of history, sociology, politics, government, literature, and linguistics; artistic expression such as novels, poetry, plays, painting, theatre, music (including the steelband and calypso which are indiginous forms), dance, and Carnival; and journalism through the media of radio, print, and television.

2 'Creole' society and culture was first defined by M.G. Smith as follows:

The creole complex has its historical base in slavery, plantation systems and colonialism. Its cultural composition mirrors its racial mixture. European and African elements predominate in fairly standard combinations and relationships. The ideal forms of institutional life such as government, religion, family and kinship, law, property, education, economy and language are of European derivation; in consequence, differing metropolitan affiliations produce differing versions of creole culture. But in their creole contexts, these institutional forms diverge from their metropolitan models in greater or lesser degree to fit local conditions.

(Smith, 1965: 5)

3 The history and different struggles of Indo-Caribbean women of Trinidad have been substantively researched by Rhoda Reddock in *Women, Labour and Politics in Trinidad and Tobago* (Ian Randle Publishers, Jamaica, 1994) and by Patricia Mohammed in *Gender Negotiations Among Indians in Trinidad 1917–1947* (forthcoming 1999).

4 The 'su-su' is a group practice of pooling money over a specified period, the sum of which is given to each donor in turn; it is a mutual saving system. The word and the concept are thought to originate from the Yoruba 'susu' (Hancock, 1980: 82; Warner-Lewis, 1991: 31; cited in Baksh-Soodeen, 1995: 155). The 'gayap' is defined as 'co-operative group labour given by neighbours and friends in some private undertaking such as farming or house-building, in return for food and drink'. The word has a possible multiple etymology, originating either from the form 'gayap' from the Amerindian language, Cumanagotan (Winer and Aguilar, 1991: 182), or from the Wolof form 'gaa nyep' meaning 'all the people; a collective' (Warner-Lewis, 1991: 169, cited in Baksh-Soodeen, 1995: 167). While these two words are specific to Trinidadian usage, other words signifying the same activities and concepts are to be found throughout the Caribbean.

References

BABB, Cecilia (1991) 'Empowering Grass Roots Women' *CAFRA News*, Vol. 5, No. 1: pp. 8–10.

BAKSH-SOODEEN, Rawwida (1995) 'A Historical Perspective on the Lexicon of Trinidadian English', Ph.D. Dissertation, St. Augustine, Trinidad and Tobago: University of the West Indies.

CHHACHHI, Amrita (1988) 'Concepts in Feminist Theory: Consensus and Controversy' in Mohammed and Shepherd (1976), pp. 76–96.

CLARKE, Edith (1957) *My Mother Who Fathered Me*, London: George Allen and Unwin.

DELMAR, Rosalind (1986) 'What is Feminism?' in Mitchell and Oakley (1986), pp. 8–33.

GREWAL, Shabnam, KAY, Jackie, LANDOR, Liliane, LEWIS, Gail, and PARMAR, Pratibha (1988) editors, *Charting the Journey: Writings by Black and Third World Women*, London: Sheba Feminist Publishers.

MATHURIN, Lucille (1975) *Rebel Woman in the British West Indies During Slavery*, Kingston: Institute of Jamaica.

MITCHELL, Juliet and OAKLEY, Ann (1986) editors, *What is Feminism?* London: Basil Blackwell.

MOHAMMED, Patricia (1999) (forthcoming) *Gender Negotiations Among Indians in Trinidad, 1917–1947*, London: Macmillan.

MOHAMMED, Patricia and SHEPHERD, Catherine (1988) editors, *Gender in Caribbean Development*, Mona, Jamaica: University of the West Indies Women and Development Studies Project.

MOHANTY, Chandra (1991a) 'Cartographies of Struggle: Third World Women and the Politics of Feminism' in Mohanty *et al.* (1991): pp. 1–47.

MOHANTY, Chandra *et al.* (1991b) editors, *Third World Women and the Politics of Feminism*, Bloomington: Indiana University Press.

NIELSEN, Joyce McCarl (1990) 'Introduction' in *Feminist Research Methods: Exemplary Readings in the Social Sciences*, Boulder: Westview Press, pp. 1–41.

OLLENBURGER, Jane and MOORE, Helen (1992) *A Sociology of Women: The Intersection of Patriarchy, Capitalism, and Colonization*, New Jersey: Prentice-Hall.

REDDOCK, Rhoda (1984) 'Women, Labour and Struggle in 20th Century Trinidad and Tobago: 1898–1960, Ph.D. Dissertation, The Netherlands: University of Amsterdam.

—— (1994) *Women, Labour and Politics in Trinidad and Tobago*, Jamaica: Ian Randle Publishers.

SMITH, M.G. (1965) *The Plural Society in the British West Indies*, Berkeley: University of California Press.

WARNER-LEWIS, Maureen (1991) *Guinea's Other Suns: The African Dynamic in Trinidad Culture*, Dover, Massachusetts: The Majority Press.

WINER, Lise and AGUILAR, E.L. (1991) 'Spanish Influence on the Lexicon of Trinidad English Creole' *New West Indian Guide*, Vol. 65, No. 3: pp. 153–91.

In Search of Our Memory:
Gender in the Netherlands Antilles*

Sonia Magdalena Cuales

FEMINIST REVIEW NO 59, SUMMER 1998, PP. 86–100

Abstract

The history of class, race and gender relations is largely under researched for the island territories of Curaçao, Bonaire, St Eustatius, Saba and St Maarten, the group of islands which comprise the Netherlands-Antilles. While there are archival sources which can depict some of this history, much of it remains submerged in our memories due to our self-imposed silences on these social issues. In this paper I extract some of this memory together with fragments of research already carried out, statistical evidence available, and some of the struggles which the feminist movement has waged in regard to oppressive legislation which discriminated against women, to provide a glimpse of this postcolonial variation which also constitutes part of the Caribbean.

Keywords

women's organizations; female headed households; Netherlands-Antilles; legislation; migration; discrimination

Introduction

The Netherlands-Antilles have a distinct character within the region. They are not always viewed as part of the Caribbean, possibly because of the long-standing links with Holland. The islands and peoples are considered Dutch in appearance, behaviour and thinking, although we see ourselves as Antillean and Caribbean. If we are more Dutch than we acknowledge, it is not surprising: over three hundred years of such close association with Holland would make anyone a captive. But a captive plant grown from another seed, from another culture, escapes at times, and in these moments of escape its roots unfold. Our gender relations have grown and developed on Caribbean soil, even though the history of our settlement and governance has been affected by many other cultures. In this paper I retrieve aspects of the society which are evolving as Antillean. The paper paints a picture of the woman of the Netherlands-Antilles and attempts to explore the gender[1] relations of the society. The term 'Antillean women' refers to the women of the Netherlands-Antilles. This area comprises five islands scattered across the Caribbean Sea: Bonaire, Curaçao, Saba, St Eustatius and St Maarten. There are some references to Aruba and Suriname, because of the historic ties and the resulting loyalty and closeness that exist among the present and former Dutch Colonies.

In order to put this paper in a general context some basic data on the Netherlands-Antilles is given in Table 1.

Table 1 *Selected demographic data on the Netherlands-Antilles*

Total population 1993	197,069		
Population growth rate 1993		2%	
Age distribution, 1992:			
Below 20 years	63,907	34%	
20–64 years	110,872	59%	
65 years and over	13,310	7%	
Households, 1993 (estimate)	60,082		
Per capita income, 1990 NAf	15,383 (=US$8,226.20)		
	Total	*Men*	*Women*
Population economically active	87,756	48,167	39,589
Employed	74,322	42,339	31,983
Unemployed	13,434	5,828	7,606
Unemployment rate	15.3%	12.0%	19.2%

Source: A Statistical Orientation on the Netherlands-Antilles, Central Statistical Office (CBS), 1994.

As in many Caribbean countries, the unemployment rate of women is higher (19.2 per cent) than that of men (12 per cent). Similar to many countries in the region, girls are performing better than boys at the primary level. In secondary and tertiary institutions, girls are enrolling in greater numbers and are gaining better results.[2]

Our memory as our history

During the past two decades, very little has been done to retrieve Antillean woman's history and record it in books or official publications to make it widely accessible. Nor has the development and history of the women's movement in the Netherlands-Antilles been systematically and analytically documented. Various explanations have been put forward to account for the scarcity of publications on the history of the Antillean woman, whether by male or female Antilleans. Joceline Clemencia, in her introduction to a collection of essays entitled *Mundu Yama Sinta Mira* (The Name of the World is Sit Down and Look) suggests that the people of Curaçao, as in other colonized countries, have been shaped by a culture of silence that manifests itself in a pervasive fear. She argues that when the people of Curaçao do express themselves, they do so in camouflaged ways (Clemencia, 1989: 7).

It has also been suggested that the Netherlands-Antilles possess a very limited capacity to undertake research and publication. There is no indigenous academic tradition and most of those who have had academic training live abroad. The small size of the islands has implications for professionals: either they are said to be overburdened, or, since they are in great demand, they may select more lucrative jobs. Research and publication do not fall into the category of lucrative employment.

There is no major body of work on the subjects of either history or gender relations. The fact is that the few reliable sources of information which do exist are often inaccessible. In addition, the existing publications have generally been written by foreigners. It is within this context that my article seeks to analyse the Antillean women from the vantage point of historical and contemporary gender relations. The dearth of documented sources also propels me to oral history and memory, for our history.

Before the United Nations women's decades, a Curaçao historian, Nolda Kenepa, did a study on the female straw-hat makers at the beginning of the twentieth century. These women produced the famous Panama hats, and it appears that they formed the first workers' organization, which can be considered a forerunner to a trade union. With the help of small studies such as this, we begin to explore some aspects of women's lives of the period. Another study on the free blacks and mulattoes (Klooster, 1994: 106) confirms that black women were engaged in low-income, working-class jobs as washerwomen, seamstresses, weavers and domestic workers as early as the eighteenth century (see Table 2).

Two more recent and important works are worthy of mention. One is the *opus magnum* by Emy Maduro, *Nos a Bai Ulanda* (We went to Holland), in which she records meticulously, from primary sources, the special case of the slave Virginie, who went to Holland (Maduro, 1986). The other is the previously mentioned *Mundu Yama Sinta Mira* (The Name of the World is Sit Down and Look). Here the authors break the silence of the Antilleans, both male and female, by writing their own stories from a feminist perspective (Ansano *et al.*, 1992).

Interestingly, feminists in Curaçao have relied on the oral tradition to

Table 2 *Main occupations of the freed slaves 1729–75*

Men	(n = 500)	%	Women	n = (85)	%
Field Slaves	129	25.8	Washerwomen	15	17.6
Sailors	82	16.4	Seamstresses	12	14.1
Carpenters	47	9.4	Weavers	10	11.8
Fishermen	32	6.4	Vendors	9	10.6
Shoemakers	30	6.0	Field Slaves	8	9.4
Cooks	16	3.2	Domestic Slaves	8	9.4
Musicians	15	3.0	Other	23	21.1
Bakers	15	3.0			
Masons	14	2.8			
Tailors	14	2.8			
Other	106	21.2			

Source: ARA.NWIC 1166 fol. 124, list of slaves belonging to citizens of Curaçao who escaped to Coro and elsewhere. Curaçao, July 7, 1775 in *New West Indian Guide*, Vol. 68, No. 384, 1994, p. 285.
Secondary source: Wim Klooster, 'Curaçao's free blacks and mulattoes in the eighteenth century', p. 285 in the *New West Indian Guide*, Vol. 68, Nos. 3&4, 1994.

videotape interviews with women. Gladys do Rego of the Union of Antillean Women (UMA) produced a video about rape, entitled Mi sa Kon bo ta Sintibu (I Know How You Feel), that has been used extensively for seminars and workshops on sexuality. In the video *Hidden Voices*, Rose Marie Allen and Jeanne Henriquez recorded interviews with four women between the ages of 60 and 80 on their daily lives, including their creative activities. Jeanne Henriquez, with a team of researchers, collected artefacts, photographs and other material on the working lives of women to produce a mobile exhibition. It is a continually expanding exhibition as it improves from comments and contributions from spectators as it travels around.

The construction of gender relations in the Netherlands-Antilles

Gender relations among the different classes and racial groupings are complex in their historical construction in the Netherlands-Antilles as they are elsewhere in the region. The racial question, always a very sensitive aspect of Caribbean life, has been avoided throughout our history, and is still being avoided in the present day. Racial factors have influenced life and reproduction in these islands to such an extent that a few relevant details must be indicated. The following diagram shows the different racial mixtures that have been identified in the islands.

The position of the different groups on the racial continuum of the

The racial continuum in the Netherlands-Antilles

Protestant	Jewish Catholic I	Catholic II
	Latino I	Latino II
White		Black

Netherlands-Antilles depends on the extent of intermarriage that had taken place with people of Latin blood, with the more light skinned mixtures with Latin being placed in a higher social category of the continuum. Mixtures of Latin and black are referred to as mulatto or mestizo.

The particular way in which slavery was experienced in the Antilles has also played its part in constructing gender relations in the Netherlands-Antilles. The Netherlands-Antilles were not part of the plantation mode of production, although they were part of Caribbean plantation society. On these islands there were no plantations. Curaçao was a slave market for the Western hemisphere. Income generating activities took place in the city, and, from time to time, the better-off retired to houses in the countryside, usually built on the top of a hill from which the surrounding space could be controlled. On their country estates, where they reared small stock such as pigs and goats, planted beans, sorghum and fruits, the more affluent ones entertained friends from the city. They employed mainly black slaves to work on the agricultural property and in the family mansions.

The history of trade in the Netherlands-Antilles has determined both the demographic development and the legal structures of the islands. This historical reality has left its mark on social relations, and equally on gender relations. Before the advent of the petroleum industry, the economy of the Antilles was based on trade and business transactions. In Curaçao during the seventeenth and eighteenth centuries, an interesting phenomenon occurred. Towards the end of the seventeenth century, this society was rapidly developing as a centre for commercial exchanges between the coastal area of what is now Venezuela and the rest of the region. This development was based primarily on the island's slave market: the commodity that was being bought and sold was labour – negroes from the West Coast of Africa and from Angola. Merchandise which was not sold remained in Curaçao where they were used for the trading company's work, or in other businesses on the island. The slaves were able to go out to work as artisans or sailors. With the persistence of the slave trade, negroes came to account for the majority of the island's population, although whites continued to be the dominant social group.

A particular social and racial mix was forged as well as a distinct set of gender relations. Black people inspired either fear or indifference in the white minority. Even so, in Curaçao there were many more manumissions (letters granting freedom), and in this way the metissage grew more rapidly than in the other countries in the region. Therefore a large group of non-whites was formed whose artisan skills and commercial astuteness enabled them to compete with the less prosperous white business people. Their assertiveness alarmed the whites. White men had unions with mulatto women, but their relationships always reflected a combination of fear and indifference.

Sexuality

Primarily to preserve distance from other groups and classes, there were intra-familial sexual relations, sometimes incestuous, among the Catholic middle-class segment of the population. The men, who had children with two or more sisters, cousins, neighbours and, perhaps also with the servants, continued to be spoiled, adored and granted privileges by all the women in the family.[3] Among members of the middle class, dances were organized in private homes or in Catholic clubs, so that young men and women could meet regularly to converse and court. In the wealthy commercial Jewish community and the Protestant community, where top public officials were to be found – both groups considered white – undoubtedly gender relations were informed largely by religious tradition.

Migration, slavery and gender relations: the case of Virginie

The first waves of migration carried mostly young men to be educated in Holland. However, historical records offer ample proof that ever since slavery, and even more so during the period of manumission, both slaves and freed slaves went to Europe, accompanying the families for whom they worked as domestic servants.

Historian-sociologist Emy Maduro highlights the case of Virginie, a slave born in Curaçao who waged an intense struggle for her freedom. Virginie argued that once she had stepped on Dutch soil while travelling as a servant with her mistress, she was entitled to her freedom. Virginie took her campaign to the highest levels and included her children, who had accompanied her, in the same petition. Her mistress was the daughter of Baron van Raders, the ex-Governor of Suriname. The case was complicated by factors such as the abolition of the slave trade, bilateral treaties on the trade, and personal and political interests. The treaty between Holland and England placed certain restrictions on Antilleans who had slaves and who wanted to transport them to another country. At one stage it became illegal to transport slaves from one colony to another. Likewise,

FEMINIST REVIEW NO 59, SUMMER 1998

slaves could only remain in the country to which the owner had taken them for a limited period of time.

When it was time for Virginie to be returned from Europe back to Curaçao, she was sent to Suriname, because no ships were scheduled to leave for Curaçao. In Suriname, Virginie presented her petition to the highest authorities. Baron van Raders launched a tenacious administrative and legal battle to ensure that Virginie was not granted her freedom. He also claimed that Virginie was too lazy and insolent to deserve her freedom (Maduro, 1986).

The interesting and perhaps unique case of Virginie shows the fighting spirit of this woman even under such inhuman circumstances, and her determination to realize her aspirations for her freedom and that of her children.

The social relations of work

The slave or ex-slave/servant who provided personal services to the mistress of the house, to the daughter, or to any other member of the family, held a key position in the household. This woman may well have been a blood relative of that family. This black *aya*, or *yaya* in Papiamento,[4] was totally responsible for raising the children (Römer, 1987). In a country where there were no real plantations, and the slaves lived and worked in the home of the owner, as *yaya*, cook, housekeeper, coachman or gardener; the interaction between blacks and whites, including boys and girls, men and women, was very close. The y*aya* had an important role to play in gender socialization. Accepted by everyone in the society, these social relations delineated through work had an impact on the overall construction of gender in Antillean society as a whole.

In analysing the complexity of such relations one must take into consideration the differences within the privileged class, comprising the Sephardic Jewish community, the white Protestants, white Catholics and, finally, the mestizos. In the course of the socio-economic history of the different groups within the islands, social structures and the power bases have also undergone change and have become more intricate.

There are many mestizo descendants of Jews and negroes (*sic*), as well as some descendants of negroes and Latinos from the South American coast or Europe. In some cases, class cuts across racial intermarriage. It is also important to consider the erosion of the old power bases and the emergence of a racial and class grouping that, before their access to education, had few opportunities for social mobility. The expanded access to higher education in the 1950s, followed by greater political and administrative participation, allowed the development of new power bases.

Social relations are characterized by an exploitative paternalism, which may be either subtle or open. Perhaps the most overt paternalism is found among a social group that operates small private businesses, the Azkenazi Jews. This group did not seek to conceal the ways in which they exploited black people, the largest yet most disadvantaged group in the country in the twentieth century. They completely misunderstood the cultural values of poor, black people, treating them with contempt and disrespect. Black and mulatto women suffered the most terrible treatment. Although there have been changes in modern society, many women continue to suffer as a sex, although this must be differentiated by race and class.

The Antillean family

Due to the intrinsic relationship between the family, sexuality and gender relations in the society, it is crucial that we understand the nature of the family in Antillean society. Although the concept of the family is defined in different ways in different societies and in different historical periods, it always refers to a social space in which both the private and public spheres intersect. Thus it fulfils productive and reproductive functions, economic, political, social, cultural and leisure functions. The family exists within a context of global and national changes to which it responds. While taking into account class differences, it has to be acknowledged that, in general, the nuclear family model has never been either popular or predominant in any social class. If it existed *de jure*, it was certainly never there *de facto*.

I have mentioned some instances of gender relations which are peculiar to the middle and upper classes, and differ according to racial grouping. In terms of the popular classes, Hoetink describes man as a migratory being, who maintains sexual relations with a number of women, leaving a son here and another there, and continuing calmly on his way (Hoetink, 1958). Numerous single mothers are the results of these relationships, a phenomenon which today astonishes and disturbs many. Even though in the contemporary period the woman may have some social space for her own escapades, the man has many more for his, and his have been accepted to a far greater degree. What emerges is a distribution of family typologies which includes a legitimate category defined by the statistical records as female headed households. In 1991, of the total 2,889 households recorded for the island of Bonaire, 27 per cent were described as female headed households. In Curaçao, of the 41,279 households, 36 per cent were female headed, and in St Maarten, of 12,164 households, 31 per cent were female headed.[5]

In general, single mothers are heads of households. However, Antillean households are headed by a woman not simply because the man has abandoned the family. The woman may opt to raise a family on her own, or the female headed home is often the result of migration. Some studies suggest that women choose this situation because of their experiences with irresponsible partners. In many cases as well, the female headed household will contain single adult males, who may have women and children in other homes while, generally, continuing to live in their mother's house. Some research, for example the work of Gladys Do Rego (1990), predicts a significant increase in the number of female headed households in future. It is not surprising to find that female headed households are a recurring phenomenon. It must also be understood that the relations of gender with regard to female headed households may not be pertinent to her emotional or sexual life, but to the material conditions of life. The laws and social services have not been designed to consider the single mother or female household head as the norm, but rather as the exception.

Overcoming the subordination of women

A significant factor maintaining women's subordination in Antillean society was women's legal status. For example, women's legal status as a minor meant that women could not sign contracts, transfer goods, or have access to loans without the consent of their partners. Following the end of the turbulent 1960s in the Netherlands-Antilles, by the 1970s the government began to show concern about women's subordination. A number of legal and social mechanisms were reviewed, including inequalities in the salaries of married men and women.

Social services were always open to political manipulation. One example in Curaçao is the peculiar approach to administering low-income housing. Before a housing foundation was set up,[6] single mothers were not eligible for a house unless they had a guarantor who signed on their behalf. The requirements for this signatory implied that he had to be a man possessing adequate economic resources. A determined struggle by twenty-four mothers culminated in the removal of this requirement. They also succeeded in partly de-politicizing the procedures for distributing low-income housing projects. In 1978 the process of de-politicizing housing policies was accelerated.

Discriminatory practices towards married and unmarried women

A discriminatory law, which was abolished in 1983, concerned female public employees. It dealt with their appointment and their civil status. Clause 6.3 of this law stipulated that a married woman could not be given a permanent civil service appointment. Her temporary appointment to the civil service was possible only in cases where there were no men or unmarried women to fill the post. Under the same law as well, a woman had to leave the civil service when she got married, or began to live with a male companion. Due to laws such as this, women had far more limited career opportunities in the public service than had men.

Differences between married and unmarried female public servants were legislated such that married women received 25 per cent less salary than either her male or unmarried counterpart. This inequality created tensions among various sectors in society and led to a constant paralysis of the education service due to massive strikes dating back to the early 1980s and prolonged unrest in the trade unions. The Union of Educational Workers waged a concerted campaign from the start of 1990. The process lasted until 1994, when the Supreme Court passed a law which brought about equal pay for all female public servants, whether married or unmarried. These changes were significant, since they signalled an environment willing to bend, and new attitudes towards gender relations in the country.

Meanwhile, the government, in an attempt to avoid a loss of revenue, formulated a new taxation scheme, that, both in principle and in practice, reintroduced gender discrimination as regards unmarried women. A large percentage of the female population are single mothers with children and heads of households who have to pay higher taxes than married women. This has yet to be dealt with by the feminist movement. Although it is clear that significant legal advances have been made in some cases with major struggles, in others there were necessary changes due to global developments in the status of women. Nonetheless, while, as in other countries, passing legislation is much easier to achieve than previously, putting such legislation into operation is another matter. Inevitably, there is usually a long delay between one stage and the next.

The kind of legislation and regulations existing as illustrated above, until recently, have led to the unfortunate situation of a very limited female representation in leadership posts and in public service managerial positions at the national level. In the middle to high level posts in public administration as at April 1995, there are 19 women to 122 men (Kompas, 1995). At the same time, however, in terms of political participation, the Netherlands-Antilles do not measure up badly against other countries in the region. The first time that two women won seats in the Netherlands-Antilles Parliament was in 1949, shortly after the introduction of universal suffrage. The country has boasted a woman as Prime Minister for almost ten years, and, between 1985 and 1995, has had four female parliamentarians, six female members of the Island Council, three female ministers, and six female Deputies. The Prime Minister came out of the ranks of the

Women's Movement, as did some of the others. It is also interesting to note that the women who occupy positions of political power have generally been young. The gender distribution of political/administrative leadership for 1995 is shown in Table 3. Although there is still a long way to go, women are now occupying posts in areas where previously they were not represented at all.

Table 3 *Select positions in the political and administrative system of the Nether-lands-Antilles held by men and women in April 1995*

Position	Women	Men	Total
Minister	1	7	8
Vice-Minister	1	2	3
Deputy	1	8	9
Acting Governor	1	4	5
Lieutenant-Governor	1	0	1
Political Leader	1	6	7
Party Chairperson	1	6	7
Government Spokesperson	1	0	1
Head of Department	5	36	41

Source: Data compiled by author, with the assistance of Aimee Kleimmoedig, April 1995.

Similarly, data for Aruba show that out of a total of 21 seats in the Aruban Parliament, over the period 1986 to 1993, women held one or two seats, and increased to three seats in the year 1993–4 (National Report of Aruba, 1994).

The women's movement

As in most Caribbean countries, the women's movement which provided the initial impetus towards overcoming the structural forms of subordi-nation of women, was preceded by another type of women's organization: clubs and women's meetings. The challenges, campaigns and achievements of the women's movement in the 1970s, 1980s and in the current period cannot be analysed without taking into account the existence of a tradition of women's meetings. This tradition has its own history.

Women pooled resources to organize activities with specific objectives, and in this way the women's organizations were formed. These organizations could be found at various social levels, and they provided women with an opportunity to develop their spiritual life, artistic creativity, cultural expression, co-operation, and solidarity with the community. The organiz-ations offered a refuge where women found understanding, affection, and support. Some of them also reinforced paternalism. In most cases, the spiritual base of these groups was the Catholic Church.

Some of the women's organizations of the 1950s and 1960s survived and coexisted in the 1970s and 1980s with the new groupings, including the feminist organizations which were then emerging. During this period, the number of organizations increased greatly. On the island of Curaçao, there were some seventy groups. In 1974, co-ordinating committees were set up in all the islands to co-ordinate activities for the International Women's Year in 1975. Three have survived to the present time. At the island level, the co-ordinating committees are members of the Island Advisory Council for Women's Affairs.

In the same year, the Union of Antillean Women (UMA) was formed, the first organization with a clearly feminist vision and perspective. UMA fought against discrimination and subordination of women and worked dynamically to bring about structural changes in Antillean society. In addition to the tradition of organizing and the spirit of accomplishing goals, various traditional groups also continued some of the archaic rules. One of these stipulates that the membership should consist only of married women, obviously still influenced by the Church. In most cases, single women, excluded from participating, are the ones who suffer more discrimination in society. Despite this rule, most women's organizations draw their membership from the working class. Even if these women are married, invariably their mothers were not.

The First Decade for Women (1976–85) enabled women's groups to develop a common objective. Notwithstanding the diversity of their interests, the more these groups combined their efforts, the more they realized that there was a common struggle against the insubordination of women, and that there was a single objective: to forge gender equality. Since that time, unfortunately, the social, economic and class contradictions among women have continued to divide various groups.

In 1980, the Women's Centre (SEDA) was established. Its primary purpose is that of human resource development and training. SEDA seeks to serve men and women at the individual level, or in their capacity as members of organizations. Its priority is to prepare women for self-reliance and self-defence. To this end, symposia, workshops, study and training seminars are organized at the organization's headquarters and in community centres. Recently, the organization has been actively involved in programmes, including legal action, concerning the incidence of violence against women and on the issue of sexual harassment. SEDA's work has been positively received in the communities, and recognized in governmental and non-governmental quarters.

FEMINIST REVIEW NO 59, SUMMER 1998

In July 1987, Informashon, Formashon i Edukashon di Seksualidat i Embaraso (INFESE) began as a research and education project on sexuality. In 1994 INFESE began offering programmes and services to young people and fathers-to-be on matters of sexuality, pregnancy and birth. The significance of this process of research and action lies in its feminist conceptualization of sexuality, reproductive health and reproductive rights. The process has not been easy, and would not have been institutionalized without vigorous feminist struggles. The impact of INFESE has been growing on many levels and in many directions.

Conclusion

The women's movement in the Antillean islands, and its feminist components, have influenced the direction and the pace of the advance made by Antillean women. The residual effects of the history of slavery, and continued migration in and out of the region, however, is still evident in the complexity of social and gender relations which exist today. A careful and systematic analysis needs to be carried out on the Netherlands-Antilles as much of this history remains hidden in our archives and our memory.

The most important achievements during the last two decades have been legal advances. Some of these have taken a long time, and in some cases, have yet to come into effect. The greatest victory in the future would be genuine respect for women as individuals and as a social group, on all levels, irrespective of social class or racial grouping. Perhaps at that point, one can start to build a society free of oppressive disequilibria.

Notes

* A version of this paper has been published in Spanish in the journal *Caribbean Studies* (Vol. 28, No. 1 (1995): 101–27) published by the Instituto de Estudios del Caribe, Facultad de Ciencas Sociales, Universidad de Puerto Rico, Recinto de Rio Piedras. The translation of the original paper was made by Jessica Byron.

1 My use of gender is derived from the ideas developed by a group of feminist academics based at the Institute of Development Studies of the University of Sussex, in England in 1978. The leader of the Sussex group, Ann Whitehead, offered a definition of the concept in an IDS seminar, in which she based her terminology on the collective debates of her colleagues. The approach studies men and women, and more specifically the relations between them. Likewise, sex is considered to be a biological term, while the category of gender is thought to be more appropriate for the Social Sciences, since it refers to the structures that evolve in the course of the history of social relations and interactions. The

concept was applied, refined and debated in the seminar on 'Social Production in the Caribbean', which took place in Rio Piedras, Puerto Rico in 1980, with widespread participation from women in the sub-region. I was one of the participants at this seminar.

2 Evidence gleaned from statistical information for the Netherlands Antilles, 1994; Belize, 1990; Jamaica, 1994; the British Virgin Islands, 1990; and Trinidad and Tobago, 1994.

3 In the eyes of the public, i.e. as far as the town gossips were concerned, many of these families lived in total harmony, and the care and mutual affection shown endured into the final stage of sharing the afflictions and difficulties of old age.

4 'Papiamento or papiamentu is the Spanish and Portuguese based creole language with a dominant Dutch vocabulary which is spoken and written in the Netherland Antillean islands of Aruba, Curacao, and Bonaire'. Richard Allsop, 1996, *A Dictionary of Caribbean English Usage*, Oxford University Press: New York.

5 Compiled from data in the National NGO Report on the Netherlands Antilles, Curacao, June, 1994.

6 In Papiamento, 'Fundashon Kas Popular' (FKP), 1978.

References

ALLEN, Rose Marie and HENRIQUEZ, Jeanne (1992) *Hidden Voices* (Voces Escondidas) Video, Curacao.

ALLSOP, Richard (1996) *A Dictionary of Caribbean English Usage*, New York: Oxford University Press.

ANSANO, Richenel, CLEMENCIA, Joceline, COOK, Jeanette and MARTIS, Eithel (1992) editors, *Mundu Yama Sinta Mira-Womanhood in Curaçao*, Curaçao.

CENTRAAL BUREAU VOOR DE STATISTIEK (CBS) (1993) *Census 1992, Third Population and Housing Census Netherlands-Antilles*, Curaçao: CBS.

CLEMENCIA, Joceline (1989) 'Het grote camouflagespel van de OPI' in *Thematische Benadering van de Poezie van Elis Juliana*, Leiden.

DO REGO-KUSTER, Gladys (1990) 'Het Afro-Caribisch Gezinsweb en de Emancipatie van de Vrouw' in *De Gids*, jrg. 153, No. 7/8, July–August, pp. 542–47.

HOETINK, Harry (1958) 'Het Patroon van de Oude Curaçaose Samenleving een Sociologische Studie', Assen.

—— (1973) *Slavery and Race Relations in the Americas, an Enquiry into their Nature and Nexus*, New York.

KARNER, Frances P. (1969) *The Sephardics of Curaçao*, Assen.

KLOOSTER, Wim (1994) 'Curaçao's free blacks and mulattoes in the eighteenth century' *New West Indian Guide* Vol. 68, No. 3&4: 283–300.

LIER, Rudolf van (1986) 'Tropische Tribaden' in *Verhandeling over homoseksualiteit en homosexele vrouwen in Suriname*, Dordrecht, Holland.

LUITEN, W.A. (1980) 'Antilliaanse Staats' in *Administratiefreshtelijke Regekingen*, No. X, Universiteit van de Nederlandse Antillen, Willemstad.

FEMINIST REVIEW NO 59, SUMMER 1998

MADURO, Emy (1986) 'Nos a Bai Ulanda' in *In het Land van de Overheerser, deel II Antillianen en Surinamers in Nederland 1634/1667–1954*, Dordrecht, pp. 135–225.

MCLEOD, Cynthia (1987) *Hoe Duur was de Suiker*, Paramaribo.

NATIONAL REPORT OF ARUBA 1994 (1995) in preparation for the Fourth World Conference on Women, to be held in Beijing (unedited/unpublished mimeo).

NATIONAL REPORT NGOs NETHERLANDS ANTILLES 1994 (1995) in preparation for the Fourth World Conference on Women, to be held in Beijing (unedited/unpublished mimeo).

PAULA, A.F. (1993) 'Vrijie Slaven' in *Sociaal-historische studie over de dualistische slaven emancipatie op Nederlands Sint Maarten*, Zutphen.

RÖMER, Rene A. (1987) *La Sociedad Curazolena; (una interpretacion sociologica)*, Caracas.

VEEN, Annemiek van der (1984) 'Hoedenvlechten als Kostwinning' in *Onderzoek naar de invloed van hoedenvlechterij op de sociaal-economische positie van vrouwen op Curaçao en Bonaire in de eerste helft van de 20ste eeuw*, Leiden.

Shattering the Illusion of Development:

The Changing Status of Women and Challenges for the Feminist Movement in Puerto Rico

Alice E. Colón-Warren and Idsa Alegría-Ortega

FEMINIST REVIEW NO 59, SUMMER 1998, PP. 101–117

Abstract

In this paper we examine the weaknesses of development strategies which have been applied in Puerto Rico. The process of industrialization by invitation, referred to as Operation Bootstrap, was instituted by the United States of America by the end of the 1940s. This involved tax incentives and subsidies for companies and was dependent on industrial peace and low wages in labor-intensive, low-wage industries, especially those of textile and clothing. Naturally, women's labor was encouraged as a result of the lower cost, as well as assumed dexterity, of the female in such areas. While these new activity areas for women also allowed other benefits in the form of legislation and increased social services, the inherent problems of rapid, labor-intensive industrialization also led to displacement and increased underemployment and impoverization of female headed families from the 1960s onwards. The paper explores some of the changes in gender relations which resulted from these policies and looks at the challenges which the feminist movement in Puerto Rico has made, particularly with regard to state processes to bring about beneficial changes in the economic, legal, political and social status of women in Puerto Rico.

Keywords

development model/strategies; feminism; status of women; reproductive health; state mobilization

In 1998, as we approach a century of United States colonialism in Puerto Rico, it is fitting that in this article we review what this has meant for gender relations and the status of women in the island. Puerto Rico has often been presented as a 'showcase of development' and 'the Shining Star of the Caribbean', having been the 'poorhouse' of the region earlier this century. Puerto Rico was put forward as a model of democracy and industrialization for underdeveloped countries in Latin America and the Caribbean. It was also highlighted, though to a lesser extent, as a model for the transformation of the status of women, women's reproductive roles and the family.

FEMINIST REVIEW NO 59, SUMMER 1998

Now that the weaknesses of these development strategies have become apparent, we need to examine both the openings and limitations which such strategies have offered for more equitable gender relations. While the prevailing political and economic policies may have facilitated women's integration into the formal economy and the public sphere, we contend that this has not been without contradictions nor without women waging their own struggles. Despite these struggles, the changes have not allowed for a 'redefinition of gender relations' nor of the traditional 'division of social functions or of the socially established separation of (public and private) spheres' (Fraser, 1989). Rather, the changes sought to integrate women as lower paid or unpaid workers in the newly evolving national and international division of labor, and to cushion the impact of consequent poverty and social inequity. Gender inequity and inequality were re-created and reinforced by a model of development which was centered neither in the needs of the people nor on equitable social relations (DAWN, 1995).

The experiences of Puerto Rican women foretold in many ways the present day experiences of women in other Caribbean and Latin American countries such as the Dominican Republic. This highlights the need for a gendered analysis of development strategies and their impact on both the public and private dimensions of gender subordination.

Struggles and opportunities: a historical overview

Puerto Rico has pioneered a development model which impacted directly on women in Latin America and the Caribbean, and became known as the early model of contemporary 'maquiladoras' (export processing zones) (Safa, 1995; Tang Nain 1995). A policy of industrialization by invitation, called Operation Bootstrap, was adopted in order to recover from the collapse of agrarian capitalism after the depression. By the end of the 1940s, reforms which included tax incentives and improved infrastructure attracted labor-intensive textile and garment industries seeking to escape higher labor costs in the United States (Dietz,1986; Safa, 1981). While these industries failed to compensate for the loss of jobs in traditional sectors, they did rely on the dexterity and lower cost of female workers. As a result women's employment declined less than that of men (Colón *et al.*, 1988).

The post-war welfare orientation of the State contributed somewhat to the changing status of women. In 1942 new legislation provided for two months maternity leave with half pay (Vicente, 1987) and, in 1952, the Puerto Rican Constitution prohibited discrimination on the basis of sex (Comisión de Derechos Civiles, 1972). From the early 1930s women activists and reformists struggled for maternal and child healthcare, birth control and home economics programs, training and certification of mid-wives, and the right to have access to information on contraception (Ramírez de Arellano and Seipp, 1983; Azize, 1990; Dávila, 1994; Fernós, 1994). By the 1950s the provision of State benefits in education, health and housing contributed to a change in women's traditionally low socio-economic status. Needs related to the domestic sphere were now recog-nized as a public responsibility. The provision of these services for women represented a minimum means of subsistence for their families, and women became less dependent on individual men (Azize, 1990; Safa 1975). Women's economic activity, their right to vote and access to political leadership, along with prevailing social services, all provided models for Latin American and Caribbean countries, and received recognition at Latin American women's fora (*El Mundo* June 1st, 1955 p.14; June 4, 1955 p.9; June 6, 1955 p.15; June 15, 1955 p.9; July 9, 1957, p.23).

Present contradictions: industrial restructuring

The flaws in Operation Bootstrap were already visible by the 1960s. In the new international division of labor, Puerto Rico became less attract-ive for labor-intensive manufacturing: local salaries had increased as a result of migration, workers' struggles intensified, a more educated and productive labor force emerged, and there were pressures from compet-ing industries in the United States. From that time on, Puerto Rico's development strategy was geared to capital intensive and high-tech phar-maceutical and electronic industries and, since the 1970s, Puerto Rico has provided intermediary financial and commercial services to North American corporations (Colón *et al.*, 1988; Dietz and Pantojas-García, 1993).

Puerto Rican women have responded to the increased educational oppor-tunities and job demands for higher qualified females. The numbers of women graduating from college increased from 5 percent of the female population in 1970, to 15 percent in 1990. Women have comprised the majority of college graduates since the 1980s in practically all academic fields, not only in the traditionally female areas (Colón-Warren, 1997).

For less educated men and women, the flight of labor-intensive manu-facturing and the move to a high-tech, financial service economy has reduced employment opportunities. Despite the expansion of corporate and government bureaucracies, and despite women's educational advance-ments, women remain at the lower levels of both administrative and pro-fessional sectors in what may turn out to be a devaluing and gendered differentiation of these occupations. The greatest concentration of women, some 35 percent, continues to be in lower paid clerical and sales jobs, and women are more likely than men to be employed in part-time jobs (Colón-Warren, 1997).

In the 1990 census 30 percent of all families reported no income-earners. With a 35 percent rate of labor force participation and an employment rate of 29 percent for females of 16 years and over, Puerto Rican women are still far below the labor market activity rate of women in most similarly industrialized developed countries (Colón-Warren, 1997). Prolonged economic instability has generated the expansion of a parallel informal economy (Petrovich and Laureano, 1987). This has created a situation of conflict which has been only partially cushioned by massive migration, welfare, and a large government bureaucracy which employs around a third of the labor force, the majority being women (Colón *et al.*, 1988; Colón-Warren, 1997).

The imposition of neoliberal economic and political policies, and the demise of a key tax incentive, have already begun to reduce corporate and government employment levels as well as cuts in social services. Women have been affected more than men. The earlier moderate increase in women's employment rate has thus resulted in their underemployment and lower earnings. The feminization of poverty observed in other countries is becoming visible in Puerto Rico (Burgos and Colberg, 1990) although unemployment and poverty is generalized and not limited to female heads of family.

The curtailment of social and economic opportunities, along with the fragmentation of communities and families, are but some of the factors which have generated an increase in illegal, violent and criminal behavior including drug trafficking. The current decade has recorded the highest rates of violent crimes and deaths in the history of Puerto Rico, a situation which has become the main concern of the population. (For diverse analyses see Pratts (1994).)

Men's power within the family has been challenged not only by women, who are more able to resist subordination as they gain some economic independence, but by the loss of their economic power. The challenge is not necessarily based on the expectation of males being providers, but on a particular man who may be labeled irresponsible. Conflict and unstable relations ensue as men are unable to fulfill expected roles, yet unwilling to relinquish their privileges in the family (Safa, 1995). The increasing divorce rates in Puerto Rico since the 1930s, among the highest in the world by the 1980s, and the increase in female headed families may reflect the economic pressures on intimate relations and consequent unstable gender roles at the individual level, while, at another level, prevailing gender ideologies go unchallenged (Muñoz and Fernández, 1988; Safa, 1995; Momsen, 1993; Bruce *et al.*, 1995). As elsewhere in the Caribbean, the alarming brutality of the increasing violence against women may be another manifestation of men's attempt to retain power under conflicting conditions (Alexander, 1994).

Challenging the view of men as the only providers may offer women some more power in the family. However, given the eroding economic opportunities for both men and women, unless there is a similar challenge to the notion of domestic work and childcare as the responsibility of women, and a challenge to gender discrimination in the labor market, women may be faced with less support from men, as well as an increase in their family responsibilities (Safa, 1995; Fernández-Kelly and Sassen, 1995). Overburdening women with economic and domestic responsibilities increases their dependency and undermines their ability to resist violence.

An environment of violence and conflict is aggravated by a strong military presence. Puerto Rico has had great strategic value for the United States military forces and the island's precarious economy has left it open to such interventions. The manufacturing of military uniforms has partly maintained whatever remains of the garment industry and associated employment of women. Though the military may appear to offer some economic alternatives, the war industry is a drain on Puerto Rico's land and its resources. The underlying military mentality of repression and authoritarianism is enmeshed with all forms of violence, particularly violence against women (Sen and Grown, 1987; Colón *et al.*, 1995).

Population control and reproductive health

Puerto Rico's Operation Bootstrap was the showcase for neomalthusian population control policies which were imposed on Third World countries as part of post-war packages of economic development. At the basis of these policies was the regulation of women's reproductive behavior, not the redefinition of gender relations.

Sterilization was practised with such zeal up to the 1970s that even its proponents admit that procedures were abused. During the 1950s and 1960s, poor Puerto Rican women were pressured to accept sterilization and were also involved in early experiments with the pill, Emko, the IUD and Depo Provera (Ramírez de Arellano and Seipp, 1983). At present, the trend towards invasive medical practices is reflected in Puerto Rico's high rate of caesarean births, among the highest in the world (Vázquez Calzada, 1990). Needless to say, population control programs have been imposed mostly on women, not on men. Priority has been given to rapid, easy, long-term methods of birth control, and to the profitability of pharmaceutical industries, rather than to women's health or their greater control over their bodies.

It is also apparent, however, that openings were provided to meet women's need to control their fertility. This has led to a steady increase in contraceptive usage since the end of the 1930s, up to a rate of 69 percent of sexually active women, according to the latest fertility survey in 1982 (Dávila, 1990; Vázquez Calzada, 1988). Despite reported regrets about sterilization, it is still the most widely used method, used by nearly 40 percent of married women in 1982 (Dávila, 1990; Vázquez Calzada, 1988). Nonetheless, women's reprodictive options are constrained by social and economic conditions.

Since the end of the 1970s, with the move to neoliberal policies of economic privatization and ideologies of the New Right, feminist and other progressive sectors in Puerto Rico have faced the pressures of the anti-abortion movement, which has attempted, without much success, to impose legislative measures limiting legal abortion or prohibiting it outright. At the beginning of the 1990s there were attacks on clinics and harassment of personnel offering abortion services, similar to those that have characterized the anti-abortion movement in the United States (Vicente, 1993; Colón et al., 1996). The attitude of politicians in Puerto Rico has traditionally been to attempt to prevent discussion of the issue on the grounds of it being too controversial, or to look the other way when abortion was illegal but still widely practised. As a result abortion is still legal, although stigmatized, and not offered as a public health service, except in cases of rape or incest (Fernós, 1994; Colón et al., 1996).

Limits in federal funding for birth control and reproductive health services have prevailed from the 1980s, under Republican administrations, to the present Democrat presidency. This has led the Puerto Rican government to take over the increasing costs of health services, but reproductive health has not been a priority. Poor women in particular have been affected (Colón et al., 1996; Dávila, 1994), as is reflected in the rise in maternal morbidity rates to 20.2 per 100,000 live births from a low of 5.3 in 1979 (Department of Health, 1991).

Political participation

The constraints to redefining gender roles in the formal political arena are still pervasive. Women have continued to increase their level of electoral participation so that in the 1996 elections they represented 53 percent of voters (Alegría, 1996b). They also work for the political parties in an infinite number of tasks such as fundraising, public relations, organizing, delegates, as well as in the low-ranked 'female' areas of cooking, cleaning and clerical work – activities fundamental to political organization (Alegría, 1996b). Currently, the proportion of women in the higher elected positions has not increased since women gained the vote in the 1930s, and has even declined in certain years in recent decades (Alegría, 1989). In 1996 the presence of women in the Legislature nearly doubled to 18 percent, with the election of six Senators and eight members to the House of Representatives. Still, in 1996, only nine women were elected as mayors, 12 percent of all mayors.

It was in 1992 that for the first time a woman, Victoria Muñoz, ran for governor. She was not elected, however, and her political adversaries attacked her in stereotypical ways, as old and weak. Another first was when Zaida Hernandez, elected to the Legislature, became the President of the House of Representatives.

The 1996 campaign also showed how male dominance has placed women in competition with each other as candidates for the same position. Lessons would have been learnt in Puerto Rican politics, if alliances had developed among these candidates that favored women and who questioned the traditional masculine ways of practising politics. Unfortunately this did not happen, for, as usual, the female candidates were judged and scrutinized more severely than male candidates by the public as well as by political analysts (Alegría, 1996b).

The second wave of feminist organizing

A second wave of feminist organizing emerged in Puerto Rico at a time when women's greater participation in the labor market and public sphere led them to recognize gender discrimination in these spheres. Discrimination was similarly highlighted by a 1972 study in Puerto Rico on the legal status of women (Comisión de Derechos Civiles, 1972). International feminist activity and the declaration of the United Nations International Women's Year also stimulated the local feminist movement. Throughout the 1970s independent feminist organizations, such as Mujer Integrate Ahora the Federación de Mujeres Puertorriqueñas and Alianza Feminista para la Liberación Humana promoted programs and activities to analyze women's subordination (Organización Puertorriqueña de la Mujer Trabajadora, 1982; Rivera Lassén, 1987).

By the end of the decade many of the early organizations had disappeared. Theoretical and political differences had developed, along with differing visions and organizational styles (López, 1987). However, feminist activity has continued. Taller Salud, a women's health collective, was formed in 1979, and by 1982 a number of other groups were established. Among the many which have been active throughout the 1980s and 1990s, there have been diverse emphases and theoretical orientations. Some focus on women and development issues, others on feminist organizing, on women and work, women's health and sexuality, lesbian concerns, race and identity issues, ecofeminism, or women and ecumenical issues. Among the groups which were active throughout the 1980s to 1990s were the Organización Puertorriqueña de la Mujer Trabajadora, Taller Salud, Feministas en Marcha, Casa Pensamiento de Mujer, Corporación para el Desarrollo de la Mujer, Coalición Puertorriqueña de Lesbianas y Homosexuales, the ecumenical group COMMADRES, Union de Mujeres Puertorriqueñas Negra and Grupo de Identidad de la Mujer Puertorriqueña Negra, and, more recently, Eva Boricua, Taller Ecofeminista Artemisa, and the Women Law Students' Organization. Organizations like Encuentro de Mujeres, Re-Unión, Inc., Teatreras donde quiera, Colectivo de Mujeres Lesbianas, Colectivo Luisa Capetillo and others, although significant during the past decade, are no longer active. Women's committees in political and labor organizations, such as Taller de Formación Politica, Frente Socialista, Mujeres Sindicalistas en Acción and the Secretaría Nacional de la Mujer Trabajadora, have also joined feminist organizations in the movement for women's rights.[1]

Throughout the 1980s, the effort to eradicate violence against women became a cohesive factor among many of these groups, programs and the State's Commission for Women's Affairs. The struggle led to the creation in 1988 of the Coordinadora Paz para la Mujer, a coordinating coalition which has brought a united voice to policy level debates. A more recent offensive against abortion rights in Puerto Rico, also led to the creation of the Grupo Pro Derechos Reproductivos, which focuses on reproductive rights.

Puerto Rican women have also participated in regional and international activities, and in organizations such as CAFRA, the Caribbean Association for Feminist Research and Action, the Latin American and Caribbean Women's Health Network, the International Women's Health Coalition, and DAWN, an international feminist research network. Not least, they have taken part in the recent United Nations conferences on human rights, population, social development, and the status of women.

State responses to mobilization

Feminist organizing has succeeded in eliciting State responses to redress gender discrimination in education, employment and women's legal status within the family. They have also mobilized to restrain the abuses of population controllers, the offensives launched by anti-abortionists and the increasing violence against women.

State responses during the 1970s focused mainly on promoting legal reforms and educational projects that would establish more egalitarian opportunities for women in the market economy, in the public sphere and in the family. During the 1970s and 1980s labor legislation was revised to disallow discrimination by sex. Maternity leave, including that which allowed Government workers full salary during leave, was legislated; family law, including property rights and custody rights, was reformed and accorded formal status (Vicente, 1987; Senado de Puerto Rico, 1984). In 1978, a judicial decision established mutual consent as a cause for divorce in response to feminist demands (Picó, 1986; Narváez, 1977).

Between 1984 and 1988 a group of feminist women were called upon to advise the President of the Senate on women's issues (Senado de Puerto Rico, 1984; Comité Asesor Asuntos de la Mujer, 1985). In 1985 workers in the private sector were offered three-quarters of their salary during maternity leave, a compromise with feminists who sought full pay. Within that period, legislation was enacted to prohibit discrimination at the workplace on the basis of sex, as well as legislation to more vigorously enforce the collection of child maintenance (Ostolaza, 1989). Reform in family legislation achieved conditions of more formal equality before the law in relation to the State and public sphere, parallel to the claim of formal economic equality in educational and occupational opportunities.

Issues of power and conflict became more evident through the analysis of violence against women, particularly during the 1980s. Shelters, crisis centres and related services had emerged since the 1970s at the Department of Health, the Women's Project of the Puerto Rican Institute of Civil Rights, Casa Protegida Julia de Burgos and, later, Casa Ruth. In the 1980s, further mobilization brought to a public level the debates about sexual harassment and domestic violence. Advanced legislation on domestic violence and sexual harassment at the workplace was passed in 1989.[2] It reflects in a comprehensive way the feminist perspective on the issue for which women have been lobbying. It represents a strong policy statement which rejects aggression in spousal relations and analyzes aggression as an expression of women's unequal status and subordination. It recognizes the particular context of emotion and intimacy in which such violence occurs and provides women with the option to pursue criminal procedures or to obtain police protection through civil procedures.

Women's health issues have been on feminist agendas since the 1970s. The group Taller Salud continues to be a pioneer in the Latin American

FEMINIST REVIEW NO 59, SUMMER 1998

Women's Health Movement challenging contraceptive and other medical policies.

Feminist activity also led to the establishment of government agencies addressing the status of women, including the creation, in 1973, of the Commission for Women's Affairs which has collaborated at times with independent groups. Women's studies groups sparked by feminist activity became part of the movement. Such women's studies projects were introduced at the University of Puerto Rico towards the end of the 1970s. Projects on equity in education were set up, as well as women's and gender committees in various universities, during the 1980s. The pioneer research unit, Centro para la Investigación y Documentación de la Mujer (CIDOM), was followed more recently by the Project Ceres (Centro de Estudios, Recursos y Servicios a la Mujer) (1984) and the Pro-Mujer project (1986), both of the University of Puerto Rico. More recently established are the Centre for Gender Studies and Research (Centro de Investigación y Estudios del Género) (1994) of the Interamerican University and the Research Network on Gender and Women in Puerto Rico (1989).

The issues of equal opportunity, violence against women and reproductive health have been central to feminist research and education. Projects within government departments, as well as local universities, continue to examine issues such as women in representational politics, discrimination in the labor market, and the way in which education, mass media and language reproduce stereotyped gender relations. Innumerable workshops and projects were conducted on these topics throughout the island from the late 1970s through the 1980s. During the 1980s and the 1990s, sexual violence and the underlying power relations and ideologies have been researched and documented (Silva *et al.*, 1990; Knudson, 1987). Research projects on reproductive health have focused on contraception, abortion issues, and HIV, among others (Colón *et al.*, 1996 Fernós, 1994; Dávila, 1990; Cunningham, 1990).

Women's struggles and feminist activity have brought into the public sphere the debate about the gendered nature of both economic (productive) and childrearing (reproductive) roles. The notions of stereotype, discrimination and sexism have become familiar to the general public. The idea has been conveyed that these involve socially imposed definitions and are neither natural nor functional. Women's capabilities outside the home have been recognized. Labor and family laws have been amended to reflect more egalitarian definitions of gender, and maternity leave reflects a recognition of childrearing. Divorce laws were changed in recognition of the fact that marital relations should be voluntary and not subject to social pressure. Currently, feminists are struggling for policy changes which would imply the recognition of violence against women.[3] Legal reform has been an important tool in women's growing awareness that they do not have to tolerate certain practices. Feminism itself has gained much wider acceptance among women, and only the most conservative would publicly state they were anti-feminist (Colón-Warren, 1995).

Challenges for women and feminism

We can thus conclude that strategies of development under colonial relations in Puerto Rico have had contradictory impacts on the status of women, opening spaces for their inclusion into the labor market and the public sphere which have mediated, and been mediated by, feminist struggles on the island. Nevertheless, given that development strategies have been geared more to integrating women in subordinate positions than to establishing more equitable social and gender relations, the achievements of the past decades have not been able to fully redefine the gendering of social functions or gender relations.

Feminist projects have brought into focus the discussion of the social and economic importance of domestic work, and the conflicts facing women when they have to fulfill a dual role when incorporated into the labor market. Feminist activity has highlighted the interconnectedness of women's participation in the domestic and the economic/public spheres, lobbying for changes such as provision of childcare. They have further proposed that roles be redefined towards more egalitarian gender relations. Organizations such as the Organización Puertorriqueña de la Mujer Trabajadora have challenged the prevalent development strategies, their impact on labor and social services, and the impact of capital intensive industrialization on occupational health and the environment. Work on female heads of household has created a model of support services required by women, specifically women in poverty (Bravo *et al.*, 1994). Issues related to women's health and reproductive needs have been made public, not in terms of population control, but of access to and quality of services, as basic to social equity. Organizations in the Coordinadora Paz para la Mujer, Grupo pro Derechos Reproductivos and Pro Familia, among others, have submitted a list of demands to the State incorporating a broader definition of reproductive health including educational services which promote gender equity.

The advancements in women's education, employment and their involvement in the public sphere in Puerto Rico have not meant a total redefinition of gendered social functions. Occupational segregation, pay differentials, the 'double day', and ideological structures that perpetuate the notion of domestic and childrearing work as women's responsibility, have all kept women sexually subjected to the control of men (Colón-Warren,

1997; Alegría-Ortega, 1996, Silva Bonilla, 1981; Alegría-Ortega, 1988, Santos Ortiz and Muñoz, 1989). The worker role is still defined in male terms while women continue to be defined mainly by their childrearing role.

The educational system and media institutions that reproduce sexist stereotypes have resisted reasonable arguments for equal opportunity, equity and the need for non-violent, non-hierarchical relations. The stereotyped definition of a citizen as male prevails, particularly in the political sphere. Here, women who show a capacity for leadership are perceived as a threat, and are accepted only if they show more traditional, motherly attitudes and do not compete for the high ranking positions (Alegría, 1996). Such stereotypes continue to undermine laws and measures introduced to address domestic violence, and they perpetuate prevalent gender hierarchies. There continues to be resistance to the implementation of such legislation among public officers and others who attempt to revert the discussion to the private sphere.

Feminist struggles also face the need to redefine social spheres so that the development process is geared more to facilitating those reproductive functions which have been defined mainly as women's responsibility (DAWN, 1995). It is difficult to promote gender equity under conditions that reproduce poverty and social inequality, that aggravate social and familial conflict and intensify the need for domestic work and housewifery, thus contributing to the definition of women as secondary workers.

It is difficult to demand equal employment opportunities and healthy conditions for women, to demand childcare and adequate public health, in a system geared to privatization and cuts in social services. Conservative views obscure the fact that the prevailing social conflict has at its base a model of development that reinforces structures of inequality. These structures are enmeshed with class, racial and other divisions, with the needs of youth and the aged, and the struggle for sexual rights.

As a final comment, we would add that, despite its linkages with established power, the State, like other social spheres, has also been an arena of struggle in which it has been possible to open some spaces for subordinate groups. There have been instances of feminist struggles being advanced by interests inside State structures. It would thus be important to have more women in elected political positions and in government decision making, provided they are committed to an agenda for gender and social equality. Ultimately, though, the strength of the struggle and the likelihood of State responses, including more women in positions of power, will depend on action by women in civil society. We would also conclude that these redefinitions of gendered functions and social spheres should be part of a redefinition of what has been known as power, development and the State.

Notes

1 For a description of some of these groups see 'Organizaciones y proyectos sobre la mujer puertorriquena' *Pensamiento Critíco*, 8 (44) May–June, 1985; La mujer en Puerto Rico, su situación actual: Breve narrativo sometido al Comité Nacional de Puerto Rico ante Beijin, ONG's, Mar del Plata, Argentina 1994.

2 Ley núm.17 del 22 de abril de 1988: Ley para prohibir el hostigamiento sexual en el empleo, imponer responsabilidades y fijar penalidades; Ley núm.54 de agosto de 1989: Ley para la prevención e intervención con la violencia doméstica.

3 As in other countries, there has been a debate, even among feminists, regarding the effectiveness of laws as a means to deal with violence against women, suggesting that they reinforce the view of women as victims and that they represent an opening to greater State control of criminalization. In brief, our position has been that the approval of the laws against sexual harassment in the workplace and domestic violence cannot be presented as the final solution to the problem of violence against women. The judicial system has proved to be extremely resistant to enforcement of these laws, and the structures of subordination that are at the basis of this behavior are still present. Nevertheless, those of us who were involved in this mobilization were taking the position that, even with the risk of strengthening the encroachment of dominant interests of the State, the personal is already social and the State is an arena of struggle that had been, in fact, acting against women (Colón-Warren, 1995).

References

ALEGRÍA Ortega, Idsa E. (1988) 'En tiempo de bolero: colonialismo y patriarcado en los melodramas y anuncios televisados' *Revista de Ciencias Sociales*, Vol. XXVII, No. 1–2, marzo–junio: 89–99.
—— (1989) 'Mujeres y elecciones 1988' *Diálogo*, febrero: 4.
—— (1996a) 'Género y política en Puerto Rico' *Puerto Rico Cooperativista*, marzo–abril: 5.
—— (1996b) 'Mujeres y elecciones 1996' presented at Roundtable Elecciones.
ALEXANDER, M. Jacqui (1994) 'Not just (any) body can be a citizen: the politics of law, sexuality and postcoloniality in Trinidad and Tobago and the Bahamas' *Feminist Review*, No. 48, Autumn: 5–23.
AZIZE, Vargas, Yamila and AVILÉS, Luis, Alberto (1990) 'Los hechos desconocidos: participación de la mujer en las profesiones de salud en Puerto Rico (1898–1930)' *Puerto Rico Health Science Journal*, Vol. 9 No. 1: 9–16.
BENNHOLDT-THOMSEN, Veronika (1988) 'Why do housewives continue to be created in the Third World too?' in Maria MIES, Veronika BENNHOLDT-THOMSEN and Claudia VON WERLHOF (1988) editors, *Women: The Last Colony* London and New Jersey: Zed Books Ltd, pp. 159–67.

BRAULIO, Mildred *et al.* (1988) 'Mujeres y legislación laboral en Puerto Rico' presented at Primer Congreso Latinoamericano de Mujer y Legislación, Managua.

BRAVO, Milagros, COLBERG, Eileen, MARTÍNEZ, Loida M., MARTÍNEZ, Maria Soledad, MÉNDEZ, Anette and SEIJO, Luisa R. (1994) 'La construcción social del genero y la subjetividad: Educación y trabajo' in Alice COLÓN (1994) editor, *Gender and Puerto Rican Women*, Río Piedras: CERES, Centro de Investigaciones Sociales, Universidad de Puerto Rico, pp. 56–83.

BRUCE, Judith, LLOYD, Cynthia B. and LEONARD, Ann (1995) *Families in Focus: New Perspectives on Mothers, Fathers and Children*, New York: The Population Council.

BURGOS, Nilsa and COLBERG, Eileen (1990) 'Mujeres solteras con jefatura de familia: Características en el hogar y en el trabajo', Rio Piedras: CERES, Centro de Investigaciones Sociales, Universidad de Puerto Rico.

COLÓN, Alice, MUÑOZ, Marya, GARCÍA, Neftalí and ALEGRÍA, Idsa (1988) 'Trayectoria de la participación laboral de las mujeres en Puerto Rico de los años 1950 a 1985: Estudios sobre la calidad de vida y la crisis económica en Puerto Rico' in *Crisis, Sociedad y Mujer: Estudio Comparativo entre paises de América (1950–1985)*, Habana, Cuba: Editorial de la Mujer, FMC.

COLÓN, Alice, FABIÁN, Ana M., MUÑOZ, Marya and VALLE, Diana (1995) 'Mujeres, desarrollo y paz en Puerto Rico' in Alice COLÓN and Ana M. FABIÁN (1995) editors, *Mujeres en el Caribe: Desarrollo, paz y movimientos comunitarios*, Rio Piedras: Instituto de Estudios del Caribe, CERES, Centro de Investigaciones Sociales, Universidad de Puerto Rico, pp. 9–28.

COLÓN, Alice, DÁVILA, Ana Luisa, FERNÓS, María Dolores and VICENTE, Esther (1996) 'Los intentos de deslegitimación del derecho al aborto en Puerto Rico' unpublished Final Report to Carlos Chagas Foundation.

COLÓN-WARREN, Alice E. (1995) 'Investigación y acción feminista en el Puerto Rico contemporáneo: Notas desde un punto en su intersección y movimiento tematico' *Caribbean Studies*, Vol. 28, No. 1, January–June: 163–95.

—— (1997) 'Reestructuración industrial, empleo y pobreza en Puerto Rico y en el Atlántico Medio de los Estados Unidos: La situación de las mujeres puertorriqueñas' *Revista de Ciencias Sociales Nueva Epoca*, Vol. 3: 135–87.

COMISIÓN DE DERECHOS CIVILES, ESTADO LIBRE ASOCIADO DE PUERTO RICO (1972) *La igualdad de derechos y oportunidades de la mujer Puertorrriqueña*, San Juan, Puerto Rico.

COMITÉ ASESOR ASUNTOS DE LA MUJER AL PRESIDENTE DEL SENADO (1985) 'Informe de progreso' sometido por Katherine Angueira, Coordinadora, 15 de abril.

CUNNINGHAM, Ineke (1990) 'La mujer y el SIDA; una visión crítica' *Puerto Rico Health Science Journal*, Vol. 9, No. 1: 47–50.

DÁVILA, Ana Luisa (1990) 'Esterilización y práctica anticonceptiva en Puerto Rico, 1982' *Puerto Rico Health Science Journal*, Vol. 9 No.1: 61–7.

—— (1994) 'Las prácticas reproductivas ante las políticas de población: Regulaciones de la fecundidad y tendencias demográficas entre las mujeres puertorriqueñas' presented at the First Conference of the Puerto Rican Studies Association, Waltham, Mass.

DAWN (1995) 'Rethinking social development: DAWN's vision' *World Development*, Vol. 23 No. 11: 2001–4.

DEPARTMENT OF HEALTH, Health Facilities and Services Administration, Office of Health Statistics (1991) *Informe Anual de Estadísticas Vitales*, San Juan, Puerto Rico.

DIETZ, James L. (1986) *Economic History of Puerto Rico. Institutional Change and Capitalist Development*, New Jersey: Princeton University Press.

DIETZ, James L. and PANTOJAS-GARCÍA, Emilio (1993) 'Puerto Rico's new role in the Caribbean: the high finance/maquiladora strategy' in Edwin MELÉNDEZ and Edgardo MELÉNDEZ (1993) editors, *Colonial Dilemma: Critical Perspectives on Contemporary Puerto Rico*, Boston, Mass: South End Press, pp. 103–15.

FERNÁNDEZ KELLY, María Patricia and SASSEN, Saskia (1995) 'Recasting women in the global economy: internationalization and changing definitions of gender' in Christine BOSE and Edna ACOSTA-BELÉN (1995) editors, *Women in the Latin American Development Process*, Philadelphia: Temple University Press, pp. 99–124.

FERNÓS, María Dolores (1994) 'El aborto como política de control poblacional en Puerto Rico' presented at the First Conference of the Puerto Rican Studies Association, Waltham, Mass.

FRASER, Nancy (1989) *Unruly Practices: Power, Discourse and Gender in Contemporary Social Theory*, Minneapolis: University of Minnesota Press.

KNUDSON, Doris (1987) 'Que nadie se entere: La esposa maltratada en Puerto Rico' in Yamila AZIZE (1987) editor, *La mujer en la sociedad puertorriqueña*, Rio Piedras: Huracán, pp. 139–53.

LÓPEZ, María M. (1987) 'Reflexiones en torno al debate feminista en Puerto Rico' *Homines*, tomo extraordinario, No. 4, febrero: 105–9.

MOMSEN, Janet H. (1993) 'Introduction' in Janet MOMSEN (1993) editor, *Women and Change in the Caribbean a Pan-Caribbean Perspective*, London: James Currey, pp. 1–12.

MUÑOZ, Marya and FERNÁNDEZ, Edwin (1988) *El divorcio en la sociedad puertorriqueña*, Río Piedras: Huracán.

NARVÁEZ, Ochoa, Evelyn (1977) 'Nuevas herramientas para nuestra liberación' *Palabra de Mujer*, Vol. 1 No. 1: 14–15.

ORGANIZACIÓN PUERTORRIQUEÑA DE LA MUJER TRABAJADORA (1982) 'Recuento histórico' documentos presentados a la Tercera conferencia de la Mujer Trabajadora, mimeo.

OSTOLAZA BEY, Margarita (1989) *Política Sexual en Puerto Rico*, Rio Piedras: Huracán.

PETCHESKY, Rosalind Pollack (1990) *Abortion and Woman's Choice. The State, Sexuality and Reproductive Freedom* rev edn, Boston: Northwestern University Press.

PETROVICH, Janice and LAUREANO, Sandra (1987) 'Towards an analysis of Puerto Rican women and the informal economy' *Homines*, tomo extraordinario, No. 4: 70–81.

PICÓ de Hernández, Isabel (1986) *Divorcio por consentimiento mutuo: su tramitación en los tribunales*, Rio Piedras: Centro de Investigaciones Sociales, Universidad de Puerto Rico.

PRATTS, Saúl J. (1994) editor, *Visiones alternas al fenómeno de la criminalidad* 2nd edn, Río Piedras: Facultad de Ciencias Sociales, Universidad de Puerto Rico.

RAMÍREZ DE ARELLANO, Annette and SEIPP, Conrad (1983) *Colonialism, Catholicism and Contraception in Puerto Rico*, Chapel Hill: University of Carolina Press.

RIVERA LASSÉN, Ana I. (1987) 'La organización de las mujeres y las organizaciones feministas en Puerto Rico (1930–1986)' (mimeo).

SAFA, Helen I. (1975) *The Urban Poor of Puerto Rico: A Study in Development and Inequality*, New York: Holt, Reinhart and Winston, Inc.

—— (1981) 'Runaway shops and female employment: the search for cheap labor' *Signs*, Vol. 7, No. 2: 418–33.

—— (1995) *The Myth of the Male Breadwinner. Women and Industrialization in the Caribbean*, Boulder, Col.: Westview Press.

SANTIAGO CENTENO, Zoraida and MARTÍNEZ RAMOS, Loida (1990) 'Puerto Rico: Logros en equidad educativa' in *Mesa redonda: Estrategias para la equidad por sexo en la educación*, San Juan: Comisión para los Asuntos de la Mujer, Oficina del Gobernador, Unidad de Investigaciones, junio, pp. 1–21.

SANTOS ORTIZ, María del C. and MUÑOZ, Marya (1989) 'An exploratory study of the expression of female sexuality: The experience of two groups of Puerto Rican women from different social backgrounds' in Cynthia García COLL and María Lourdes MATTEI (1989) editors, *The Psycho-social Development of Puerto Rican Women*, New York: Praeger pp. 140–65.

SEN, Gita and GROWN, Caren (1987) *Development, Crises, and Alternative Visions: Third World Women's Perspectives*, New York: Monthly Review Press.

SENADO DE PUERTO RICO, Estado Libre Asociado de Puerto Rico (1984) Informe de la Comisión Especial de Asuntos de la Mujer sobre el estudio de la problemática de la mujer puertorriqueña.

SILVA BONILLA, Ruth (1981) 'El lenguaje como mediación ideológica entre la experiencia y la conciencia de las mujeres trabajadoras en Puerto Rico' *Revista de Ciencias Sociales*, Vol. XXIII, marzo–junio: 23–50.

SILVA, Ruth *et al.* (1990) *Hay amores que matan. La violencia contra las mujeres en la vida conyugal*, Río Piedras: Huracán.

TANG NAIN, Gemma (1995) 'The impact of prevalent economic strategies on women's lives in the English-speaking Caribbean: woman's responses and community projects of economic development' in Alice COLÓN and Ana M. FABIÁN (1995) editors, *Mujeres en el Caribe: Desarrollo, Paz y Movimientos Comunitarios*, Rio Piedras: Instituto de Estudios del Caribe y (CERES) Centro de Investigaciones Sociales, Universidad de Puerto Rico, pp. 55–74.

VÁZQUEZ CALZADA, José L (1988) *La población de Puerto Rico y su trayectoria histórica*, Rio Piedras: Raga Offset Printing Service.

—— (1990) 'El impacto de los partos por cesárea sobre la fecundidad en Puerto Rico' *Puerto Rico Health Science Journal*, Vol. 9 No. 1: 69–73.

VICENTE, Esther (1987) 'Las mujeres y el cambio en la norma jurídica' in Yamila

AZIZE (1987) editor, *La mujer en Puerto Rico*, Rio Piedras: Huracán, pp. 171–91.

—— (1993) 'El aborto derecho fundamental' *Pensamiento Crítico*, Vol. 16 No. 23: 5–7.

'Fanm Se Poto Mitan:

Haitian Woman, the Pillar of Society

Marie-José N'Zengou-Tayo

FEMINIST REVIEW NO 59, SUMMER 1998, PP. 118–142

Abstract

In this paper Marie-Jose N'zengou-Tayo draws on a variety of sources, both historical and contemporary, to describe the journey of Haitian women from nineteenth-century post-War of Independence, to present-day Haitian society.

The paper is divided in two sections. In the first, the author traces a brief social history of women, quoting anthropological and sociological studies from the 1930s to the 1970s. She begins with rural peasant women noting their significant involvement in farming, marketing and in the internal food trade sector. The development of polygamy and common law unions as the most common form of conjugal union is seen as a practical response to survival in rural Haiti. The author notes the major impact on women's lives of continued political upheavals, violent repression, rural degradation and migration to the cities. Opportunities for employment in a deprived urban setting, and women's initiatives in income generating are also described under the Duvalier regimes. A brief overview of the lives of the middle class is included, although there is a paucity of research in this area available to the author. Violence against women is a regular threat facing domestic workers, and a means of repression used by the state against women across classes.

In the second section N'Zengou-Tayo addresses the literary representation of Haitian women by both female and male Haitian writers. The paper examines how female writers have developed subversive narrative strategies to shape a female identity in order to break away from the stereotypes portrayed in men's writing.

N'Zengou-Tayo concludes that the tremendous contribution of Haitian women to their society has neither been recognized nor documented. Despite this, the resilience of Haitian women, whether in their daily lives or in their writing, has enabled them to make strides towards improving their lives.

Keywords

migration; rural; conjugal unions; women's writing; class; violence against women

On the 3rd April 1986, a demonstration took place in Port-au-Prince which drew Haitian women of all ages and social backgrounds into the streets. Haitian economist Mireille Neptune-Anglade, in *L'Autre moitie du developpemement*, considered this event a sign of changes taking place in Haitian women's consciousness (Neptune-Anglade, 1986). Seven years later in 1993, a documentary featuring interviews with representatives of women's organizations revealed the tremendous changes that had taken place in the lives of Haitian women in less than a decade in their overall development and educational progress (CPEDAV, 1993). More recently, the impact of the 1991–4 period on women's traditional activities, the return to democratic order, and the creation of a Ministry of Women's Affairs, call for a re-examination of the status of Haitian women.

This paper seeks to gather the scattered knowledge about Haitian women. First of all it will trace a brief social history of women, and then examine their literary representation by male and female Haitian writers, in an attempt to identify how female writers voiced and shaped a female identity by breaking away from male stereotypes.

Haitian women and their society

The political instability which characterizes Haitian history, due to the violent confrontation of two opposing views of the state (Moïse, 1989), has contributed to the division of the country into two separate worlds. This, along with massive rural migration to the cities in the second half of the twentieth century, has split Haiti into two worlds which live side by side, but which are economically far apart. The urban dollar economy is characterized by consumption of imported manufactured goods and advanced technology, while the 'gourde' economy of rural Haiti is one of scarcity and low consumption (Barthélémy, 1988; Rouzier, 1989). This economic separation is mirrored by class divisions which operate differently in urban and rural areas. These differences affect women's status and require a distinction to be made between rural and urban women.

Women in a rural Haiti

Ever since the early days of the Haitian Republic in the early years of the nineteenth century, peasants held a different status from city dwellers. This differential status was dictated by the need to maintain the plantation system. Legislation passed in 1825 which accorded Haitian peasants second-class citizen status was never revoked, though it was amended by successive governments. From 1945, the law stipulated that 'Paysans' was to appear on a peasant's birth certificate. This infamous law which perpetuated a social stigma was repealed just ten years ago, and the repeal implemented only in 1995.

Gender differences arise in childrearing practices and in access to education. In relation to education, rural women are at a great disadvantage. In 1938, only one in ten children of school age attended state or private schools. There were only 8,282 girls among the 30,000 students attending state-run rural schools (Dartigue, 1938: 24). Girls' access to schooling has never been a priority in rural Haiti. Girls start their household apprenticeship very early, sometimes as early as age 7, caring for younger brothers and sisters, carrying water, helping with cooking and marketing. Boys start helping their fathers in the fields at age 10 (Bastien, 1951: 84). Though parents would like to see their children learn to read and write, insufficient income and the pressure of farmwork always lead to children's irregular school attendance and a high drop-out rate. In a survey conducted in the late 1970s and early 1980s, rural sociologist Jacomina P. de Regt, noted that 'even young children can make a substantial contribution to the operation of the household by caring for siblings, working in the fields, or selling newspapers in the streets' (1984: 121). She also found that girls were enrolled less frequently than boys, although their rate of enrolment grew slightly faster than that of boys (1984: 120).

Figure 1 Premiére communion de Marie-José Dartigue faite en la chapelle de Saint-Louis-Rois-de-France.

Rural women are also the first to suffer from inadequate health care. Pulmonary tuberculosis is common among rural women (Farmer, 1994) and Neptune-Anglade notes this could be linked to insufficient food intake (1986, quoting Laviolette, 1982). Moreover, antenatal clinics are insufficient in rural areas and pregnancy becomes a health hazard for the peasant woman as

> une diète misérable jumelée à l'urgence de travailler jusqu'à l'accouchement pour simplement survivre, engendre souvent des anémies nutritionnelles prononcées.
>
> (Neptune-Anglade, 1986: 65)

> (an insufficient diet and the need to work right up to the time of birth in order to survive, often provokes nutritional anaemia.)

Another aspect of life in rural Haiti is the prevalence of Customary Law over Statute Law (Haiti's legal system is based on Roman Law). Thus, although Civil Law requires that all children receive an equal share of their inheritance regardless of their sex, Mireille Neptune-Anglade noted in 1986 that traditional practices of inheritance, along with excessive division of the land, resulted in women's increasing exclusion from land ownership (1986: 15). Yet notably, up to the early 1950s, women used to receive an equal share of the land that made up their dowry (Bastien, 1951).

Rural women gain social status through marriage rather than common law unions, and from their marketing activities rather than agricultural activities of sowing, weeding and harvesting. Though common law union and polygamy are the most common conjugal patterns (Price-Mars, 1928; Dartigue, 1937; Bastien, 1951; Moral, 1961; Lowenthal, 1984; Neptune-Anglade, 1987), religious/legal marriage confers prestige on the peasant couple. In a survey of 884 households conducted in 1938, Maurice Dartigue observed

> Bien que le mariage sanctionné par l'Église et l'État ait un grand prestige aux yeux des paysans, comme l'indique la déclaration de quelques-uns d'entre eux qui auraient voulu avoir assez de moyens pour se marier (et se distinguer ainsi des autres), le plaçage n'est pas moins une union stable où se rencontrent les caractéristiques et les fonctions de la famille.
>
> (Dartigue, 1938:1)

> (Though marriage sanctioned by both Church and State carries much prestige in the eyes of the peasants, as confirmed by those who say they would like to have enough money to get married and 'distinguish themselves from the others', common law union is nevertheless a stable union in which all the characteristics and functions of the family can be identified.)

The prestige is more important for women. Bastien reports a quarrel between women in which being married was a sign of one's superiority over the other:

'Il nous est souvent arriveé d'entendre au cours de querelles entre femmes des sorties comme celle-ci: 'Mais regardez, je porte une bague et mon mariage a coûté cinquante dollars. Vous, vous n'êtes qu'une *femme-jardin*!'

(1951: 100)

(Often during some quarrels among women, we heard them hurling this insult: 'So look, I wear a ring and my wedding cost fifty dollars. You, you are only a "femme-jardin"' [garden-woman]!)

(Translation: Dayan, 1995)

The Catholic Church tried to promote free collective wedding ceremonies but met little success as peasants felt humiliated by these 'barefoot' weddings. In addition, considerable savings are required to meet the traditional expenses associated with this event (Price-Mars, 1928; Dartigue, 1938); consequently few peasants are able to afford legal marriage. When they manage to get married, the ceremony often takes place after several years of common law union and marks both personal and social achievement for the family.

Anthropologists have commented on polygamous unions in rural Haiti, and see polygamy as a survival of African tradition. On the other hand, it is considered a practical response to the need for labour to manage scattered farming plots. This second explanation accounts for the distinction between 'fanm marie' (spouse), 'fanm kay' (house woman) and 'fanm jadin' (garden woman). In rural Haiti, though class differences are not as obvious as in the cities, there is a social hierarchy among peasant women. As Drexel Woodson was informed: 'Tout mounn se mounn, men tout mounn pa menm.' (All people are people, but all people aren't the same) (Dayan, 1995).

Class distinctions are marked also by the amount of cash women can generate in their marketing activities. Thus the 'Madan Sara', and small shop-('boutique')-keepers are above the ordinary market women and roadside retailers. Neptune-Anglade offers a gendered economic interpretation of the polygamous rural common-law unions, as unions which symbolize the 'social contract of our poverty' (1986: 52) with two complementary objectives:

procurer à l'homme une force de travail pour la production et la commercialisation, et fournir à la famille ainsi constituée à partir de ce type d'union les moyens de sa survie économique.

Dans cette association, l'homme fournit la terre et la femme une grande partie du travail. L'absentéisme de l'homme est consubstantiel à cette union insérée dans un ensemble d'unions . . . mais, la crise actuelle de la structure agraire fait diminuer le nombre de femmes qu'un homme pourrait se permettre 'd'établir'; le travail des femmes dans l'agriculture tend à diminuer comme le nombre

d'hommes à plusieurs foyers à la fois, même si le modèle consensuel et polyga-
mique est encore largement dominant.

(Neptune-Anglade, 1986: 68)

(to provide men with labour for production and distribution and provide the
family based on this type of union with the means for economic survival.

To this partnership, the male partner brings the land and the female, a large
share of the labour. The man's absenteeism is the corollary to this union, which
in turn is part of a wider network of unions . . . however, with the current crisis
in the agricultural sector, a man would have to reduce the number of women
he could 'set up' [settle with]; there are fewer women working in farming, and
fewer men able to maintain several co-existing households, even though the
common law and polygamous pattern is still prevalent.)

It is worth noting that women control the money earned through marketing operations. They set the quantities to be sold from the harvest as well
as the prices. They make decisions about household expenditure and the
purchase of manufactured goods. Bastien commented on this financial
freedom as a sign that rural women were far more advanced in terms of
financial independence and entrepreneurial skills than their urban middle-
class counterparts who were not working (1951:123). André Corten,
quoting Mintz (1960), noted the recurring pattern of rural women's contribution to the household budget, a situation that was reinforced by seasonal migration. In the absence of their companions, women were in
charge of the household budget and had to find means of supplementing
this insufficient income (1986: 82).

From a feminist viewpoint, it could be said that for a Haitian woman,
common law union and religious/legal marriage mean loss of her identity
as she loses her name and is then addressed as 'Madan X', with 'X' being
her husband's first name. (This practice is not limited to rural society and
transcends class divisions.) It also means an increased workload. Neptune-
Anglade talks about the disproportionate workload of women (1986: 17)
which for the peasant woman implies land cultivation and marketing activities as well as household chores. In 1938, Dartigue's survey indicated that

un certain nombre de paysans peuvent travailler comme journalier sur les routes
publiques ou dans des usines pendant que *les femmes s'occupent des champs.*
Dans d'autres cas, *la femme augmente les revenus du foyer par son travail
comme blanchisseuse, commerçante de détail ou revendeuse, charcutière,* etc.

(1938: 10; italics mine)

(several peasants may work as seasonal workers in road building or in factories
while women till the fields. In other cases, women help to increase the household income by working as laundress, retailer, pork butcheress, etc.)

Long before Neptune-Anglade, Haitian anthropologist Rémy Bastien marvelled at the work that was expected from a peasant's wife (1951: 117–42). As he interviewed a peasant about his life, the latter was angry with his wife and complained about her 'laziness'. Bastien discovered that she was considered lazy because, unlike her female neighbours, she was unable to undertake any commercial activity ('un petit commerce') in addition to her normal household chores and the care of three young children (Bastien, 1951: 117–18). Thirty-seven years later nothing much had changed for the peasant woman when, in 1987, a participant at a workshop described the considerable contribution of women to the economy of the north-western region. She noted that women are entirely responsible for the household economy, organizing the family, raising children, working in the fields and gardens; and that 90 per cent are involved in some form of commercial enterprise, and spend most of the day at the market which they reach on foot or by donkey (Larosilière, 1988: 16).

Though peasant women help with farming (sowing, weeding and harvesting) the particular domain of activity reserved for them is marketing. As noted by Neptune-Anglade:

> il est quelque chose de particulier à Haïti que la littérature scientifique fait émerger depuis plus de deux décennies et que les démarches comparatives confirment comme spécifique au cas haïtien: c'est l'ampleur, l'omniprésence, la dominance de la femme dans la commercialisation interne des vivres. On dirait, au niveau du constat empirique quotidien, que le commerce intérieur des vivres, les circuits de sa commercialisation, les lieux de sa transaction, les agents de sa redistribution, . . . sont affaires de femmes.
>
> (1986: 19)

> (There is something peculiar to Haiti that has emerged consistently in scientific literature for two decades and is confirmed by comparative approaches: this is the widespread and dominant presence of women in the internal food sector. It is as if the food trade, distribution systems, marketplaces, retailing . . . were all women's business.)

To understand the major change that occurred in rural women's lives one has to remember that in 1938, 60 per cent of the women in Dartigue's survey were engaged in agriculture as their *main* activity (Dartigue, 1938: 35). In those days, marketing was secondary to sewing, laundering, beef and pork butchery, bakery, hat and basket making, and speculating on coffee and acting as 'middlewoman' in the coffee trade. Neptune-Anglade points out that there are no gendered studies of the commercial food trade despite the abundant literature on the marketing of goods in Haiti (1986: 20). Also missing from labour studies are approaches which link paid labour to domestic labour (Neptune-Anglade, 1986: 21).

The late 1980s saw a tremendous effort on the part of women to gain education through literacy classes and from 1987 to 1989 women out-numbered men in the literacy groups based in Croix-des-Bouquets, a small town not far from Port-au-Prince. A documentary entitled *This Other Haiti* (1992) showed women's struggle to obtain education and their significant involvement in the 'Mouvement Paysan Papay' in the north-eastern region. Among the various peasants interviewed for the documentary, a leading figure, Mme Irama, 'emerges as one of the backbone figures of the Peasant Movement of Papay . . . Mme Irama walks tall and speaks without a trace of self-pity as she describes her arrest' (Patricia Hatfield (1993), in a review of the documentary).

More recently, the 1993 CPEDAV documentary mentioned earlier, entitled *Fanm organize men nou* (Organized Women Here We Are), shows a rural women's group tilling the soil during a 'coumbite' (collective agricultural work). In view of earlier findings on the exclusion of women from land ownership, and in view of the fact that tilling the soil with a hoe was a man's job, this all-female coumbite is unusual. Indeed, these women represent an association which had managed with great difficulty to obtain land on lease or to farm as sharecroppers. They had decided to plant and harvest by themselves without the help of their husbands or partners.

The most striking events in recent years have been the attempts made by rural women to organize themselves. In spite of difficulties encountered and the violence during the 1991–4 period of repression, rural women never gave up though they were frequent victims of sexual abuse by 'attachés' (former 'macoutes' or police auxiliaries), 'chefs de section' (rural police officers) and soldiers. The National Coalition for Haitian Refugees, a non-profit organization based in New York, as well as Paul Farmer's 1994 book, *The Uses of Haiti*, recount several cases of violence against peasant women, and the disruption of their lives during the period. Through Farmer's account of Acephie's story (1994: 321–44) one can assess the severe degradation that occurred in rural Haiti since Price-Mars' *So Spoke the Uncle* (1928). Lack of infrastructure, lack of water, defor-estation, along with increased pressure on land (noted earlier) which led to the exclusion of women from land ownership, all resulted in massive migration of women to the city. Here, women are engaged in paid work either in a domestic context or as vendors ('Madan Sara'). Neptune-Anglade predicted in 1986 that external migration of women would be the next trend among the rural masses. Indeed, though men still outnumbered women among the boatpeople, the number of women steadily increased (Charles, 1982; Icart, 1986).

In conclusion, this section on rural Haitian women may well give a grim impression of these women's lives. Nevertheless, Haitian rural women have

FEMINIST REVIEW NO 59, SUMMER 1998

not given up hope of improving their circumstances. Their traditional resilience is now strengthened by a fighting spirit of 'vaillance'. Recent work by the Ministry of Women's Affairs, the existence of Enfofanm, Kayfanm and many women's organizations at the grassroots level prove that women are struggling to emerge from the economic and historical 'invisibility' (Neptune-Anglade, 1986: 103, 109) that was their lot. Contemporary peasant women are taking steps to change the condition of their lives.

Urban women

In the cities, Western sociological categories of working/middle/upper class apply, as does Statute Law. At the bottom of the social ladder we find the recent female rural migrants who are unemployed and frequently single parents. In the slums of Port-au-Prince, Cap-Haïtien, Gonaïves and Port-de-Paix, these rural women try to adjust to their new situation which Gérarda Elysée (in Jean-Jacques *et al.*, 1988: 21) describes as follows:

> il s'agit de femmes qui ont dû quitter la campagne pour émigrer vers la ville, qui ont perdu terre et bétail, qui ont de plus perdu confiance en elles-mêmes. Elles arrivent en ville avec deux ou trois enfants sur les bras sans savoir où donner de la tête. Elles doivent s'adapter au milieu urbain dans des conditions les plus dures.

> (They are women who have had to leave rural areas and migrate to the city. They have lost their land and cattle, they have lost self-confidence. They arrive in town with two or three children in their care and they don't know what to do. They have to adjust to an urban setting in very harsh circumstances.)

They very often have to resort to prostitution in order to survive. Alternatively, they earn a living by retailing goods such as 'kinkay' (trinkets), food, sweets, cheap jewellery, clothing, haberdashery. Vending constitutes a 'fiercely competitive occupation' according to Simon M. Fass (1990: 77) who studied the Saint-Martin area of Port-au-Prince from 1974 to 1976. Income generation is very uncertain as not much capital is invested. In addition, any unforeseen event such as illness, political unrest, strikes, or lack of marketing expertise may drive these women out of business within a matter of days or weeks.

As in the rural areas, most traders in the cities are women. According to Fass '[their] most common difficulty . . . was childbirth and illness. . . . A birth meant a brief period out of the market in order to nurse, and a trader's illness, or that of a trader's immediate family often had the same effect' (1990: 80). They would then face difficulty in re-entering the market as 'they had lost their niche' (Fass, 1990: 81).

Women working in the trade sector were willing to finance men's activities in the manufacturing sector based on the assumption that these activities would increase earning for the household (Fass, 1990: 86). Whereas 'few women in trade received support from their husbands, [while] most women in manufacturing got started that way' (Fass, 1990: 86). One could say that women were more willing to 'capitalize' men than the other way around. As far as family structure in urban areas is concerned, Fass observes that 'only men with substantial means maintained one or more extra households' and that many of these 'were Macoutes, and many of the women they supported served as informers' (1990: 91).

The 1970s saw the development of an urban type of 'Madan Sara' who would travel to Puerto Rico, Curaçao, St Martin and Panama and bring back clothes, shoes, underwear, etc. These could be sold at a low cost since these goods did not attract customs duties and were in fact smuggled in as personal belongings. These distributors became so prevalent that a new market at the north entrance of Port-au-Prince (Marche Tête-Boeuf) was devoted to their business. Today, all the streets surrounding the Iron Market are invaded by street vendors retailing new and used smuggled goods.

Working-class women are either domestic workers or factory workers. At the beginning of the century, domestic workers were employed on a feudal basis: daughters of sharecroppers were sent to town to work in the household of their father's landlord. They would be attached to the family for their lifetime, unless they were fired by the mistress of the house for misconduct or disrespect.[1] These domestic workers risked facing sexual harassment by their masters or masters' son(s) (Chauvet, 1957; Lhérisson, 1905, 1966). In present day Haiti, young peasant girls are sent to work as domestic servants in lower middle-class or working-class households, while young adults are employed by upper middle- and middle-class households. These jobs are now considered temporary rather than lifetime attachments. Domestic workers accept these jobs in order to accumulate just enough capital to start a commercial activity (Fass, 1990).

Women constituted the large majority of the labour force in the assembly industries that were attracted to Haiti by the Duvalier Government's incentives (low wages, tax exemption, etc.). A survey conducted by André Corten in 1986 show a female workforce in baseball and softball manufacturing (Haiti was then the world's foremost producer of baseballs), in apparel and shoemaking, and in needlework. Though the minimum wage was US$1 per day (i.e. five gourdes), few earned that much. In some cases workers are paid by piece work. In the baseball industry, for example, women workers said that by starting at 5.00 a.m. and bringing additional

FEMINIST REVIEW NO 59, SUMMER 1998

work home, with the help of their family they were able to earn almost US$2 per day (Corten, 1986: 157). In clandestine interviews conducted by New York based Haitian journalist, Ben Dupuis, for a documentary entitled *Bitter Cane*, women in the baseball factory spoke of the intensive workpace, low pay and sexual harassment.

Factory workers who live at Carrefour, a middle-class and slum area in the south of the city, face transportation problems since they have to take an early 'tap-tap' (bus or open passenger van/truck) to reach the industrial zone. They have to wake up very early in order to have everything ready for their family before leaving. Fetching water and cooking can be very time consuming and require strenuous work (Fass, 1990). Usually, young girls (sometimes they are servant children or 'restavek') are sent to the standpipe to collect water. When water is cut off, it means going farther in search of water, or buying water from a street seller. In 1986 and 1987 attempts were made to organize and educate female factory workers and the association 'Fanm ouvriyez' (Women Workers) was created. A family planning and health centre and literacy programmes were put in place as well as a canteen project involving street food vendors in order to improve hygiene and quality.

During the post-Duvalier period, and due to the political instability of the country, many assembly industries closed down. It is estimated that some 30,000 to 60,000 jobs were lost during the 1986–94 period. More attractive conditions offered in other countries of the region (Dominican Republic, Costa Rica, Mexico, etc.) accelerated the relocation of many assembly industries that had mushroomed in Haiti during the Duvalier era. Female factory workers were the first victims of these lay-offs. This meant they either had to return to the marketplace or the street as vendors, find a job as a domestic worker or take up prostitution. During the 1991–4 embargo against the Haitian *de facto* government, fierce competition for selling smuggled goods, like gasoline and other imported commodities, pushed women out of the trade to make way for men. Women in slum areas had to face sexual abuse and sometimes trade sex for financial support and protection. The Macoutes had been replaced by 'Attachés' and/or drug traffickers and when these, and the army, raided slums women often were victims of rape. A Human Rights Watch report, entitled *Rape in Haiti: A Weapon of Terror*, documents numerous cases in which rape was used as an instrument of torture against women. The introduction to the report states:

> Our findings, combined with recent reports from local human rights monitors, the press and the UN/OAS Civilian Mission in Port-au-Prince, all point to a disturbing pattern of rape by police and attachés acting with impunity. HRW

[Human Rights Watch] and NCHR [National Coalition for Haitian Refugees] found that military forces and attachés use rape and sexual assault to punish and intimidate women for their actual and imputed political beliefs, or to terrorize them during violent sweeps of pro-Aristide neighborhoods. Rape also functions as punishment for the political beliefs and activities of the victim's male relatives.

(HRW/NCHR 1994: 3)

Haitian traditional attitudes towards female sexuality and virginity makes rape a traumatic experience. Though prostitution is widespread in the cities as a means of survival for poor women, and though common law and polygamous unions are the norm, virginity is still the yardstick of female honour. Forty-three years after Bastien's findings on the issue of virginity for girls (Bastien, 1951) a Haitian human rights activist explained to the HRW/NCHR team that:

When a girl is about to get married, members on both sides of the family are anxious to know if she is a virgin. If she is not, this is a dishonor for the girl and especially for the family. You lose your honor when you have been violated.

(HRW/NCHR 1994: 21)

Other reports record the humiliation of raped women and the forced silence that follows. A document published in 1993 by the Lafontant Joseph Center for the Promotion of Human Rights analyses the psychological impact of rape on women as they are 'obliged to repress [their] pain and live with [their] frustrations'.

Middle-class women have not attracted as much scholarly attention as their peasant and working-class counterparts. To comment on their situation, I rely heavily on personal observation, testimonies by female writers and scattered information. Middle-class women's lives were strongly influenced by French Bourgeois ideology that shaped Haitian society prior to the American Occupation (1915–34). Under the Occupation, American influence infiltrated the Haitian way of life (through technology and consumer goods). Today, the Haitian middle class is cosmopolitan due in large part to the influence of migration. This takes the form of both personal and family migration, and short visits abroad to migrant relatives living in Europe, Canada and the United States, among other countries.

Middle-class women accessed education very early. However, while state schools for boys were created in the early days of Independence (Henri Christophe's reign 1807, Petion's Government, 1807), girls were educated only in private convent schools and had limited access to higher education. Up to 1945, girls' schooling ended at the level of 'Brevet' (roughly equivalent to the O-level) and their prospects for further education were either in Home Economics or Teachers' Training College (such as 'Ecole Elie

Dubois'). Privately run Business Schools (Ecole Maurice Laroche) offered training in office procedures, book-keeping and accounts. Before the 1930s, professional opportunities were very limited. Middle-class married women were not expected to work and young women were supposed to prepare themselves (through needlework and home economics) for their wedding and be on the lookout for the wealthy husband, preferably white and foreign, who would offer them an easy life. Haitian literature is filled with portrayals of such women coached by calculating mothers, hunting rich husbands (Hibbert, 1910; Lhérisson 1905, 1966). In 1974, Ertha Pascal Trouillot published a two-page list of legislation which restricted married women.[2] Then in 1982 women's prior status of Minor was revoked but only women who married after the enactment of the law benefited because of the principle of non-retroactivity in Haitian law.

At first, Haitian women writers and feminist activists emerged from the middle and upper middle class. Influenced by North American, Latin American and European feminists, they tried to organize themselves and lobby for civil and political equality. The 22nd February 1934 saw the launching of the first women's civil rights movement, 'La Ligue féminine d'action sociale' (Women's League for Social Action) which campaigned for access to higher education and voting rights. The political circumstances of the 1930–55 period gave women the opportunity to organize and to voice their complaints. The period saw some gains for women as they subsequently gained access to the Baccalaureat (A-levels examination), then to the University (the Medical School) and in 1950 they

Figure 2   1968 Girls convent school in Haiti.

obtained the right to vote. Haitian historian Claude Moïse dates women's increasing involvement in politics from 1929 (1990: 287). He considers the 1950 Constitution as a victory for the women's movement after the major setback of 1946 when the Government had revoked women's eligibility for political appointment (Moïse, 1990: 287–8). Moïse writes:

> Du point de vue du droit public, la grand nouveauté de la Constitution de 1950 est sans aucun doute l'accession de la femme à l'exercice de ses droits politiques.
> (1990: 318)

(From the viewpoint of public law, the great innovation in the 1950 Constitution is undoubtedly women's access to their political rights.)

In a footnote he acknowledges the part played by the Women's movement, La Ligue féminine d'action sociale, in this struggle:

> Le fer de lance du mouvement d'émancipation des femmes est constitué par la *Ligue féminine d'action sociale* qui, depuis sa fondation en 1934, ne rate pas une occasion tant sur le théâtre national, dans le cadre des luttes de pouvoirs, que sur les tribunes internationales, de promouvoir les revendications pour l'égalité civil et politique en Haïti. *La Voix des femmes*, organe de la Ligue et *La Semeuse* fondée en 1937 par Jeanne Pérez témoignent de l'action féministe sur une longue période.
> (Moïse 1990: 319, footnote)

(The women's emancipation movement was spearheaded by *La Ligue féminine d'action sociale* (The Women's League for Social Action) which never missed an opportunity since its creation in 1934 to promote their claims for civil and political equality in Haiti, both at the national level – within the framework of power struggles – and at the international level. *La Voix des femmes* (Women's Voice), the League's magazine, and *La Semeuse* (The Female Sower) created in 1937 by Jeanne Perez are the symbols of feminist action over a long period.)

During the François Duvalier era, the women's movement went undercover. Most of its outspoken leaders went into exile and the remaining members turned the movement into a kind charitable organization in order to avoid persecution by the government. The movement survived the Duvaliers' dictatorships but failed to attract the younger generation. Even after 1986 it remained mostly middle-class oriented and rather conservative.

The François Duvalier dictatorship was ruthless against women from the opposition, as documented by Carolle Charles. However, according to Ertha Pascal-Trouillot (1974), the 1961 François Duvalier Labour Law was very progressive concerning women's emancipation although the fact that the measures were never enforced hindered women's progress as promoted by this law. She also points out the contradiction between Labour Law and Civil Law since the former allowed transactions at the workplace that were not allowed by the latter in civil society (Pascal-Trouillot, 1974: 16). Married women experienced more restrictions than unmarried ones: a married woman would need her husband's authorization to present a case in court. Similarly, the Social Security Act passed in 1967 offered better protection to working women (Pascal-Trouillot, 1974: 18,19). The contradictions of the Duvalier dictatorship were also apparent in the corruption at the National Insurance Office and its collapse in 1987.

On the pretence of promoting equality between men and women, François Duvalier created a female section to his 'Macoute' corps, named after Marie-Jeanne, a heroine of the Haitian War of Independence. These militia women were nicknamed 'Fiyèt Lalo', the name of a sorceress in a popular song. Mrs Max Adolphe, chief of his Militia staff was well known for her cruelty. The Duvalier dictatorship encouraged violence against women and used rape as torture against the wives and daughters of political opponents. This violence was to be overshadowed only by the 1991–4 repression.

The Jean-Claude Duvalier dictatorship (1971–86) started with an apparent liberalization during the period up to 1980. The restrictive legislation identified by Ertha Pascal-Trouillot was rather loosely enforced particularly for business activities, although in some cases it was used against wives of disappeared opponents to the regime and in cases of marital disputes and divorces.

Most contemporary upper- and middle-class women are involved in some form of professional activity. They hold executive positions in the trade and banking sectors at par with their male counterparts, although there are still some occupations that are predominantly male, particularly in the field of applied sciences. Women's groups speak out against the fact that very few women hold an elected position. The Ministry of Women Affairs in the Preval Government is said to have been established as a result of much lobbying by women's organizations.[3]

Middle-class women have also excelled in the fine arts, in dance and painting. Young women enrolled very early on at the 'Centre d'art' created by Dewitt Peters and some became prominent painters such as Luce Turnier, Marie-Josée Nadal and Rose-Marie Desruisseaux. Others, such as Yvonne Sylvain, abandoned painting to pursue medical studies; she became the first female gynaecologist-obstetrician in Haiti. They are few in numbers: Haitian middle-class education discourages artistic skills among women and, moreover, women artists are frequently considered deviant, bringing shame to their families (Poujol-Oriol, 1996).

Haitian women and their literary representation

From its inception, Haitian literature was politically motivated (committed). Emerging after the National Independence war, caught in the early civil wars (1807) and the fear of a French invasion, early writings reflect the violence of the times. French revolutionary discourses strongly influenced their rhetoric (Gouraige,1960: 13,14) and the literary representation of Haitian women immediately took on a symbolic value. The first Haitian novel, *Stella* (1859) by Emeric Bergeaud, uses a female protagonist as an allegoric figure of Freedom. Stella is the daughter of a white planter who is saved by two brothers, one mulatto, the other black, during the slave uprising of 1791. She helps them in the War of Independence and once the war is over, reveals that she was 'Freedom' before disappearing to Heaven, leaving a message of solidarity and brotherhood.

A similar pattern prevailed in poetry, creating a literary equation 'Woman = Haiti = Freedom'. During the colonial era, women were evoked in the traditional rhetorical framework of French love poetry. 'Lisette quitté la plaine', a poem recorded by Moreau de Saint-Méry in his *Description de la partie occidentale de Saint-Domingue* (1797–8), illustrates this type of representation. After Independence, it was not until the poems of Alcibiade Fleury-Battier[4] that one finds tropical images being used to portray women, albeit with European features. It is with the noted poet Oswald Durand, in the latter part of the century, that an ethnic characterization of Haitian women appears in Haitian literature. A womanizer, Oswald Durand is the first to introduce black Haitian women in his poetry and to comment on the various ethnic types which existed in the country. According to Gouraige (1960), he was the first if not the only poet to celebrate the female body and the peasant women. His most famous poem 'Choucoune', written in Haitian Creole, celebrates the 'Marabout', a dark skin mulatto woman with straight hair, considered the perfect mix of African and European beauty. During the American Occupation, Durand's example was followed by the poets of the 'Indigenous' Movement. (This was a cultural and literary movement of resistance to the Occupation which promoted the African heritage in Haitian culture and the peasant culture that until then had been ignored. The ideology of the Movement was articulated by Jean Price-Mars in two major books, *Ainsi parla l'oncle*, (1928) and *La Vocation de l'élite* (1919).) The most famous poem celebrating the black woman is Emile Roumer's 'Marabout de mon coeur' (My Beloved 'Marabout'). In this poem, the persona declares his love to his 'Marabout' using Haitian fruit and food imagery in an extended metaphor strongly marked with orality.

FEMINIST REVIEW NO 59, SUMMER 1998

The first Haitian novels were set in Europe and their female protagonists were mostly Europeans (French, usually, or Italian). With the emergence of realism as a literary movement, a more nationalistic approach influenced the novels with stories set in Haiti. Novels published at the beginning of the twentieth century criticized Haitian political life and offered a vivid description of the society and its mores. Female characters come from the emerging middle class. They fall in two categories: married women (mothers and dutiful spouses) and maidens whose future is threatened by political instability. Generally in these fictions married women are portrayed as unsophisticated, dedicated, strong-willed and devoted to their families. It is interesting to contrast early portrayals of Haitian women in Frédéric Marcelin's novels from 1901 to 1903, to later characterizations by Fernand Hibbert, between 1905 and 1923. In the works of Hibbert women appear cynical and anxious to 'whiten' their offspring and to climb the social ladder by marrying a white foreigner. Hibbert's bourgeois characters are corrupt (by money and politics). Husbands have lost their authority over ambitious and vain women who spend lavishly the money earned in dubious deals with the government. By the beginning of the twentieth century, novelists turned Haitian upper-class women into myths. These portrayals survived until the 1940s and 1950s since we find similar descriptions, with specific reference to Hibbert's works, in *Les Arbres musiciens* (The Musician Trees), a novel by famous Haitian writer Jacques Stéphen Alexis published in 1957. To be fair to these unscrupulous women, one must remember the political and economic instability of the period which saw many Haitian-owned businesses failing while foreign-owned ones received compensation for damages and loss incurred in civil wars.

With the 1915 American Occupation, Haitian women again became literary political symbols. During this period Haiti was once more feminized with an interesting paradigm of the black peasant woman as the symbol of the country's exploitation and resilience. In contrast, the mulatto maiden became the symbol of the upper class ready to make compromises with the Occupier. J. Michael Dash (1989) offers a very perceptive analysis of Haitian literature of this period in *Haiti and the United States*: 'Haitians found within Haiti a new muse. An earthy, sensual, uninhibited 'terre-femme' who could satisfy the new longings. Quite often this female figure was a prostitute whose experience was a microcosm of the national one' (p. 63, 1996 edition).

Haitian critic Régine Latortue shows how the novelists of this period, and even later, systematically developed a paradigm of strength and resilience to represent (and we would add, to idealize) peasant and working-class women. Strength is equated to beauty in most fictions. Physical descriptions borrow from the tropical fauna and flora and landscapes are described using female attributes. This imagery is not specific to male writers: similar ones appear in the work of Marie (Vieux) Chauvet and Marie-Thérèse Colimon, two leading Haitian female writers. Latortue notes that as symbols of life and nature, Haitian working-class women become almost literally the food necessary to men's survival (1984: 67). In these texts, there is a fusion/confusion between nature and women. In her conclusion, Latortue draws a parallel between these descriptions of peasant/working-class women and their contribution to the country's economy. She draws attention to the emergence of symbols associating sex with eating (as further analysed more recently by Laroche, 1997). In these texts she identifies an emerging mythology of new 'goddesses' associating strength with beauty, resilience with grace (Latortue 1984: 69).

While men's writings were published in the early years of Haitian Independence, women's writings do not emerge before the second half of the nineteenth century. Moreover, prior to the twentieth century, the few educated women who became famous all had something in common. They either had received an education in France and/or had upper- or middle-class origins, such as Virginie Sampeur (1839–1919) and Ida Faubert (1883–1969). In most cases, they were themselves educators, as was Virginie Sampeur. In addition, they had the opportunity to attend [male] literary circles through family contacts. This helped them to develop their writing skills. Virginie Sampeur, one of the earliest Haitian women poets, was the divorced wife of the famous poet Oswald Durand and Mrs Courtois, one of the first female journalists, was married to leading journalist and writer Félix Courtois. Ida Faubert, whose literary skills were acknowledged and encouraged by Haitian male writers of her time, was the daughter of Président Lysius Félicité Salomon and had been educated in France (Charles, 1980). This pattern still exists though contemporary women writers are mostly from the middle class.

Publications by Haitian women writers are far fewer than those of their male counterparts. For instance, an anthology of Haitian poetry published in 1978 included four female poets out of sixty-one selected authors (Condé, 1979: 81). There are two reasons for this discrepancy. One is limited access to higher education, as noted earlier. Women whose parents could afford to send them to France received a shallow, if refined, convent education. The second reason relates to the conditions of publishing which prevail in Haiti. Though Haiti has a record of publications (18,000 books in 1986[5]), what is less known is that most of these works were published through vanity press. To date, there is no well organized publishing house in Haiti. Women, of course, were at a disadvantage as far as publishing was concerned since they would need a generous husband or family to put up the requisite funds. Paulette Poujol Auriol had to wait almost ten years between her first and second book because she had to get returns from her first book in order to publish the second. In an interview with Maryse Condé in 1979, Marie-Thérèse Colimon revealed that her first novel lay in a drawer for thirteen years and was published only in 1974 when she won the France-Haiti literary competition (Condé, 1979: 117). Her second book, a collection of short stories was published in 1979.

In terms of international recognition, Haitian women writers are not as famous as their male counterparts. Marie Vieux Chauvet is an exception, mostly due to the circumstances surrounding the publication in 1968 of her masterpiece, *Amour, Colère Folie*. After the book was published, Chauvet was forced into exile by her husband's family who bought all the copies of the book from the publisher. Marie-Thérèse Colimon and Paulette Poujol-Oriol managed to make their name known abroad by winning a literary award; other female writers of the Haitian Diaspora are known in the literary circles of their adoptive countries (Liliane Devieux-Dehoux, Ghislaine Rey-Charlier, and more recently, Lilas Desquiron) Jan J. [Gigi] Dominique and Yanick Lahens who emerged more recently, are currently living in Haiti after studying abroad. The 1990s also saw the emergence of Haitian writings in English among the US-based Haitian diaspora. Edwidge Danticat is the most renowned as her first novel *Breath Eyes Memory* (1994) was widely acclaimed and translated in French as *Le Cri de l'oiseau rouge* (1996).

The question that arises is what differentiates women's from men's writings in Haitian literature. Like their (male) fellow writers, women writers are concerned with the social, economic and political circumstances of their country. The difference between the two rests in their approach. As suggested by Maryse Condé, Haitian women concern themselves with politics only when this impacts on their private lives (1979: 82). Like other female authors in the region, they are interested in writing about their childhood,[6] however, these stories deal less with individual concerns and more with the broader society. For instance in Lahens' short story 'The Blue Room', the young protagonist's childhood is shattered by the Duvalier dictatorship. This experience is recounted through directly witnessing the adults' fear and through an encounter with a political opponent hiding in her own house. While male writers offer a broader view of the society and its politics, women focus more on matters which impact on the private space. In addition, women writers are less lyrical than their male counterparts, their descriptions more sober and straightforward.

Another characteristic of Haitian women's writing can be found in the choice of narrative techniques. Women's fiction privileges the use of first person narration or the form of the diary. In third-person narration, they rely on introspection to give an insight into the main character. Given the nature of women's representation by male writers, we could add that women's fiction attempted a redefinition of the self during the post-Occupation period (cf. Chancy, 1997). This is particularly true of writers emerging in the 1930s and involved in the first women's organization (La Ligue féminine d'action sociale) such as Cléanthe Desgraves-Valcin, Annie Desroy, Marie-Thérèse Colimon, among others. Feminist ideas spread in Haiti during the 1930s and culminated in women's activism and demonstrations for voting rights in the 1950s. Nevertheless, if this political activism can be considered influenced by Western feminism, it does not transpire much in women's fiction. Very little Haitian women's writing openly tackles feminist issues, particularly issues pertaining to gender and sex. Therefore women writers have developed narrative strategies in order to voice, sometimes in muffled tones, their views on specific aspects of women's lives. Chancy (1997: 77) notes that:

> The most transgressive aspects of women's lives – their tenacity, their use of violence to attain liberation, their expression of sexual desire, to name but a few – are therefore told at a slant, as if there are secrets to be whispered and preciously preserved.

The use of a neurotic protagonist as a narrative voice is one of these strategies. Claire Clamont in Marie Chauvet's *Amour* (1968) and Paul/Lili in Jan J. Dominique's *Mémoire d'une amnésique* (1984) are examples of female characters who can speak the 'truth' about the (middle-class) female condition precisely *because of* their neurosis.[7] Haitian women's fictions, from this viewpoint, are more innovative as they had to '[reshape] the parameters of textual representation' (Chancy, 1997: 77), creating in more recent publications (Dominique) a 'postmodern effect'. Women writers sometimes use images or metaphors introduced by their male fellow writers as shown by Régine Latortue in her analysis of the representation of the black woman in Haitian fiction (Chancy, 1997: 68). However, they subvert these stereotypes by showing the dark side of these poetic metaphors. Their fiction reveals, without self-pity or complacency, the high price paid for standing up as the backbone of the country.

The traditional invisibility of women in Haitian society meant that women writers, who were more outspoken on feminist issues, ran the risk of alienating themselves from their class, from literary circles and even their family. As noted earlier, Marie Chauvet was forced into exile. Less known is the case of Nadine Magloire, who published two provocative books (*Le Mal de Vivre* (The Uneasiness of Life) in 1968 and *Autopsie in vivo: Le Sexe mythique* (Autopsy in vivo: The Mythical Sex) in 1975) dealing with sexual freedom and women's work and artistic creativity. In an interview with

Nicole Aax-Rouparis, she explains how these two books alienated her from Haitian feminists and intellectuals, and why she lives today in semi-seclusion in Montreal, Canada.[8]

Conclusion

Haitian women have struggled to make their voice heard. An analysis of their social condition shows that whatever their class, their tremendous contribution to their country and to the economy has never been thoroughly assessed. This social and economic 'invisibility' has been reproduced in the field of culture. As writers and artists, they are seen as deviant and marginalized. However, these women have challenged quietly yet decisively male stereotypes concerning them. Coming from a tradition in which women always had to summon their forces in silence and hold firm in the face of adversity, they have developed narrative strategies intertwining double discourse, *double entendre*, silence and words. They have tried to redefine themselves, subverting the dominant male discourse that sought to silence them. The new narrative strategies they crafted have enriched the body of Haitian literature. Most of these writers were at the same time involved in social activism and feminist struggles. They paid a dear price during the Duvaliers' dictatorship. Today, despite the volatile political climate and the harsh conditions of life in Haiti, women writers are trying to create a protected space from which will emerge new prospects for their country.

Notes

1 Personal communication: Mainmaine, with grand-mère Salnave; Ti Mène, with the Sangosse family; Lucienne, with the Dartigue family.

2 'Droit et Privilèges de la femme dans la législation civile et sociale d'Haïti,' *Conjonction*, No. 124; 'Femmes Haïtiennes', Août 1974, pp. 9–21.

3 Private conversations with women activists in October 1996. It was then said that former President Aristide was more open to women's claims and encouraged their organizations. He also appointed several female ministers in his government.

4 Born 1843, died 1883; his collection 'Sous les bambous' (Under the Bamboo Trees) was published in 1981.

5 David Norton in 'Haitian Publishers: Open New Chapters', in ISLA, Oakland California, August 1, 1987, p. 1014, col. 2. Quoted by Mireille Milfort de Ariza, p. 192, in 'L'Haitien face à la valeur sociale et aux domaines d'emploi du créole et du français,' *Anales del Caribe*, La Habana: Casa de las Americas, No. 13, 1994, pp. 191–9.

6 JacquelineTurian Cardozo's *On ne se guérit pas de son enfance* (Childhood Is Not Easy to Forget), J.J. Dominique's *Mémoire d'une amnésique* (Memories of an Amnesiac), Yanick Lahens' 'La Chambre Bleue' (The Blue Room) or Edwidge Danticat's *Breath Eyes Memories*. Cf. English translation of 'La Chambre Bleue' in Charles Rowell's anthology *Ancestral House*, Boulder, Col.: Westview Press, 1995.

7 Cf. Evelyn O'Callaghan's analysis of the recurrent pattern of 'neurotic/mad' female protagonists in fictions by Caribbean women writers in *Woman Version . . .* , Chap. 2, 'Mad Woman Version,' pp. 36–48.

8 Cf. Nicole Aax-Rouparis' Interview with Nadine Magloire in 1992 (Aax-Rouparis, 1997b). Also by the same author, 'Voix/voies migrantes haïtiennes: Nadine Magloire, de la parole au silence' (Haitian Migrant Voices and Paths: Nadine Magloire, from Speech to Silence) (Aax-Rouparis, 1997a).

References

AAX-ROUPARIS, Nicole (1997a) 'Voix/voies migrantes haïtiennes: Nadine Magloire, de la parole au silence' (Haitian migrant voices and paths: Nadine Magloire, from speech to silence) in **Rinne** and **Vitiello** (1997) pp. 53–62.

—— (1997b) 'Entrevue avec Nadine Magloire. Montréal, Novembre 1992. Nadine Magloire : "Une exilée de l'intérieur"' in **Rinne** and **Vitiello** (1997) pp. 63–8.

ALEXIS, Jacques Stephen [1957](1984) *Les Arbres musiciens* (The Musician Trees), Paris: Gallimard.

AYITI FANM (HAITI WOMAN) (1996) Monthly publication by Enfofanm, founded in 1990, Chief Editor: Clorinde Zéphir, Port-au-Prince. Vol. 6, Nos. 18, 19, 20, April, May and June.

BARTHÉLÉMY, Gérard (1988) *Le Pays en-dehors* (The Estranged Countryside), Port-au-Prince: Henri Deschamps.

BASTIEN, Rémy [1951](1985) *Le Paysan haïtien et sa famille* (The Haitian Peasant and His Family), Paris: ACCT/Karthala. (Originally published in Spanish as *La Familia rural haitiana*, Mexico: Libra.)

Bitter Cane (1984) Documentary film, 1 hour, New York.

BERGEAUD, Emeric (Posthumous, 1859) *Stella*, Paris: Maison E. Dentu.

CHANCY, Myriam (1997) *Framing Silence: Revolutionary Novels by Haitian Women*, New Brunswick, NJ: Rutgers University Press.

CHARLES, Carolle (1995) 'Gender and politics in contemporary Haiti: the Duvalierist state, transnationalism, and the emergence of a new feminism (1980–1990)' *FS / Feminist Studies*, Vol. 21, No. 1, Spring.

CHARLES, Christophe Philippe (1980) *La Poésie féminine haïtienne* (Poetry by Haitian Women), Port-au-Prince: Ed. Choucoune.

CHARLES, Jean-Claude (1982) *De Si jolies petites plages* (Such Beautiful Small Beaches), Paris: Stock/2.

CHAUVET, Marie (Vieux) (1957) *Fonds des nègres*, Port-au-Prince: Henri Deschamps.

—— (1968) *Amour, Colère, Folie*, Paris: Gallimard.

CONDÉ, Maryse (1979) *La Parole des femmes: Essai sur les romancières des Antilles de langue française*, Paris: L'Harmattan.

CORTEN, André (1986) *Port-au-Sucre: Prolétariat et Prolétarisations – Haïti et République dominicaine* (Sugar Port: Proletariat and Proletarization – Haiti and the Dominican Republic), Montreal: CIDIHCA.

CPEDAV (SOLER, René, MANGIN, Claire and PORCENA, Gina) (1993) *Fanm oganize men nou* (Here We Are, Organized Women), Documentary, 35 minutes, first aired on Télé Haiti on International Women's Day, 8 March 1993, Haiti/Canada.

DANTICAT, Edwidge (1994) *Breath Eyes Memory*, New York: Soho Press.

—— (1997) *Le Cri de l'oiseau rouge*, Paris: Presses Pocket. (French Translation by Nicole Tisserand).

DARTIGUE, Maurice (1938) *Conditions rurales en Haïti* (Peasants' Conditions in Haiti), Port-au-Prince: Service National de la Production Agricole et de l'Enseignement Rural, Bulletin No. 13, Imprimerie de l'Etat.

DASH, J. Michael (1989) *Haiti and the United States: National Stereotypes and the Literary Imagination*, Basingstoke/London: Macmillan, 2nd edn, 1996.

DAYAN, Joan (1995) *Haiti, History and the Gods*, Berkeley/Los Angeles/London: University of California Press – A Centennial Book.

DOMINIQUE, Jan J. [Gigi] (1984) *Mémoire d'une amnésique*, Port-au-Prince: Ed. Henri Deschamps.

FARMER, Paul (1994) *The Uses of Haiti*, Monroe/Maine (USA): Common Courage Press.

FASS, Simon (1990) *Political Economy in Haiti: The Drama of Survival*, New Brunswick (USA)/London (UK): Transaction Press, 1st publication, 1988.

GOURAIGE, Ghislain (1960) *Histoire de la littérature haïtienne (De l'Indépendance à nos jours)*, Port-au-Prince: Imprimerie N.A. Théodore.

GREGOIRE ISIDORE, Ginette (1997) Participant in the documentary *Fanm oganize men nou*, personal communication (March).

HAITI INSIGHT (1991–4, 1996) National Coalition for Haitian Refugees' Newsletter, New York. Since 1996 National Coalition for Haitian Rights.

HATFIELD, Patricia (1993) 'Getting to the Heart of Haiti' from promotional leaflet for D. Korb's *This Other Haiti*.

HIBBERT, Fernand [1910](1988) *Masques et Visages* (Masks and Faces), Port-au-Prince: Ed. Henri Deschamps.

—— [1910](1988) *Le Manuscrit de mon ami* (My Friend's Diary), Port-au-Prince: Ed. Henri Deschamps.

—— [1923](1988) *Les Simulacres* (The Pretenders), Port-au-Prince: Ed. Henri Deschamps.

—— [1906](1988) *Les Thazar*, Port-au-Prince: Ed. Henri Deschamps.

HRW/NCHR (Human Rights Watch/National Coalition for Haitian Refugees) (1994) *Rape in Haiti: A Weapon of Terror*, Washington/New York: HRW-Americas/NCHR, Vol. 6, No. 8 (July), 30 pages.

ICART, Jean-Claude (1987) *Négriers d'eux mêmes*. (Self-Enslavement), Montréal: Les Editions du CIDIHCA.

JEAN-JACQUES, Maryse, FABIEN, Ghislaine, THEBAUD, Edele and LAROSIL-LIERE, Michèle (1988) *Femme: Organisation et Lutte* (Women: Organizations and Struggles), Port-au-Prince: Centre de Recherche et de Formation Economique et Sociale pour le Développement (CRESFED).

KORB, David (1993) *This Other Haiti*, Documentary, New York: Ciné Soleil.

LAHENS, Yanick (1978) 'Le Paraître féminin, sa structure, sa stratégie dans le roman de Fernand Hibbert: *Les Thazar*' (Female appearance: structure and strategy in Fernand Hibbert's novel: *Les Thazar Conjonction*, Nos. 136–7, Février, Port-au-Prince: Institut Français d'Haïti, pp. 42–55.

—— (1995) 'The Blue Room' in **Charles Rowell** (1995) editor, *Ancestral House*, Boulder, Col.: Westview Press; translated from French by Kathleen Balutansky; originally published in the collection *Tante Résia et les Dieux*, Paris: L'Harmattan, 1996.

LAROCHE, Maximilien (1997) *Bizango: Essai de mythologie haïtienne* (Bizango: Essay on Haitian Mythology), Laval: GRELCA, Coll. Essais, No. 14, Université Laval.

LAROSILLIERE, Michèle (1988) 'A la Campagne, les femmes deviennent de plus en plus conscientes de leur situation et de la nécessité d'en sortir . . .'. (Increasing awareness among women in the countryside . . .) in **Jean-Jacques** *et al.* (1988) pp. 15–17.

LATORTUE, Régine (1984) 'Le Discours de la nature: la femme noire dans la littérature haïtienne' (Nature's discourse: black women in Haitian literature) *Notre Librairie*, 'Caraïbes: Afrique et Imaginaire Literaire' (The Caribbean: Africa and the Literary Imagination) No. 73, janvier–mars, Paris: CLEF, pp. 65–9.

LAVIOLETTE, Lionel (1982) 'Les Problèmes nutritionnels de la femme rurale' in *La Femme rurale en Haïti et dans la Caraïbe, traditions et innovations*. Collection du CHISS (Centre Haitien d'Investigations en Sciences Sociales), Port-au-Prince, pp. 139–53; quoted in Neptune-Anglade, 1986.

LHERISSON, Justin (1978) *La Famille des Pitite-Caille* (The Pitite-Caille Family)[1926] *Suivi de Zoune chez sa nainnaine* (Zoune at her Godmother's)[1906], Paris: Editions Caribéennes.

LOWENTHAL, Ira (1984) 'Labor, Sexuality and the Conjugal Contract in Rural Haiti.' in **Charles R. Foster** and **Albert Valdman**. *Haiti – Today and Tomorrow*, Lanham/New York/London: University Press of America: pp. 15–33.

MAGLOIRE, Nadine (1968) *Le Mal de Vivre*, Port-au-Prince: Editions du Verseau.

—— (1975) *Autopsie in vivo: le Sexe mythique*, Port-au-Prince: Editions du Verseau.

MILFORT de ARIZA, Mireille (1994) in 'L'Haitien face à la valeur sociale et aux domaines d'emploi du créole et du français' *Anales del Caribe*, La Habana: Casa de las Americas, No. 13, pp. 191–9.

MINTZ, Sidney W. (1960) *Worked in the Cane. A Puerto Rican History*, New Haven: Yale University. (Quoted in Corten, 1986).

MOISE, Claude (1989) *Constitutions et luttes de pouvoir en Haiti (1804–1987)* (Constitutions and Power Struggles in Haiti (1804–1987) Vol. I (1804–1915), Montréal: CIDIHCA.

—— (1990) *De l'Occupation étrangère à la dictature macoute* (From Foreign Occupation to Macoute Dictatorship) Vol. II (1915–1987), Montréal: CIDIHCA.

MORAL, Paul (1961) *Le Paysan haïtien (Étude sur la vie rurale en Haïti)*, Paris: Maisonneuve et Larose Ed.

MOREAU de SAINT-MÉRY [1797](1958) *Description topographique, physique, civile, politique et historique de la partie française de l'isle de Saint Domingue*, Paris: Larose, Société d'Histoire des colonies françaises. (3 volumes).

NEPTUNE-ANGLADE, Mireille (1986) *L'Autre moitié du développement* (The Second Half of Development), Pétionville: Editions des Alizés.

O'CALLAGHAN, Evelyn (1993) *Woman Version: Theoretical Approaches to West Indian Fiction by Women*, London/Basingstoke: Macmillan – Warwick University Caribbean Studies.

PASCAL-TROUILLOT, Ertha (1974) 'Droit et Privilèges de la femme dans la législation civile et sociale d'Haïti' (Women's rights and privileges in Haitian social and civil legislation) *Conjonction*, No. 124, 'Femmes Haïtiennes' Août, pp. 9–21.

POMPILUS, Pradel and FIC (Frères de l'Instruction Chrétienne) (BERROU, Raphaël) (1961) *Manuel illustré d'Histoire de la littérature haïtienne*, Port-au-Prince: Ed. Henri Deschamps.

POUJOL-ORIOL, Paulette (1996) Le Rôle des femmes haïtiennes en littérature (Haitian women's role in literature) unpublished paper at the Eighth Annual Conference of the Haitian Studies Association, 30 October–2 November, 1996, Delugé, Haiti.

PRICE-MARS, Jean (1919) *La Vocation de l'élite*.

—— (1928) *Ainsi parla l'oncle*, from English translation by Magdaline W. Shannon (1983) *So Spoke the Uncle*, Colorado Springs: Three Continents Press, 1994.

REGT, Jacomina P. de (1984) 'Basic education in Haiti' in **Charles R. Foster** and **Albert Valdman** (1984) editors, *Haiti – Today and Tomorrow*, Lanham/New York/London: University Press of America, pp. 119–39.

ROUZIER, Philippe (1989) *En Deux ans comme en deux siècles* (In Two Years As In Two Centuries), Port-au-Prince: Henri Deschamps/CIDIHCA.

RINNE, Suzanne and VITIELLO, Joëlle (1997) editors, *Elles écrivent des Antilles (Haïti, Guadeloupe, Martinique)* (They Write from the Antilles (Haiti, Guadeloupe, Martinique), Paris: L'Harmattan.

SHELTON, Marie-Denise (1993) *Image de la Société dans le roman haïtien*, Paris: L'Harmattan.

Gendered Testimonies:

Autobiographies, Diaries and Letters by Women as Sources for Caribbean History[1]

Bridget Brereton

FEMINIST REVIEW NO 59, SUMMER 1998, PP. 143–163

Abstract

Although history has been one of the main disciplines through which we can understand gender, the paucity of data written or recorded by women makes it more difficult for the historian to research women's lives in the past. In the Caribbean, this task has been made easier by the discovery of a few key sources which allow an insight into the private sphere of Caribbean women's lives. These records of women who have lived in the Caribbean since the 1800s consist of memoirs, diaries and letters. The autobiographical writings include the extraordinary record of Mary Prince, a Bermuda-born enslaved African woman. Other sources which have been examined are the diaries of women who were members of the élite in the society, and educated women who worked either in professions or through the church to assist others in their societies. Through her examination of the testimonies of these women, the author reveals aspects of childhood, motherhood, marriage and sexual abuses which different women – free and unfree, white, black or coloured – experienced. The glimpses allow us to see Caribbean women who have lived with and challenged the definitions of femininity allowed them in the past. It demonstrates that the distinctions created between women's private and public lives were as artificial then as they are at present.

Keywords

engendering history; sources; testimony; domesticity; sexuality; education

Over the last quarter of a century, historians have been engaged in the effort to rescue women of the past from their invisibility in the traditional record. This work of recovery and retrieval has made possible the redefinition of 'history' to include aspects of life previously seen as non-historical; they were seen as 'natural' and (therefore) timeless and unchanging, especially family relations, domesticity and sexuality. It has made it possible – indeed, imperative – for us to insert gender and gender relations into our work as historians, to 'engender history'.

These achievements have depended on finding sources which speak to

143

women's experiences in past societies. Historians are always prisoners to their sources and, by and large, women's voices have been silenced in the records of the past. Women have left far fewer traces than men in the historical records; most of what they created has vanished forever, and men have monopolized the written word as well as the public arena. Of course, the mainstream records which historians use may contain rich data about women and gender relations, and such records have been fruitfully mined by researchers asking different questions and bringing different perspectives. These include autobiographies, diaries and private letters written by men, which often yield excellent data about gender relations; Thomas Thistlewood's extraordinary Jamaican diaries come immediately to mind. Yet the evidence is usually scattered and problematic, and the records are often silent about the real lives of women.

This is why historians concerned to engender history have sought to capture the actual voices of real women, and to make their testimony, whether written or oral, central to their reconstruction of the past.

Oral history allows for the retrieval of life stories of women (and men) as they themselves conceptualize and tell them: real people, real lives. Its importance for reconstructing women's history is clear enough; as a French scholar puts it, 'women have spoken a great deal more than they have written'.[2] This dictum is even more true for Caribbean women than for Europeans. In the 1989 Elsa Goveia lecture, Blanca Silvestrini, the Puerto Rican historian, urged us to accept women's voices and their lives as they tell them (whether in oral or written testimonies) and to make them central to the writing of history.[3] Several scholars working in Caribbean history have taken up Silvestrini's challenge. Patricia Mohammed, for instance, made oral history central to her brilliant study of gender relations in the Indo-Trinidadian community in the first half of the twentieth century. She sees the method as critical, not only because many of her 'subjects' were illiterate or without access to the written word, but because she was seeking evidence on how women and men redefined and reconstructed gender in their private and family lives.[4]

Women's voices may also be captured through fiction. Literary sources, generally discounted by social historians as being too unreliable because they are generated by the artistic imagination, may be rich in materials. Elizabeth Fox-Genovese has argued that Toni Morrison's great novel *Beloved* evokes the story of women's experience of slavery in two ways. It depicts the feelings of a woman who endured slavery and is thus a source for the 'elusive psychological "facts"'.[5] It is a 'source for another history, namely the history of the elusiveness of women's experience of slavery until our own time': the history of why and how the story was repressed.

Though women have left far fewer traces in the written record than men, 'personal documents' left by literate women are a key source for women's history, a channel for the transmission of their own voices. They include autobiographical writings and memoirs, diaries and journals, private and family correspondence. Family papers and letters, Joan Scott notes, 'have revealed information about the texture of women's lives and family relationships'. Women are 'the scribes of the family', and their letters are rich sources for 'commonplace events and private life' which are the core of most people's lives. Diaries were often important outlets for self-expression for women whose lives might be very circumscribed. Autobiographies and memoirs contain the life histories of literate women. These 'personal documents' have been important sources in the engendering of European and American history.[6] I suggest that we can explore similar materials as sources of gendered testimony for Caribbean history; I shall limit my discussion to the English-speaking Caribbean.

There are few such sources. The great majority of Caribbean women up to the present century were outside the documentary culture, as were most men. Most of the women who wrote memoirs, journals or letters – those which have survived because eventually published, or found in private or public archival collections – were either outsiders, British for the most part, or belonged to the white Creole elite.[7] Black and Indian women were largely silent, in literary terms, until well into the twentieth century. Except for the celebrated autobiographies by Mary Prince and Mary Seacole, writings by black Caribbean women of the nineteenth century – letters, diaries, memoirs, fiction – have not often been located or used as sources.

Unlike oral history testimonies, these written personal documents have an inherent bias towards the privileged: letters, diaries, memoirs were much less likely to be generated by poorer women, were less likely to survive or to be published. This bias, of course, exists for European or American history too; Anna Davin notes that few nineteenth-century British workers wrote memoirs, and 'of women there are almost none'.[8] In the Caribbean case, some of the authors of these documents were British women, such as Lady Nugent, engaged in the imperialist enterprise even if in a subordinate role. Though this fact does not negate their value as sources of gendered testimony about Caribbean society, we need to note, as Evelyn O'Callaghan does, that their writings give us access to the voice of the colonizer's 'other half', even if women's position in the essentially patriarchal colonial project was often marginal.[9]

I shall examine in this essay some memoirs, diaries and letters by women who lived in the Caribbean since the early 1800s; most, but not all, have been published. They include five autobiographical writings. That by Mary

Prince, a Bermuda-born enslaved African-Caribbean woman, occupies a unique position in Caribbean historiography. It is the only extant work written by an enslaved woman from the British Caribbean and the first autobiography by a Caribbean woman. Born around 1788, Prince worked in Bermuda, the Turks Islands and Antigua, before coming to London with her owners in 1828, where she walked out of slavery. Mary Seacole's autobiography was first published in 1857. She was a mixed-race Jamaican born in the early 1800s who became famous as a nurse in the Crimean War. We have three memoirs all written by Trinidadian women born between 1888 and 1902: Yseult Bridges, a member of an elite French Creole family, wrote a memoir of her childhood in the late nineteenth century; Anna Mahase Sr. described her life as a student, teacher, wife and mother in Trinidad's Christian Indian community; and Olga Comma Maynard, a prominent Afro-Trinidadian teacher and writer, has recently published an autobiography.[10]

I also look at the diaries of three women. By far the best known is that of Maria Nugent, the British-American wife of a governor of Jamaica who lived there between 1801 and 1805: it was published after her death, though she certainly did not write with publication in mind. From Trinidad, I examine two unpublished diaries: Amelia Gomez, the Grenada-born wife of a prominent Venezuelan/Trinidadian lawyer, wrote a diary in the early 1840s, part of which has survived; and Adella Archibald, a Canadian missionary and teacher who lived and worked in Trinidad between 1889 and 1934, left a diary for 1930–6.[11] Finally, I read the letters of three women, British and Canadian, who lived in the Caribbean during the last century. Elizabeth Fenwick was a well-educated Englishwoman who ran a girls' school in Barbados between 1814 and 1821; her letters to a friend at home were subsequently published, over one hundred years later. Many letters by Sarah Morton, who lived in Trinidad between 1867 and 1912, were published as part of her biography of her husband, John Morton, the pioneer Canadian Presbyterian missionary to the Indians of the island. Finally Susan Rawle, wife of the Anglican Bishop of Trinidad in the 1870s and 1880s, wrote many letters to her relatives in England which have survived.[12]

How far can these memoirs, diaries and private letters by women help us to reconstruct the history of the region over the last two centuries? They all permit us to listen to women's voices and women's experiences (mediated, of course, by national origin, ethnicity and class), in contrast to the vast majority of written sources on the post-Columbian Caribbean which have been generated by men. Like oral testimonies, they often tell a life-story as the subject herself saw it, emphasizing the activities and emotions important to her own lived experience; they are potentially rich in experiential material. Though less democratic than oral testimony, they take us further back. Of course, as with all personal testimony, the shift from the specific and individual incidents, experiences and emotions to generalizations about society is often problematic for the historian. Diaries, private letters, memoirs (written or oral) are essentially individual as well as culturally and socially determined. What Mohammed says about oral testimonies could equally apply to the kinds of documents I examine: they are 'the lived examples of reality, which may or may not typify the norm, but which bring alive the actual people who have lived through and made this moment in history'. And Silvestrini reminds us that traditionally, historians have only 'listened' to the few individuals whose testimony made up the great bulk of conventional sources.[13]

One of the greatest insights of women's history is that no sharp rift existed (or exists) between women's 'public' and 'private' lives, and that the 'private sphere' has been much more central to the lives of women than of men in most human societies. Personal documents like diaries, memoirs and letters can illuminate this sphere, and help historians of the Caribbean to reconstruct it. Testimony by women (written or oral) often reveals the centrality of personal and familial relationships in their lives, and the whole world of experience and emotion generated by them. Historians have more or less accepted by now that such matters are legitimate (and necessary) subjects for their enquiry.

In examining my sample of personal documents by women, I shall be looking for testimony on their gendered life experiences, experiences probably different from those of men because of gender roles and expectations. I want to see how far these documents yield gendered perceptions of Caribbean society over the past two hundred years.

The centrality of the 'private sphere' to women's lives is reflected in most of our texts; they are a rich source of data on motherhood and marriage, health and sexuality, domestic life and household management, and the rearing and education of girls.

Mary Prince gave us a glimpse of the childhood of a slave girl in Bermuda at the end of the eighteenth century. In the relatively benevolent household of her first owner, Mrs Williams, she grew up with her mother, also a domestic, and her siblings. Mrs Williams' daughter made her a pet; 'she used to lead me about by the hand, and call me her little nigger. This was the happiest period of my life; for I was too young to understand rightly my condition as a slave, and too thoughtless and full of spirits to look forward to the days of toil and sorrow'. Prince's education consisted of instruction in the full range of domestic tasks, as well as care of livestock, from her various owners and fellow domestics. In her late 30s, she was taught to read by the wives of Moravian missionaries in Antigua; she records with pride 'I got on very fast'.[14]

Mary Seacole, born around 1805 to a white father and a free black Jamaican mother, was trained in medical and nursing skills by her mother, Mrs Grant. Mrs Grant was a noted 'doctress', a traditional healer, held in high esteem by Kingston's military men who frequented her lodging-house as much for medical care as for accommodations. Seacole acted as her assistant from the age of 12, and took over her lodging-house (along with her sister Laura Grant) on her mother's death. Mrs Grant exemplified the enterprising, independent, free black woman, making her way in a racist and sexist society, and Seacole's remarkable career owed much to this Jamaican tradition. She is explicit in her pride that she always earned her own bread and succeeded in life on her own.[15]

Both Maria Nugent and Elizabeth Fenwick saw how slavery corrupted the rearing of white children in the Caribbean. Nugent knew how hard it would be to prevent her little son, surrounded by domestics obliged to gratify his every whim, from 'thinking himself a little king at least, and then will come arrogance, and all the petty vices of little tyrants'. Children were 'injudiciously treated' in every respect and were made 'truly unamiable, by being most absurdly indulged'. Fenwick dreaded, for her grandchildren in Barbados, 'the sensual indulgences and luxury that most Children here are allowed'.[16]

Many élite girls attended schools for 'young ladies' of the kind run by Fenwick and her daughter in Bridgetown between 1814 and 1821. No mixed-race girls were admitted. The pupils, who stayed until they were 17 or so, studied writing, arithmetic, geography, history, music, dancing and French. Generally, though, élite parents tried to send their girls to England for a 'polish'. Nugent noted how Miss Israell of Clarendon, educated at a 'fashionable' London school, was forever consumed with anxiety lest her rustic parents embarrass her. In the 1890s, Yseult Guppy went to a private girls' school in Port of Spain run by an English lady; the teachers were young Creole women, badly paid, undereducated, and lacking any notion of how to teach. All the pupils were white. When the family moved to the country, Yseult received desultory tuition at home from her scholarly father. Then, at 14, came the inevitable: she was shipped off to England to be 'finished' before entering 'Society', to eradicate 'the insidious singsong Creole accent' and acquire that 'poise and complexion . . . which would enhance her chance of making a "good match". . . the whole object of a woman's existence'.[17]

Anna Chandisingh (later Mahase), second-generation Indo-Trinidadian[18] born into a Christian home in 1889, received a more useful education from the Canadian Presbyterian Mission. She attended the Mission-run primary school of which her father was headmaster, then spent four years in the Mission's Home for Girls in Tunapuna. She went in 1915 to the Girls' High School in San Fernando, studying for the teaching examinations; she and four other girls were the nucleus of the female section of the Mission-run Naparima Training College for Teachers. They studied along with the young men:

> To me it was a novelty, young East Indian men and girls in their teens, sitting and studying in one common room. It was the first of its kind . . . These were the days of the beginning of the emancipation of our East Indian girls and women.

Anna eventually passed the Third Class Teachers' Examination, and could begin her career (at 18) as a certified teacher in Mission schools. Her auto-biographical account of her education is usefully supplemented by Sarah Morton's letters and Adella Archibald's diary; both women pioneered the Canadian Mission's work with girls and women. Morton described the operation of the first Home for Girls, which she founded: the teenaged girls studied academic subjects, including Hindi and English, and religion; 'all the housewifely arts' were taught, including 'the mysteries of English dishes'; and the girls gardened, did all the housework and laundry, and cleaned the near-by Mission church. Many entries in Archibald's diary covering 1930–5 concern the Indo-Trinidadian women who became 'bible-women' (catechists) and teachers after their education in the Mission's primary schools, Homes for Girls and Training College.[19]

Anna Mahase's contemporary, Olga Comma (Maynard), was the daughter of an African-Trinidadian headmaster. She grew up in Belmont, a middle-class suburb of Port of Spain. Here she was socialized into gender roles. 'There was never any little girls on the roadway. There were many small boys, with torn trousers, rolling barrel hoops. . . . Little girls seemed to be kept inside to play with their dolls or to help clean the house.' On Saturdays, while her brothers ran errands like buying the coals, she cob-webbed and swept, or fed the latest baby sibling. She attended her father's elementary school, then the Tranquillity Girls' Higher Class, a sort of quasi-secondary school attached to a primary and 'model' school. She left this to become a pupil teacher at her father's school, receiving 5 dollars a month, and studying for the teacher's certificate on her own; she never went to Training College, but had a successful career as an elementary school teacher, with a fourteen-year break (1932–46) when she was forced to resign on marriage.[20]

So much of women's lives was lived in the 'private sphere'; and mother-hood is often central to that sphere. Maria Nugent gave birth to two infants in Jamaica. She wrote a lively account of her first 'Creole confinement' in 1802. As if a labour of two and a half days, oppressive heat, semidarkness and mosquitoes were not misery enough,

> the old black nurse brought a cargo of herbs, and wished to try various charms, to expedite the birth of the child, and told me so many stories of pinching and tying women to the bed-post, to hasten matters, that sometimes, in spite of my agony, I could not help laughing, and, at others, I was really in a fright, for fear she would try some of her experiments upon me. But the (English) maids took all her herbs from her, and made her remove all the smoking apparatus she had prepared for my benefit.

On the morning after the birth of her son, she was allowed a warm bath (she must have had an enlightened doctor); she spent three weeks in her bedroom, then resumed normal life. She engaged the wife of an Irish soldier as a wet-nurse, though she was upset that the heat, and her public duties, prevented her from nursing the baby herself ('why should I not be a mother indeed?') The inoculation of the baby against smallpox was a source of great anxiety; and Nugent tried to keep the baby away from the black domestics as much as possible, vowing that 'none of the blackies' should ever give him 'a morsel'. Her second confinement, in 1803, was easy: 'my illness was literally nothing, for I was actually speaking and walking towards the sofa, the instant before it was all over'.[21]

Amelia Gomez, in Trinidad in the early 1840s, was less fortunate. In 1841, after a long illness, she

> became worse and lost my hopes of giving my dear Husband a little son or daughter . . . I have been very much debilitated and have suffered more in that respect than I ever did before having been twice bled, and kept on a low diet.

She soon became pregnant again, and had a rough time 'being very much unwell and obliged to keep to my bed for some days and afterwards constantly to be in a recumbent position, the least effort disposing me to lose my second hope of being again a mother'. She had 'seven months close confinement on my sofa', an 'imprisonment' spent 'working and reading', worried at the 'fatigue and annoyance' her husband endured by being 'obliged to attend to the menage'. She gave birth to a 'fine handsome boy' in September 1842; 'I was much favoured by the Almighty in my hour of trial'. Gomez was constantly worried about the health of Richard, her son by her first marriage, and for several weeks in 1843 her diary is filled with references to his imminent departure for school in England (he was about 11). He was to travel alone, in the care of the ship's captain and his wife, to his mother's great anxiety. 'Every hour as it passed brought me nearer to the time of parting with my dear child', she wrote a few days before he left; 'this has indeed been a sore trial to me'.[22]

Mary Prince was childless; at least, there is no mention in her text of her ever giving birth. Was she made sterile by the repeated physical abuse to which she was subjected all through her childbearing years, as her modern editor speculates? As a teenager she witnessed the murderous flogging of a pregnant fellow domestic, Hetty, followed by the birth of a dead infant and Hetty's own death. Motherhood, in Prince's text, is pure tragedy. She describes her mother's misery when she, along with two sisters, was sold away at the age of 12:

> The black morning at length came; it came too soon for my poor mother and us. Whilst she was putting on us the new osnaburgs in which we were to be sold, she said, in a sorrowful voice, (I shall never forget it!) 'See, I am shrouding my poor children; what a task for a mother!' . . . 'I am going to carry my little chickens to market' (these were her exact words) 'take your last look of them'.

Slave mothers, Prince knew, 'could only weep and mourn over their children'; testimony to the 'implacable war against motherhood' waged by the slave system.[23] Slavery militated against marriage of the morally responsible kind, too; at the age of 38, Prince married a free black carpenter. He tried to buy his wife's freedom, but her owners refused, and Prince records in her usual terse style 'I had not much happiness in my marriage, owing to my being a slave. It made my husband sad to see me so ill-treated'. After only two years of marriage, she left him in Antigua when (still a slave) she accompanied her owners to Britain, and may never have been reunited with him.[24]

For élite girls, marriage was, of course, the only acceptable destiny. Yseult Bridges' French Creole mother, Alice Rostant Guppy, monitored likely white bachelors with meticulous care. She firmly believed that marriage, children and home were 'the very foundations' of a woman's life, and that love would follow marriage and motherhood, not the reverse. Both Yseult and her sister Ruth were married at eighteen to well-connected Englishmen working in Trinidad who were considerably older than the two girls. At the close of the nineteenth century, élite girls in Trinidad entered the marriage sweepstake at the annual Debutantes' Ball at Government House, and Bridges gives an amusing description of the drama surrounding Ruth's preparation for this event, on which 'her whole future' might depend. Not getting married meant failure, and relegation 'to the background of the home, there to live parasitically or to eke out a genteel existence in some ladylike way'. Mary Seacole's deliberate choice for independence as a single woman, a young widow ('and here I may take the opportunity of explaining that it was from a confidence in my own powers, and not at all from necessity, that I remained an unprotected female'), seems to have been unthinkable for élite white girls of the time, except for those who took the veil. And even the fiercely independent Seacole, whose whole life challenged nineteenth-century gender roles, represented herself as morally upright and ladylike; she carefully disassociated herself from the 'low' women she met in Panama, a place which, she said, 'was not agreeable for a woman with the least delicacy or refinement'.[25]

In the writings of Anna Mahase, Sarah Morton and Adella Archibald, we can trace the changes in marriage patterns and life chances for girls of the Indo-Trinidadian community. Mahase's mother, Rookabai, was a Hindu child bride in India who ran away from a traditional marriage at the age of 12 to a much older man (she was especially upset about his moustache). Defying the whole social and gender structure of traditional India, she emigrated to Trinidad in the 1880s. Here she came under the influence of the Canadian Presbyterian Mission. Converted, she acquired a new name (Elizabeth Burns), and went through a second arranged marriage to a promising young teacher, Anna's father. The missionaries actively sponsored (or vetoed) matches among their young converts. As Morton makes clear, the main purpose of the Homes for Girls run by the Mission was to prepare suitable brides for its teachers and catechists, and the teenaged pupils were married off at 15 or 16 to approved young men. She wrote in 1891

> many masculine eyes are turned anxiously in the direction of our Home. . . . We wish to keep our present pupils a little longer, for their own sakes. We shall then intimate to the expectants that they may advance their suit and the result will be to make room for new ones.

Morton was actively engaged in 'persuading' the girls to make the right choice, and, she wrote, 'I recall only one marriage arranged in the Home proved a really unhappy one'.

Anna Mahase might well have entered into a similar arranged marriage, as did most of her fellow pupils at the Home for Girls in Tunapuna, around 1914. A young teacher working in Princes Town 'asked for' her, but the missionaries vetoed the match because their policy was not to permit 'Tunapuna girls' to marry 'in the Princes Town field'. Then the missionary's wife arranged a match with a teacher. She had never spoken to the young man, but 'I did not mind because he belonged to a Christian family . . . so I decided in my mind that all would be well'. Nothing came of this, and Anna was still single at 18, in her first teaching job. She met Kenneth Mahase, a student teacher, and a discreet but clearly western-type courtship began. The two young people studied together and passed the teachers' examinations together. Once Kenneth was appointed as a head-teacher, they were married; Anna was 20. The missionaries approved, but this was no arranged marriage. By then (1919), the work of the Canadian Presbyterian Mission in many villages throughout Trinidad had given some

Indian girls an opportunity for education, for deferment of marriage, for mixing with boys during adolescence in schools and in the Training College. Ideas of choice in marriage, even if still limited, could begin to develop, first among the Christian Indian community. Ironically, this meant that the missionaries lost a degree of control over their young converts' options. Adella Archibald, in the early 1930s, records a few marriages of Presbyterian girls to men she disapproved of, and mentions a young woman, a trained teacher from a 'nice Christian family', who went 'off the track' and produced an illegitimate baby. Archibald tried to help her get a job 'as it was not advisable for her to take up teaching' in a Mission school.[26]

The health of husbands, children and friends was a constant preoccupation for many of these women. The Caribbean was a dangerous place for European residents at least up to the end of the nineteenth century, and fear of disease and sudden death pervades the journal and letters of Nugent and Fenwick. The latter wrote frequently about her grandchildren's many illnesses and the swift deaths of young pupils and friends. Her daughter was in constant ill health, and her beloved son, only 20, succumbed to yellow fever after an illness of just three days. 'We who seek for gain in these climates', she wrote, 'have terrible penalties awaiting us'. Nugent, too, worried endlessly about her husband's and her infants' health, and many journal entries recorded the illnesses and deaths of white people personally known to her. The many doctors who attended at King's House in Spanish Town (Jamaica's capital at the time) are familiar characters in her journal. She noted that white women in Jamaica were far more successful in keeping their health than the men; unlike the women, who were generally temperate in their habits, the men 'really eat like cormorants and drink like porpoises'. Fenwick found the same situation in Barbados: 'nothing is so common here as old Ladies of 80 to 100 years of age. The men shorten their period by intemperance and sensuality'. She was terrified that her son might slip into the almost universal 'habit of drinking'. Her son-in-law was a drunkard.[27]

In the latter decades of the century, Sarah Morton and Susan Rawle both worried about the health hazards of residence in Trinidad. Morton, her husband and their four children (three born in the island) all suffered severely from malaria and 'ague' in their first three years. She had two dangerous bouts of malaria in her first three years in the mission house at Iere Village, and in 1877 she nearly died from a serious disease (she does not name it in her letters) which forced her to spend over a year in Canada. Her letters to her husband in Trinidad indicate that she expected to die. Though Rawle says little in her letters to her sister in England about her own health, she often worries about English clergymen and their families getting malaria or yellow fever, especially during the 1881 epidemic. She also wrote about the health problems of the local population, noting with surprise the prevalence of tuberculosis; 'it is astonishing how tender the coloured people are especially & what little things give them colds'. Like Nugent and Fenwick before her, Rawle noted that 'drink is the greatest temptation out here & is very fatal', especially among young men. She applauded the work of the local temperance movement, though irritated by the 'humbug and overstraining of things' by its leaders. As in Britain and America, the temperance movement appealed especially to women, who recognized how drinking threatened their domestic world.[28]

Elite women were threatened, too, by sexual liaisons between white men and brown and black women, enslaved and free. Fenwick, writing in 1815 and no doubt influenced by the humanitarianism which had spread widely in educated British circles since the 1780s, showed some sympathy for the women involved in these relationships and their children. 'It is a horrid & disgraceful System', she wrote;

> the female slaves are really encouraged to prostitution because their children are the property of the owner of the mothers. . . . What is still more horrible, the Gentlemen are greatly addicted to their women slaves & give the fruit of their licentiousness to their white children as slaves. I strongly suspect that a very fine Mulatto boy about 14 who comes here to help wait on two young Ladies, our pupils, is their own brother. . . . It is a common case & not thought of as an enormity.[29]

Maria Nugent swiftly became aware of the sexual politics of Jamaica: the black 'chere amie', the 'mulatto ladies' who said they were 'daughters of Members of the Assembly, officers, etc, etc'. She concluded that 'white men of all descriptions, married or single, live in a state of licentiousness with their female slaves'. Though she was sympathetic to the children of these unions, especially the daughters, most of her concern was directed to the young white men who risked 'ruin' from their 'horrid connections' and 'improper lives'. Many journal entries describe her unsuccessful attempts to keep the British officers in the governor's staff from these entanglements. Driving around Spanish Town, Nugent encountered 'several of the unfor-tunate half-black progeny of some of our staff; all of fine muslin, lace etc. . . . What ruin for these worse than thoughtless young men!' On the evidence of her journal, she spared few thoughts for the young men's willing or coerced prey.[30]

Sexual abuse is a submerged sub-text in Mary Prince's narrative; extreme reticence characterizes her treatment of the subject. She explicitly de-scribes only one episode of sexual abuse, when she defied the advances of Mr D—, her third owner:

He had an ugly fashion of stripping himself quite naked and ordering me then to wash him in a tub. This was worse to me than all the licks . . . I defended myself, for I thought it was high time to do so. I then told him I would not live longer with him, for he was a very indecent man . . . with no shame for his servants, no shame for his own flesh.

After this act of defiance, she got herself sold to new owners: 'the truth is, I did not wish to be any longer the slave of my indecent master'. Prince presents herself as the active and courageous defender of her 'virtue', not as a passive victim. Moreover, her account shows that female slaves were capable, despite their own sexual jeopardy, of empathizing with white women victimized by male power. Prince herself risked serious injury in order to defend Mr D——'s daughter from her father's brutal beatings.[31]

Household management was, of course, the task of women, and for élite women in the Caribbean, control of the domestics, whether slave or free, was pivotal to their daily existence. It was one of the few forms of power they possessed, and defiance of their authority by the servants was seen as an assault on their status as women of the ruling caste. Yet they depended on the domestics, and interacted with them on a level of daily intimacy. The domestics intruded constantly into the personal and domestic lives – the real lives – of the white women. These relations of intimate enmity are salient in several of our texts.[32]

Nugent found the vast establishment at King's House to be disorderly and chaotic; but the domestics responded well when she met with them and promised them 'every kindness'. An evangelically minded Christian, she devoted a great deal of effort to religious instruction of the domestics, preparing a 'little Catechism' for them and seeing to their and their children's baptism. She delighted the King's House slaves by dancing with 'an old negro man' at a fete for the servants, 'exactly the same as I would have done at a servants' hall birthday in England', to the horror (of course) of the Creole ladies. A British aristocrat, secure in her caste status, she dealt with her slave domestics with a degree of tolerance and civility. But as she travelled around Jamaica, staying on plantations, she found many disorderly houses with crowds of dirty and badly clothed servants. The Creole ladies were 'perfect viragoes; they never speak but in the most imperious manner to their servants, and are constantly finding fault'. 'The continual scolding at the servants', Nugent wrote, 'is to me the most distressing thing in the world'.[33]

Elizabeth Fenwick found dealing with her domestics in Bridgetown an appalling task. The management of her household, she wrote, involved 'annoyances & fatigue . . . that the mistress of an English family, with even the worst of English servants, can form no idea of'. Her slave domestics, hired from their owners, were lazy, self-willed and dishonest; 'pilfering seems habitual & instinctive among domestic slaves'. Keeping house for her daughters, Fenwick told her English friend,

> I was several times almost mad with the provocations their dirt, disobedience & dishonesty caused me. . . . You would be astonished to hear me scold, – I do so, I assure you, & that with a vehemence which on reflection surprises and pains me.

With no sense of irony, Fenwick complained of 'the slavery of managing a family in the West Indies with Negro Domestics'. Just after the end of slavery, Amelia Gomez often complained to her diary about servant troubles; 'this evil increases', she wrote, 'quite wearing to the spirits, as well as the body, it leaves no leisure for any agreeable occupation or even for necessary duties'.[34]

It is Mary Prince who provides a unique testimony from the other side of the barricades. She was employed mainly as a domestic for most of her working life in the Caribbean (*c.* 1788–1828). Three of her four owners treated her, and her fellow domestics, with extreme brutality. Captain and Mrs I— of Bermuda, who bought her when she was about 12, routinely tortured their domestics, and murdered Hetty, a pregnant 'French' slave who died after an atrocious flogging ('the manner of it filled me with horror', Prince recorded). Mrs. I— flogged and beat Prince with her own hands; 'she was a fearful women and a savage mistress to her slaves'. Prince had to do cleaning and general housework, child minding, and milking and general care of the livestock; 'there was no end to my toils – no end to my blows'. Her last owners, the Woods of Antigua, constantly abused her both verbally and physically, yet she was their chief 'confidential servant' who was left in sole charge of the household during their frequent absences from home, and they refused to sell her despite several offers. The ability to control Prince, a woman of manifest dignity and intelligence, was clearly critical to the Woods' sense of power and status. When she got married at the age of 38 to a free black, both the Woods were furious; they could not tolerate her assertion of a right to a separate and autonomous personal and sexual life. Mr Wood flogged her, and Mrs Wood said 'she would not have nigger men about the yards and premises, or allow a nigger man's clothes to be washed in the same tub where hers were washed'.[35]

Growing up in a white Creole household in Trinidad fifty years after the end of slavery, Yseult Bridges recalls the black domestics and retainers as idealized servants of the old world. Her mother was a domestic tyrant, obsessively critical of her many servants, directing their lives with the arrogant self-confidence of a slave-owner's daughter. The servants (at least in Yseult's nostalgic memory) were utterly loyal; she shows no recognition of the degradation and self-contempt at the heart of these traditional relationships. Zabette, for instance, born a slave, had been wet-nurse to the Rostant babies and head domestic in the Rostant country house; she identified whole-heartedly with the white family, and liked to tell stories of the wonderful old days of slavery and high living on the patriarchal French Creole estates. Only rarely does a darker note creep into Bridges' memories of the servants. When her mother's maid was seduced by the handyman's son, both were instantly dismissed, the girl evicted pregnant and penniless; so much for paternalism. Though Bridges recalls the servants as affectionate presences in her childhood, blacks outside the domestic setting were vaguely menacing. She recounts what was, perhaps, the classic nightmare of the white Creole girl: As a child of 9 or 10, she was walking alone in a rough part of Port of Spain, when she was stopped by a black man who must have assumed she was lost.

> To my horror a huge negro stepped in front of me, grinning, and barred my way. 'Let me pass', I said, trying to assume an imperious air. . . . The negro grinned still more widely . . . I was now getting frightened. He gave a loud guffaw, echoed from all sides from the crowd that was collecting now, hemming me in, from the ragged children prancing around me. They gaped and jabbered, and the smell of their unwashed skin and clothes was rank and nauseating. My knees went weak, my stomach seemed to cleave to my spine. . . . The big negro man took a step towards me with his hand outstretched, intending to grip me by the arm . . . I think I must have been on the point of fainting . . .

when she was 'rescued' by a kindly (and masterful) Englishman.[36]

The diaries and letters of Morton, Rawle and Archibald often mention the difficulties of managing their households, though these women (all connected to the Anglican or Presbyterian churches) are generally appreciative of their various domestics. Morton told her relatives at home in Canada about the novel aspects of housekeeping in the tropics (ants, snakes, flies, as well as problems with the helpers), and the loneliness and monotony of life for the young wife in an isolated mission house (in Iere Village deep in rural southern Trinidad). When they moved to a house in San Fernando the kitchen was an old mulestall; 'no doubt the mule had been fairly comfortable there, but cook and I were not'. She wrote home in 1876:

> My cook has left me to nurse a sick child; Willie [her baby son] has the mumps and cries a great deal; a silver spoon is lost; I often wish I had some one to attend to the house and let me teach the Indians.

Archibald, who lived in Trinidad for about forty-five years as a teacher and mission worker, seems (on the evidence of her diary) to have had warm relationships with her (mainly Indian) domestics, such as Thelma Bahadur, whose wedding she attended and whom she frequently visited after her marriage.[37]

In her autobiography, Olga Maynard gives an interesting account of house-keeping in a black headteacher's family in Port of Spain at the opening of the twentieth century. The large household (Olga's mother had twelve children, four of whom died as infants) employed one helper. An essential feature of domestic life was the many vendors (mostly women) who sold foodstuffs from door to door, each day: a black woman sold sticks of chocolate for the breakfast tea each morning; a 'veiled Indian woman' sold milk from a pail, by the dip; an elderly Indian woman had vegetables and fruits carried on a wooden tray on her head; the fishwife sang her wares in French Creole. The 'old-time kitchen', detached from the house, was the centre of the housewife's activities, and Maynard gives a detailed description of such a kitchen, with its coal-pot fire, its coffee mill and cocoa stone (for grinding the coffee and cocoa beans), its 3-foot wooden mortar and pestle for pounding plantain or breadfruit. Maynard lived in Tobago during the Second World War, and describes how difficult it was to feed a family in the face of constant shortages of imported food. Butter, cheese, tinned food, Cow & Gate milk (she had young children), onions, all disappeared, and flour came and went (she would line up for hours to get maybe 2 pounds of discoloured flour with weevils). Housewives tried hard to prepare decent meals; fried green bananas substituted for bread, plantains 'threatened to grow out of our ears', honey took the place of sugar. When Maynard returned to teaching in Trinidad in 1946, she employed a 'maid of all work' to help, but she spent most of her evenings after school preparing dinner, and the next day's breakfast and lunch.[38]

For middle- and upper-class Caribbean women, the idea, derived from European gender ideology, that they should be largely confined to the 'private sphere' had considerable force. It was never of any real relevance to working-class women after the end of slavery, far less to female slaves. Mary Seacole stands out as the great nineteenth-century exception: her extraordinary life was lived almost entirely in the public arena, indeed in a largely masculine arena, though she presents herself as a feminine person of 'delicacy and refinement'. Maynard and Mahase, each born at the turn of the nineteenth century to headmaster fathers, had satisfying careers as teachers; Mahase was not forced to resign on her marriage in 1919, thanks to the intervention of the Canadian Mission, and combined teaching with raising a large family; Maynard had to resign in 1932 but returned to teaching in 1946 when the Trinidad government quietly reversed its policy. But for women of the white élite, working outside the home was usually unacceptable before the 1920s, except for unfortunate spinsters or widows, as Bridges noted of her family's social circles. Religious and charitable activities provided one of the few socially sanctioned opportunities for these women to enter the 'public sphere', in the Caribbean as in Europe.

A good example is Amelia Gomez. Her social life consisted of an endless round of private visits, dinners and luncheons, but a large part of her diary describes her participation in the life of the Roman Catholic church (she was a convert from Anglicanism) and its charitable work. Susan Rawle organized Anglican ladies of Port of Spain into a 'working party' to make objects to sell for charity; 'the ladies seem to like it so far', she told her sister, '& it is a good thing to get them out & lead them to take some interest, if ever so little, in something outside themselves'. Some of her ladies taught Sunday school, others were involved in the temperance movement or worked with her in the 'Young Women's Help Society' which she founded to help girls 'to keep the right course'. Both Rawle and Morton, as the wives of senior clergymen working in Trinidad, functioned in effect as full-time assistant missionaries, with (of course) neither status nor salary from their churches. Morton, coming to the island as a young wife, raising her four children in mission houses often in fairly remote villages far from Port of Spain, struggled against chronic ill-health, loneliness, social isolation and exhaustion. But she was always fully involved in the Mission's work, especially in its attempt to reach the Indo-Trinidadian girls and women. She mastered Hindi after a few years, and she spent most of her time visiting Indian women in their barracks and cottages, teaching classes for girls and women, and running the residential Home for Girls which she founded; her daughter Agnes also became fully involved in all these activities after she left school in Canada. Unlike Morton, Adella Archibald was a salaried employee of the Canadian Women's Missionary Society (of the Presbyterian Church), charged with teaching in Mission schools and working with women. She first came to Trinidad in 1889 as a young woman of 20, retiring in 1934. Since she was not an ordained minister, of course, both her salary and her status in the church were lower than the clergymen's, but she did have a recognized position, and her forty-five years of work in Trinidad clearly won her considerable respect. The missionary endeavour, like the colonial enterprise to which it was so closely linked, was definitely a male project (even patriarchal), but it provided real opportunities for some women, albeit in subordinate roles.[39]

Through the writings of Morton, Archibald and Mahase, we can trace the impact of the Canadian Mission on the lives of Indo-Trinidadian women, as schooling and western values gradually changed life-chances for many of them. Archibald's diary gives a detailed account of the innumerable 'women's meetings' she held, in Indian villages or homesteads, or estate housing, all over southern Trinidad in the early 1930s. Most of the women attending were Hindus or Muslims. With the help of Indo-Trinidadian biblewomen, she ran Sunday schools and organized groups of girls and women. Literacy and schooling for the children were, of course, key incentives for Indian women to respond positively. At a meeting of twenty-two women in Penal, for example, they asked Archibald to organize them, and to set up a reading class 'as a number, even of the young women, are not able to read' (this was 1930). By then the Mission had a network of coeducational primary schools in virtually every area where Indians lived, as well as a girls' secondary school (Naparima Girls' High School), a female Training College, and a residential Home for Girls. By then, too, a number of Indian women, educated and trained in the Mission's institutions, had emerged as biblewomen, trained teachers and professionals. Many entries in Archibald's diaries record her pride in these women's achievements.[40]

The influence of the Mission's work with women – largely carried out by women, Canadian and Indo-Trinidadian – gradually changed their lives, by providing western education for many, by allowing for postponement of marriage and mixing between adolescent boys and girls, and by spreading western notions of love and courtship and western ideologies of gender. Morton encountered (and sparred with) a Brahmin father who remonstrated with her 'if you teach a boy you will get some good of it, but a girl is not yours; she is some other man's; why should you trouble with her?' Gradually, such attitudes became less acceptable in the Indo-Trinidadian community, and a life like that of Anna Mahase, born in 1899 – western schooling, a career as a trained teacher, a western-type marriage – became possible, if only for a few.[41]

These autobiographies, diaries and letters by women provide some rich testimony about women's historical experiences in the Caribbean. They often speak to the real quality and texture of women's lives, so much of them played out in the private and domestic spheres. Along with oral testimonies, and the mainstream of historical records generated in the vast majority by men, they may help to reconstruct the Caribbean past in a more nuanced way – in short, they may help to engender this region's history.

Notes

1 A slightly different version of this essay was published under the same title as the 1994 Elsa Goveia Memorial Lecture (UWI, Jamaica, 1994). The author and editor thank the Department of History, The University of the West Indies, Mona, Jamaica, for permission to republish.

2 M. Perrot, 'Making history: women in France', in S.J. Kleinberg (ed.), *Retrieving Women's History* (Paris, 1992), 50. The essays in this collection by Perrot, A. Davin and J.W. Scott include useful discussions on sources for women's history.

3 Blanca Silvestrini, *Women and Resistance: Herstory in Contemporary Caribbean History*, 1989 Elsa Goveia Memorial Lecture (UWI, Jamaica). Elsa Goveia was a distinguished West Indian who pioneered research and teaching in Caribbean history at the University of the West Indies. She died in 1980 and is commemorated in a series of annual lectures at the Mona (Jamaica) campus of the University.

4 P. Mohammed, 'A social history of post-migrant Indians in Trinidad from 1917 to 1947; a gender perspective', PhD, Institute of Social Studies, The Hague, 1993, especially 52–68; see also Mohammed, 'Structures of experience: gender, ethnicity and class in the lives of two East Indian women', in K. Yelvington (ed.), *Trinidad Ethnicity* (Knoxville, 1993), 208–34.

5 E. Fox-Genovese, *Unspeakable Things Unspoken: Ghosts and Memories in the Narratives of Afro-American Women*, 1992 Elsa Goveia Memorial Lecture (UWI, Jamaica).

6 J.W. Scott, 'The problem of invisibility', in Kleinberg, 10; Perrot, 47–9.

7 'Creole' is used in the accepted Caribbean sense of 'born in the Caribbean'.

8 A. Davin, 'Redressing the balance or transforming the art? The British experience', in Kleinberg, 70.

9 See E. O'Callaghan, *Woman Version: Theoretical Approaches to West Indian Fiction by Women* (London, 1993), 17–28.

10 Mary Prince. *The History of Mary Prince A West Indian Slave: Related by Herself*, edited by Moira Ferguson (London, 1987; first published 1831); Mary Seacole, *Wonderful Adventures of Mrs. Seacole in Many Lands*, edited by Z. Anderson and A. Dewjee (Bristol, 1984; first published 1857); Y. Bridges, *Child of the Tropics: Victorian Memoirs*, edited by N. Guppy (London, 1980); A. Mahase, *My Mother's Daughter: The Autobiography of Anna Mahase Snr. 1899–1978* (Claxton Bay, Trinidad, 1992); Olga Comma Maynard, *My Yesterdays* (Port of Spain, 1992). For comparison with Prince's text, see Harriet Jacobs, *Incidents in the Life of a Slave Girl, Written by Herself*, edited by Jean Fagin Yellin (Cambridge, Mass., 1987; first published 1861). Jacobs was a former American slave.

11 Maria Nugent, *Lady Nugent's Journal of Her Residence in Jamaica from 1801 to 1805*, edited by P. Wright (Kingston, 1966); 'Unpublished Diary of Amelia Gumbs Gomez 1841–43', typescript and notes by Michael Pocock; 'Unpublished Diary of Adella Archibald 1930–36', typescript by Gordon J. Archibald. I had intended to include Edna Manley's diaries, published in 1989. But they tell the life-story of such an extraordinary woman, who lived so much in the public sphere, that I found it difficult to incorporate them into the discussion.

Edna Manley was an eminent Jamaican artist and 'mother' of modern Jamaican sculpture and painting. She was also the wife of Norman Manley and the mother of Michael Manley.

12 A.F. Fenwick (ed.), *The Fate of the Fenwicks: Letters to Mary Hays, 1798–1828* (London, 1927), 161–217; S.E. Morton, *John Morton of Trinidad* (Toronto, 1916); unpublished letters by Susan Rawle, 1857–86, Rawle Mss File 8, Correspondence, Trinidad, Rhodes House Library, University of Oxford.

13 Mohammed, 'Social History', 66; Silvestrini, 16. For a perceptive discussion of this issue as it relates to oral history, see Mary Chamberlain, 'Gender and memory: oral history and women's history', in *Engendering History: Caribbean Women in Historical Perspective*, ed. V. Shepherd, B. Brereton, B. Bailey (Kingston, 1995), 94–110.

14 Prince, 47–8, 73.

15 Seacole, 55–7. For the Jamaican tradition of brown and black women keeping hotels which doubled as nursing homes, see A. Josephs, 'Mary Seacole: Jamaican nurse and "Doctress", 1805/10–1881', *Jamaican Historical Review* XVII, 1991, 48–65.

16 Nugent, 146–7; Fenwick, 200.

17 Fenwick, 167–9, 191, 202; Nugent, 58; Bridges, 97, 116–20, 157.

18 The term 'Indo-Trinidadian' refers to immigrants who came from India to Trinidad between 1845 and 1917, and their locally born descendants.

19 Mahase, 20–8, 32–4; Morton, 343–9; Archibald Diary, e.g. entries of 5/8/1930, 21/10/1930, 8/12/1930, 6/4/1931, 16/3/1932, 12/5/1932, 30/12/1933.

20 Maynard, 4, 43–8, 104, 108–11. Female public servants, including teachers, were obliged to resign on marriage in Trinidad. Though the colonial government relaxed this rule around 1946, it was not revoked until the early 1960s.

21 Nugent, 123–32, 118–22, 198–9, 174–9.

22 Gomez Diary, entries of 14/9/1841, undated (probably October 1842), 8/1/1843, 17/4/1843, 7/5/1843, 10/5/1843.

23 Caribbean plantation slavery meant low fertility rates for enslaved women, forced separation of families, and appallingly high infant and child mortality rates.

24 Prince, 50–3, 74–5; Fox-Genovese, 11.

25 Bridges, 157–66; Seacole, 59–61, 100.

26 For this and the preceding paragraph, Mahase 3–5, 11–20, 22–44; Morton, 347–52; Archibald Diary, e.g. entries of 4/7/1931, 17/3/1932; cf. Mohammed, 'Social history', 152–3.

27 Nugent, 186, 59, 81; Fenwick, 182–7, 196–7, 204, 171, 173-74, 193.

28 Morton, 86–91, 138–40, 173–84; Rawle letters to her sister, 23/5/1882, 24/6/1882, 6/8/1882, 10/6/1886, 29/9/1886.

29 Fenwick, 169–70. Fenwick's correspondent, Mary Hays, a radical British writer, had published an anti-slavery novel, *The Memoirs of Emma Courtney*, in 1796. See Moira Ferguson, *Subject to Others: British Women Writers and Colonial Slavery*, 1670–1834 (New York, 1992), 194–6.

30 Nugent, 12, 29, 30, 68, 78, 86–6, 172–3, 214.

31 Prince, 67–8, 71–4, 48.

32 cf. O'Callaghan, 26–7.

33 Nugent, 11, 12, 234, 156, 80, 82, 59.

34 Fenwick, 163–4, 167, 168, 175, 188–9; Gomez Diary, e.g. entry of 16/4/1843.

35 Prince, 52–60, 69–78.

36 Bridges, 27, 32, 46–64, 82, 181, 188–91, 112–113. A sensitive fictional portrayal of the Madam–servant relationship in a French Creole family very like that of Bridges can be found in *Witchbroom* (London, 1992) by the Trinidadian writer Lawrence Scott.

37 Morton, 42–9, 97, 157–8; Archibald Diary, e.g. entries of 17/6/1931, 4/7/1931.

38 Maynard, 4–6, 79–80, 93–4, 100–4, 110, 115.

39 Gomez Diary, *passim*; Rawle to her sister, 6/4/1878, 23/5/1882, 5/9/1883; Morton, 67, 83–4, 223–58, 340–54, 355.

40 Archibald Diary, *passim*; quotation, entry of 10/9/1930.

41 Morton, 257–58.

Masculinity and the Dance of the Dragon:
Reading Lovelace Discursively[1]

Linden Lewis

FEMINIST REVIEW NO 59, SUMMER 1998, PP. 164–185

Abstract

The exploration and examination of the construction of masculinity is increasingly emerging as an integrated part of the study of gender in society in general, and in the Caribbean in particular. We are constantly in search for new sources of material which tell us about the ways in which men construct their masculinity in Caribbean society. In this paper I draw on the imagery and ideas provided by the literary text. I interrogate the novel *The Dragon Can't Dance*, written by Trinidadian novelist Earl Lovelace. The writer uses the metaphor of the dragon, the costume donned by the main protagonist Aldrick in the yearly Carnival masquerade, as a mask which disguises the need for Aldrick to confront his own masculinity under poor, urban conditions in Trinidad. In the struggles and confrontations between urban working–class men and women in the community of Calvary in Trinidad, the novelist teases out the different constructions of masculinity in the various characters he portrays. I explore the novel, focusing particularly on the ways in which this construction is embedded in the struggles over issues of identity, ethnicity, reputation and honor. While the novelist is clearly able to read into the mind of the male in society, his renditions of the female are not so incisive. However, this is not a shortcoming as the women, though not as well-rounded characters in the novel, play key roles in the definition and shaping of masculinities. This reading of the novel illustrates that the literary text suggests itself as a critical site for further explorations of the illusive data on gender and especially that on masculinity.

Keywords

Caribbean masculinity; manhood; literary sources; identity; honor

Earl Lovelace's classic novel *The Dragon Can't Dance*, is a cultural *tour de force* of the political sociology of the Caribbean, and more specifically of the Trinidadian, working-class struggle for survival. It details the difficulties faced by a people in constructing and negotiating notions of community, and of establishing reproductive modalities of self-affirmation and survival under difficult circumstances. The novel is a richly textured analysis of the social relationships between men and women, as well as within these gendered categories. Lovelace examines, and in some ways contests, the presumption of liminality in the Trinidad carnival.

Moreover, the author explores the unmasking of human pretensions in the aftermath of carnival, which would have served to obscure and defer the pain and suffering of life in the slums of Trinidad. At all times Lovelace is mindful of class origins, status aspirations and contradictions in this very gripping tale of being and nothingness. The people whose lives are revealed in this novel fight to rescue their humanity from the abyss of poverty. In the Yard, many are unable to sell their labor power while others have long since given up on the idea of work in its formal sense.

There is however another dimension to this fascinating novel which is often overlooked. *The Dragon Can't Dance* represents a truly nuanced discourse on the construction and negotiation of masculinity in the Caribbean, and more specifically in Trinidad. What is remarkable about this novel is that it was written in 1979; Lovelace was therefore ahead of his time in this regard. This paper focuses on the various conceptualizations of masculinity in the novel, in particular the struggle over issues of identity, reputation and honor in the construction of masculinity. These issues lie at the heart of the novel, thus this paper opens up for further consideration the place of such texts as a site for exploring a popular and academic understanding of the role of gender in Caribbean society.

The setting of the novel

Most of what transpires in *The Dragon Can't Dance* takes place in Calvary Hill and on Alice Street. The name Calvary is not fortuitous. Calvary has biblical resonances as a site of torture, suffering and testing, redemption, transformation and hope. Lovelace perhaps intended to imply to the reader that Calvary Hill was entirely a place of hopelessness. Indeed, most of the main characters of the novel undergo some type of transformation and renewal in the course of the book. Lovelace does not sugar-coat the severity of the problems of living there. He notes of Calvary Hill that it is a place 'where the sun set on starvation and rise on potholed roads, thrones for stray dogs that you could play banjo on their rib bones, holding garbage piled high like cathedral spire, sparkling with flies buzzing like torpedoes' (1979: 23).

Calvary is also a place where people make their own history every day. In a sense, it is the site of the people's theater, an arena in which children imitate 'the grown-up laughter and big-man pose of their elders' (1979: 24). From the very outset Lovelace deals with gender socialization and gendered performances. The 'cool pose' [2] of the young and older men on the street –

FEMINIST REVIEW NO 59, SUMMER 1998

the place for which Lovelace uses the military metaphor of the 'battlefield' (1979: 26) – becomes another construction of male identity. Lovelace also draws our attention to the 'lime'. The lime is a space for hanging out and shooting the breeze, often an informal space for male bonding in the Caribbean. The lime, as Lovelace explores, can also be a space of ritual male harassment of women,[3] a place where male intent and desire are voiced openly without regard for the embarrassment or discomfort they may cause to others, mainly women. Indeed, the corner hang-out becomes a place where young men are harassed by the police for loitering and congregating, and they respond with a certain defiance. The young men in turn, molest passing school girls – an activity which many view as innocuous.

Varieties of masculine construction

In a remarkably anti-essentialist fashion, Lovelace presents several versions of masculinity through his four principal characters. The central charac-ter, Aldrick Prospect, the Dragon master, can be placed at times firmly into a hegemonic type of masculinity, while at other times he seems more sen-sitive, reflective and caring. Belasco John, Fisheye, represents the stereo-typical muscular manhood, trapped by a mindscape of warriorhood and the politics of the body. There is also Pariag, the young Indian man who yearns for acceptance and recognition in the Yard: his is a struggle for iden-tity which is mediated not only by considerations of class but also of race and ethnic culture. Lastly there is the calypsonian, Philo, whose social mobility alienates him from his male friends, while granting him other types of privilege. Philo represents the Dandy (The Dan or the 'Dan Gorgon') whose cool pose masks the underlying pain of his class origins, and a low-achieving, alcoholic father. It masks an insatiable desire for Miss Cleothilda, who for the most part is just out of his reach.

Aldrick Prospect – the Dragon Man

Aldrick Prospect, the main character of *The Dragon Can't Dance*, is some-what of an anti-hero. His father Sam Prospect moved from Manzanilla to Port of Spain without any clear purpose, except a vague notion of freeing himself from the constraints of his place of origin and with a conviction that his manhood was somehow bound up with this idea of freedom. Sam Prospect left his children a somewhat dubious legacy, a sense of 'miracles and manness[4] this surviving on nothing and standing up still on your own two feet to be counted as somebody in a world where people were people, were human, by the amount of their property' (1979: 55). It is this same sense of groping for freedom and identity which Aldrick notices in his uncle, Freddie, with whom he is raised (1979: 55).

Figure 1 Construction of masculinity 1: Guyana.

Figure 2 Construction of masculinity
2: Dominica.

This purposelessness is refined and perfected by Aldrick. Lovelace describes his habits in the following account:

> not knowing where his next meal was coming from, [he] would get up at midday from sleep, yawn, stretch, then start to think of where he might get something to eat, his brain working in the same smooth unhurried nonchalance with which he moved his feet, a slow cruising crawl which he quickened only at Carnival.
>
> (1979: 25)

Aldrick by his very lifestyle rejects hegemonic notions of masculinity which advance an instrumentalist and goal-oriented (type of) ideology. Owing to his economic situation he does not wish to lay claim to a breadwinner role, an important but always contested notion of masculinity in the Caribbean (see Safa, 1994).

Other men seem to accept Aldrick and respect what he represents among them. Some women also seem unconcerned by his inability to fulfill commonly accepted definitions of the role of man. Aldrick recognizes his own limitations when he reflects:

> 'Me? Married! I can't afford a woman. You don't see how I living? No chair, a little bed in a little room. A woman want things. I ain't have nothing here except my dragon costume to put on for Carnival.'
>
> (1979: 46)

It is noteworthy how in the above, it is not the financial arrangements of relationships in contemporary society that become a matter of concern for Aldrick, but rather the economic costs of having a woman in his life. There is also an implication of female extravagance (at work here as subtext). Aldrick's ability to survive is a source of puzzlement to Sylvia, the young woman he becomes obsessed with:

> 'I could ask you a question? Don't get vexed, you know.'
> 'What could get me vex?' he said.
> 'How? How you make out? I mean, how you manage not working nowhere and you always have women coming to your place?'
> He paused. 'I don't know.'
> 'Well,' she said, 'you not so bad looking.'
> 'You ain't so bad looking yourself,' he said.
>
> (1979: 48)

Perhaps Sam Prospect's notion of 'miracle and manness' goes a long way to explain Aldrick's survival strategy and his appeal to women. As Cornwall and Lindisfarne have noted, even though hegemonic discourses of masculinity may suppress, they rarely totally censor contradictory subjectivities (1994: 45).

Aldrick lives his life through the mask of the Dragon, a carnival costume which he makes, discards and rebuilds every year and which everyone recognizes as exquisite: 'Every year I make a new costume. The costume this year ain't the one I had last year. When I finish I always throw them away' (1979: 47). For Aldrick, the Dragon is a construction and extension of his identity as a man. Indeed, the making of the Dragon is a metaphor for the construction and reconstruction of masculine identity.

> the making of his dragon costume was to him always a new miracle, a new test not only of his skill but of his faith: for though he knew exactly what he had to do, it was only by faith that he could bring alive from these scraps of cloth and tin that dragon, its mouth breathing fire, its tail threshing the ground, its nine chains rattling, that would contain the beauty and threat and terror that was the message he took each year to Port of Spain. It was in this message that he asserted before the world his self. It was through it that he demanded that others see him, recognize his personhood, be warned of his dangerousness.
>
> (1979: 49–50)

Though some aspects of the Dragon may be quite real for Aldrick, it is also part farce. The Dragon for all its ferocity could not really dance. It threatens, it menaces, it might even conjure up fear but its danger is always symbolic, Aldrick eventually recognizes this fact.

The love of his life, Sylvia, has stirred emotions in him that he has suppressed for a long time, emotions which force him to come to terms with the fact that the Dragon had begun to control the way he thought and behaved. When he suited up for the carnival that year, he felt it to be his last. He had grown tired of being the Dragon. After two days of revelling in the carnival, he rested, taking off the head of the Dragon costume. Cartey observed:

> As the revels of Carnival come to an end, the head of the mask, the dragon, which has danced so proudly, which has danced the warrior dance, lies discarded by its dragon dancer, Aldrick. Symbolically the head has gotten too heavy for him and, now powerless, it lies apart, void of its function, its role.
>
> (1991: 459)

Having made the decision not to play mass (masquerade) in the next carnival he is forced to come to terms with the dilemmas which this poses:

> He had tried to think of it, but his mind just wouldn't focus on Carnival. It scared him. Just the thought of not playing dragon made him feel naked and empty. It was as if he had outgrown it or something. But, what was he without the dragon? Who was he? What was there to define himself? What would he be able to point to and say: This is Aldrick? What?
>
> (Lovelace, 1979: 164)

Aldrick recognizes the inadequacy of the way he had constructed his masculinity, an inadequacy which he feels most strongly in relation to

FEMINIST REVIEW NO 59, SUMMER 1998

Sylvia, the girl/woman who tantalizes his brain, stirs his loins and occasions deep reflection in him.

Sylvia the Dragon tamer

Sylvia is one of the seven children of Miss Olive who lives in the Yard in Calvary Hill. Sylvia, still only 17, is 'ripening like a mango rose' (1979: 37), an object of desire but also a symbol of hope and promise. Many young men had demonstrated a sexual interest in her, while the older men and all the women recognize a certain defiance in her personality, a spirit of freedom and a sense of not surrendering to the strictures of her environment. Lovelace however removes any romantic illusions about this character when he declares that 'whoredom was her destiny if not her calling' (1979: 40).

Sylvia has made a big impression on Aldrick.

> To him she was the most dangerous female person on the Hill, for she possessed, he suspected, the ability not only to capture him in passion but to enslave him in caring, to bring into his world those ideas of love and home and children that he had spent his whole life avoiding.
>
> (1979: 45)

Aldrick recognizes his vulnerability and is uncomfortable with this young woman's potential hold on him, so he keeps his distance from her. She possesses the power to tame the dragon. The more Aldrick distances himself from Sylvia, the more anguish it causes him, to the point where his good friend Philo, speculates:

> It's Sylvia, not so? Philo said with that sympathetic grin, joined to him how men are joined together in their pursuit of a woman they all desire but against whom one, the one she chooses goes forth as hunter.
>
> (1979: 114–15)

Here masculinity and male bonding are predicated on a notion of conquest in which man is the proverbial hunter and woman the hunted, the trophy at the end of the chase. Indeed some Caribbean men pursue women in this manner and some women expect to be similarly pursued. Aldrick muses about the impact Sylvia has on his cool pose:

> You know, I used to say to myself: Aldrick, you living the life. If it have one man in the world living the life is you – no wife, no child, no boss, no job. You could get up any hour of the day you want to, cuss who you want. Anywhere you go people like you. You is a favourite in the world. Anybody will give you a dollar just so. And for Carnival you's the best dragon in the whole fucking world . . . and now this little stupid girl, this girl . . .
>
> (1979: 115)

Sylvia is perceived by Aldrick as disrupting and disturbing his autonomy, a carefully crafted universe. She is fundamentally threatening to his status quo in a way which reduces his control over his own destiny. Love for Aldrick is essentially ensnaring.

Aldrick faces two problems in relation to Sylvia. First, though Sylvia is clearly interested and basically offers herself to him, he lacks the confidence to take on the responsibility of a relationship. His economic circumstances inhibit him but, more significantly, the possible loss of control over himself paralyzes him emotionally. Consequently, he does not communicate his interest and desire to Sylvia, even though she may long have discerned his feelings. When Sylvia comes to his door he feels acutely vulnerable and recognizes that she is contesting his masculinity:

> He couldn't let this girl come and stand before his door and be more woman than he was man. He couldn't let her come with that virginal and bridal and lady-like dignity and hope, that not only concerned him – indeed, went beyond being a challenge to him, was a statement of her promise to living, to her own hopes – and make a joke of it.
>
> (1979: 57)

The second problem Aldrick faces in relation to Sylvia is her growing impatience. Unable to wait for Aldrick she forges a pragmatic relationship with the rent collector, Mr Guy. This is a relationship which, though not initially instigated by Sylvia's mother, could not have continued without her complicity.

Mr Guy is an old lecher. He has exploited the economic deprivation of Sylvia's mother by seducing her daughter in exchange for turning a blind eye to the mother's defaulting on rent payments. When Aldrick discovers the relationship between Sylvia and Guy, he reflects partly in frustration, partly in envy: 'So Guy is the man,' he thought. 'Guy! The son-fa-bitch, stepping around like a proper gentleman and screwing all the little girls on the Hill! Guy!' (1979: 45). Aldrick later reflects on Sylvia's pragmatism rationalizing that 'Maybe she had not so much chosen Guy as refused the impotence of dragons' (1979: 217).

Sylvia becomes less tolerant of Aldrick's entreaties and he grows tired of being snubbed by her. At one point in the Yard they confront each other, but Aldrick is unable to articulate his feelings:

> 'Talk,' she said, impatient already, knees bent backward, arms akimbo. 'I listening.' And before he could get a word out, she was sweeping off: 'You ask me to listen, I stand up. Why you don't talk? You know what! Aldrick, you don't have nothing to say.'
> 'You know what you want, Sylvia,' he said, his anger overpowering him, 'you want a good fuck.'

'Well, you is one man not going to give it to me.'

(1979: 166–7)

The scene above has been played out between men and women millions of times in the Caribbean. On the one hand, women adopt a certain kind of sassiness, as evident in Sylvia's retort, perhaps more as a defense mechanism against the insensitivity of men. Here woman challenges man to assert his masculinity, then mocks his failure to do so, while man resorts to the paradigm which views sex as a panacea.

As Aldrick becomes more introspective and withdraws from life in the Yard, he seeks solace at the corner with Fisheye and some other disaffected men. He becomes embroiled in the rescue of a dying warriorhood[5] of Calvary Hill. Later he becomes involved in an abortive rebellion organized by the men at the corner. Lovelace is retelling the story of the 1970 Black Power uprisings in Trinidad as parody. Clinging to a form of masculinity that privileges warriorhood and intimidation, Fisheye, Aldrick and a few sycophants of Calvary Hill embark on an ill-conceived demonstration of resistance. The People's Liberation Army, as they call themselves, have no people to liberate but themselves (1979: 188), it is but another type of Dragon dance, threatening, menacing even, but essentially powerless. Warriorhood in the context of the Hill, is no longer viable. The warriors themselves are impotent: they cannot commit to one another, let alone the 'people'.

All nine men are imprisoned for various lengths of time. Aldrick receives five years in prison for his part in the rebellion, and it is in this period of confinement that he essentially comes to terms with himself and his masculinity and experiences an epiphany. He becomes more reflective and his life seems to acquire more purpose. Lovelace here gives his character a more traditional type of masculinity, one that is more in line with the gendered status quo. Aldrick renegotiates his manhood in prison and is now 'better' prepared to re-enter civil society, for his spirit of insurgency had been reconfigured. Aldrick approaches Sylvia on his release from prison, to declare his love for her, to convey to her how much he had changed, and to try and establish the kind of relationship with her which he was clearly unable to handle before. This is Aldrick, the Dragon unmasked as it were, yet more himself than the pose could ever be. 'Now I know I ain't a dragon . . . Funny, eh? Years. And now I know I is more than just to play a masquerade once a year for two days, to live for two days,' he said (1979: 212).

During Aldrick's imprisonment Mr Guy decides to marry Sylvia. Stunned and dismayed Aldrick pleads with her not to surrender the spirit of freedom and hope which she embodies.

'You don't want nobody to take care of you, to hide you, to imprison you. You want to be a self that is free, girl; to grow, girl; to be, to be yourself, girl.'

(1979: 216)

There is a quality of ambivalence in this passage. Though Aldrick appears to be making a progressive and sensitive admonition to Sylvia, it is somewhat self-serving. Firstly, he hopes that the quality of freedom in her that he most admires would sideline Mr Guy and open a window of opportunity for himself. Secondly, Aldrick adopts a distinctly patronizing posture towards Sylvia. He, and not Sylvia, discerns the need to protect her defiance and seeks to rescue Sylvia's personhood, from herself – a self which seems unaware of its own existence, even disinterested. She remains (a symbol) – a catalyst for his self-reflection or prize to be won. The reader never encounters her consciousness. Hence, the text reinstates the male gaze, where the man determines what is best for the female subject: 'he [Aldrick] had come to Sylvia, not to claim her, but to help her claim herself' (1979: 217).

In the end, as Sylvia abandons the security provided by Mr Guy for an unknown existence with Aldrick, the reformed Dragon, her autonomy could be in jeopardy. Could not Sylvia have pursued another option which involved neither dragons nor sponsors? Though Lovelace attempts to fashion a male character who is sensitive at some levels, and with whom readers could empathize, he ends up retelling a time-honored patriarchal tale. This is a tale in which the woman capitulates in the end, and the 'star boy' wins the girl, even though as a sort of consolation, she has 'tamed' the Dragon, somewhat.

Fisheye and muscular manhood

Belasco John, alias Fisheye (so named because of his bulging eyes), is in many ways Aldrick's opposite. Fisheye represents a different type of masculinity, and indeed performs the more traditional hegemonic male role on Calvary Hill. For Fisheye, masculinity is inextricably bound up with physicality and violence. Fisheye is trapped in his own physical self, imprisoned in his narrow understanding of the politics of the body, and consequently does not mature. Nor does he move beyond living his warriorhood. Indeed, it is Fisheye who refuses to use the bottle of aftershave cologne given to him by his girlfriend 'because a man not supposed to smell so' (1979: 71). Fisheye's position points to some of the ways in which masculinity is externalized to embrace seemingly unrelated matters.

In a certain sense, Fisheye was destined to become the man he is. He is a transplant from Moruga, southern Trinidad, descending from a line of tall strong men who were good with their fists (1979: 62). His father, a proficient stickfighter turned preacher, had taught him and his brothers the ancient art of stick fighting; hence, from very young, Fisheye conflates the culture of intimidation and violence with the performance of masculinity. By the time he arrives in Port of Spain, therefore, he already has a sense of how he will negotiate masculine honor and reputation.

> for when he came to Port of Spain to live just after the war, he was, at eighteen, already too young, too strong, too eager to prove himself a man to have escaped the violence in which men were tried and tested in that town.
>
> (1979: 62)

Fisheye works very hard in the first months that he lives in Port of Spain, not just to meet his immediate financial needs but because he likes the feeling and display of strength in his arms. Hard work, muscle and sweat are the standards Fisheye uses to measure his masculinity in relation to other men.

> He had taken to working exceedingly hard just for the joy of feeling it gave his muscles. His co-workers viewed his behavior somewhat differently however. Fisheye learnt from a friend that the other men were deliberately leaving all the work for him to do. 'Well, we see like you feel you could kill work', Lonie reported, 'so we say "okay, go ahead", to see if work really going to dead.'
>
> (1979: 63)

It seems as though Fisheye finds himself through violence, through a 'hyperactive virility displaying itself in all its pathology' (Badinter, 1995: 20).

> He didn't know what it was in his head. At nights he couldn't sleep, lay awake tossing, feeling a sense of uselessness, feeling as if he was here, and life, real life, was in some region far away from him, and to make sure that he was himself he would have to get up and go and burst a man head.
>
> (1979: 64)

Evidently Fisheye confides to his friend Lonnie this compulsion of his. Lonnie, wishing to commiserate with Fisheye's dilemma, suggests it might be the 'devil' directing his actions:

> 'Same thing used to happen to me before I had this girl I now living with. You have to get a girl or some kinda thing to get you so tired that you can't think.'
>
> (1979: 64)

In this incredibly sexist exchange, Lonnie crassly suggests that Fisheye establish a relationship with a woman, not on the basis of mutual compatibility, or caring, but as a diversion. She would serve to satisfy Fisheye sexually, while performing the more important function of draining him of excessive energy and testosterone-induced behavior. While Lonnie's objectification of womanhood is captured in his comment: 'You have to get a girl or some kinda thing . . .' it may very well be that Lonnie could be hinting that a 'real' man is incomplete without a woman.

After a term in jail, Fisheye returns to society without any noticeable change. He seeks confrontation but does not encounter much opposition by which to prove his manhood (1979: 67). Even Fisheye's participation in the Calvary Hill steelband is an activity rooted in brawn rather than musical skill. He carries the three-note boom – a huge three foot steel drum traditionally carried by the strongest man in the band (1979: 68). It is therefore in the fierce territorial rivalry of the steelband culture that Fisheye finally finds solace.

> In this war, in this army, Fisheye at last found the place where he could be a man, where his strength and quickness had meaning and he could feel pride in belonging and purpose to his living, and where he had all the battles he had dreamed of, and more, to fight.
>
> (1979: 68)

The steelband in this novel is yet another metaphor for the construction of masculinity. The fashioning of melody in the crucible of steel drums, wooden sticks, rubber tips and fire, constituted the alchemy through which young boys became men, and where they experienced their 'manness' and enacted their warriorhood. Fisheye continues to do battle under the cover of steelband rivalry, until one day his lady, Yvonne, is prompted to ask him:

> 'You mean you will go on fighting one another? Why you can't join up?'
> 'And fight who?'
> 'Fight the people who keeping down black people. Fight the government.'
>
> (1979: 73)

Fisheye does not conceive of his resistance as being directed in any way. It is as though narrow hegemonic masculinity is incapable of discerning alternative strategies of resistance. Yvonne's suggestion resonates with him and he begins to envision himself as some sort of general in this new army (1979: 73). It is particularly instructive that it is Yvonne, a woman, who brings Fisheye to this realization. Lovelace appears here to be demonstrating the complementarity of femininity and masculinity. He proffers femininity as the voice of reason, attempting to prevail upon the wanton violence of misdirected masculinity. Yvonne's next suggestion is interpreted by Fisheye as a contestation of his masculinity.

> 'If you don't do something with life, Belasco, life going to do something with you', she warned. 'If you intend to spend all your days as a bad John, I could get a decent man.'
>
> (1979: 78)

Fisheye responds in typical fashion by striking Yvonne to the ground. Fisheye's visceral reaction points to what he perhaps conceives as an entitlement, that is, the monopolization of her desire. He could not imagine himself being replaced by some other man with so-called respectability, a man with a different class background from that of a 'Bad John' and perhaps a different type of masculinity. Interestingly, when Fisheye is with a woman, he appears more civil, more humane, at least temporarily. Nevertheless, even here, he is dependent on others to construct his identity for him. Fisheye reads her comment as an insult and rebuke, if not a betrayal. This leads him back to where he started: he employs violence against his second girlfriend Daphne. Fisheye is clearly a batterer. Indeed, this is how some men measure their manhood and exercise control over the women in their lives. Fisheye becomes more miserable than ever – the 'devil' in him is represented by this misguided equation of masculinity and physical prowess – he is unable to transcend this dilemma.

An interesting encounter between Fisheye and Aldrick provides some insight into the nature of male negotiation of territory and spheres of influence. Aldrick, acting on behalf of his dragon-making acolyte, the young Basil who turns out to be Fisheye's son, approaches the latter with a sort of empty braggadocio:

> 'I just bringing home your little son. I hear you does beat him for nothing.'
> 'So what?'
> 'So', he plunged on, for he was aware of the boy standing tensely beside him.
> 'So, I come to warn you. If you beat him again I going straight to the gym and lift some weights and learn some jujitsu and come back for you.'
> 'I ain't making joke tonight', Fisheye said coldly.
> 'If you think is joke I making, touch him', Aldrick said, maintaining his tone.
>
> (1979: 86)

The above illustrates the way different types of masculinity may collide but avoid destroying each other. This aggressive, anticipatory and conciliatory humour is the means by which men say to each other what they have to say, while avoiding conflict (Lovelace, 1979: 86).

Even in terms of hegemonic masculinity, hypermasculinity as it were, Fisheye had gone beyond the boundary of acceptability. Jail was the only response the community had for this caliber of warrior. Fisheye received seven years for his participation in the rebellion yet never reformed. He never quite understood the changes which had begun to seize the Hill. Perhaps he was never interested in such issues nor capable of discerning such developments. In the end, Fisheye represents the least progressive and least hopeful aspect of life on the Hill, and arguably the most flawed and fossilized representation of masculinity in the *The Dragon Can't Dance*.

Pariag – the search for Indian manhood

Unlike the other central male characters in this novel, Pariag, or Boya as he was more familiarly called, seems to be groping simultaneously with the definition of his masculinity and his ethnic identity. Pariag seems to be in search of himself in the world, and the reason he

> had come to the city to live was so that he could join up with people, be part of something bigger than just New Lands sugar estate, be more than just a little country Indian, cutting sugar-cane in the day, cutting grass for the cattle in the evening, and, on Sundays, playing all fours in front the play-ground with Seenath, Bali and Ramjohn.
>
> (1979: 91)

Pariag is on a mission to prove his manhood in terms that are perhaps more ambitious than all the other male characters: a manhood that could be recognized and accepted outside of its Indian context. He had hoped to transcend race and culture in this search for self, 'he longed to go beyond the cows and grass and cane, out beyond the droning chant of pundit, into a world where people could see him, and he could be somebody in their eyes' (1979: 92). Lovelace essentially defines Pariag against the grain, against the common stereotypes of Indian masculinity, just as he had mapped Aldrick's masculine defiance.

Pariag's views on choosing a mate astound his father. Responding to familial pressures to get married Pariag first indicates that he did not think he was ready. 'And besides, I want to choose a girl for myself. I is the one going to have to live with she' (1979: 93). His father was vitriolic in his riposte:

> 'For yourself?' his father asked. 'For yourself?' 'You think you getting married for yourself?' 'You think I get married for myself?' 'You hear how you talking already and you ain't even leave this house yet.'
>
> (1979: 93)

There are many cultural and racial issues to be unpacked here, such as the economics of marriage, and traditional notions of extended kinship relations which are forged through marriage. Hence the need for parents to guide, if not determine, the matter. The fact that Pariag ends up visiting, with a view to marrying, the young woman who had been selected for him, is testimony to the weight of the culture and its traditions. The machismo which Pariag displays in his first encounter with this young woman is quite arresting.

> 'What you name?' he asked her, kinda tough.
> 'Dolly', she said. She was trembling.

FEMINIST REVIEW NO 59, SUMMER 1998

'I is Boya. You ever . . . you ever went to Port of Spain?' as if he himself was familiar with the city.

. . .

'You going to have to live in Port of Spain', he said.

(1979: 94)

Pariag assumes that such a move would be immediately acceptable to Dolly. Lovelace describes these two young people in stereotypically (Indian) terms. Dolly, 'slim like a rice stalk, with hair down to her waist' (1979: 93) and teeth which jut out beneath her upper lip, immediately comes across to the reader as passive, unworldly and meek. Pariag, in contrast, appears self-assured, if not arrogant, wanting to establish his familial authority immediately, and worldly at least in his own imagination. Indeed, Pariag clearly feels that marrying Dolly was tantamount to doing her a huge favor.

When Pariag and Dolly move to live in Calvary Hill they are the only two people of Indian descent in the Yard, present but socially invisible. The one thing that Pariag wants most is to be accepted by the people on Alice Street but they ignore him. Pariag and Dolly are in the Yard but not of the Yard. Fisheye as guardian of the Hill, hits upon a plan of demanding a sort of tribute of a shilling from Pariag. They enter into a strange commercial pact. Though Pariag did not like this extortion, 'in some strange kind of way he felt that it joined him more firmly to the Hill' (1979: 103). He reveals to Dolly the arrangement with Fisheye, to which she replies:

'You don't see that you is Indian and they is Creole', Dolly said to him, when he told her about it. 'No, Dolly, No. It ain't that. They don't know me. They don't know the kinda man I is.'

(1979: 103)

As with Yvonne, Fisheye's former girlfriend, and Sylvia, Dolly's voice is one of reason and stability. Dolly offers similar counsel after the Christmas revellers had bypassed their house: 'They don't want your friendship, Boya', Dolly told him. 'They go by everybody and they leave you out. You don't see' (1979: 105). As was customary, Pariag did not buy this explanation.

'You know what it is Dolly', he said to her when they were in bed.
'They not seeing me, that is what it is. That is it; they don't see me. You see?'
'How they could not see you?'
'Well, I ain't big. I mean, I ain't have no huge muscles, and I don't sound tough, and I ain't tough, and I can't fight, and don't know how to play steelband or sing calypso, and I don't know much about Carnival . . . you see?'

(1979: 105)

Pariag's declaration is quite remarkable: here is Pariag, openly admitting both to himself and his wife, all that is lacking in his masculinity. Many

Caribbean men might fear a loss of respect, status and honor from such a confession to their wives or women and may therefore suppress all that Pariag so freely shares. He must have tremendous confidence in his relationship with his wife, or in his ability to overcome these perceived deficiencies. Moreover, what Pariag defines above is a specific rendition of Afro-Caribbean and, more specifically, Afro-Trinidadian masculinity. Calypso, carnival and steelband are predominantly, though not exclusively, 'creole' and hence Black cultural signifiers. Pariag is wittingly or unwittingly defining himself in relation to Black masculinity within the Yard. He suggests that his impaired masculinity could be overcome by the acquisition of some object which has the capacity to confer male status. Since a car was out of his immediate reach, he settles for a bicycle. This acquisition immediately gives him a sense of importance and recognition, but it also becomes a bone of contention in the Yard.

The bike is interpreted as an ostentatious and divisive display, among folk who are equal in their poverty and nothingness. Pariag's act is read by the folk in the Yard as 'dangerous'. The acquisition serves to bruise Pariag's ego and identity rather than recover it. 'In less than an hour the fact of Pariag's new bicycle had settled upon the Yard like a death' (1979: 113). The people in the Yard choose Aldrick to punish Pariag for his apparent capriciousness, for it is Aldrick who most eminently embodies the reality and philosophy of non-possession as a way of life (Lovelace, 1979: 119). Aldrick for his part, 'wasn't so sure that to buy a bicycle was such a sacrilege' (1979: 119). In fact, Aldrick is very perceptive about how Mr Guy and Cleothilda were manipulating this issue of the bike:

'Everybody rushing me as if they in such a hurry. I want to catch a breath, I want to see what I doing on this fucking Hill. Let the Indian buy his bike. Guy and Cleothilda ain't fooling me. The Indian is a threat to them, he ain't no threat to me.'

(1979: 124)

When they fail to get Aldrick to move against Pariag, someone smashes his bike during the night. This event becomes a turning point in Pariag's life. Not only did he protest this destruction by confronting everyone in the Yard over it, but the next day his quiet defiance earned him respect and recognition by all. Ramchand comments on this event in the novel:

However different from Pariag the members of the Yard consider themselves, even they respond to the challenging dignity of the Indian, seeing him for the first time, ironically, just when they have violated him by smashing the bicycle.
(1988: 11)

With his determination not to report the incident to the police and his defiant walk of the bike through the community, Pariag signals the

FEMINIST REVIEW NO 59, SUMMER 1998

renegotiation of his masculinity and honor in the Yard. Pariag senses a new found recognition of himself and his standing on the Hill. Paradoxically, the damage to his bike had also symbolically marked an end to his efforts to integrate with the folks in the Yard. He was 'Finished with the Hill' (1979: 156).

The incident forces Pariag to look inward at his relationship with Dolly, which hitherto he has taken for granted. His emotional distance from Dolly is connected to a general male inexpressiveness to which Lovelace draws attention. Aldrick agonized over Sylvia's remark while jumping up in the band, 'I have my man'. He wanted to cry if he had known how, and admitted to himself: 'I have to learn to feel' (1979: 145). Fisheye too reaches a point when he 'wished he could cry, but he didn't know how to' (1979: 79). Pariag was unable to communicate his deepest fears and anxieties to Dolly. 'He thought about a lot of things to say, but he didn't have the words to say them' (1979: 156). Like Aldrick, he eventually reaches a point where he did find the words to reach out to the uncomplaining Dolly. He invites her to go to see an Indian movie. Dolly is overwhelmed by the invitation and weeps without even answering; 'he realized that this was the first place he had asked her to go to, and he found that he had water in his eyes too' (1979: 157). Pariag had begun to look within himself rather than to seek the approval of others and in so doing he noticed Dolly was right there, willing to be a part of his journey of identity and discovery. Previous to Pariag's overture to Dolly, and even subsequent to that night in bed with her, he did not seem to think that he could share his deeper thoughts, dreams and frustrations with Dolly. He had always seen himself as superior and more worldly than she. It brings him to this point in his life.

Still concerned with gaining approval in the Yard, Pariag rationalizes to Dolly:

> 'They see one part of me and they take that to be the whole me. They take the part of me that they see.'
>
> (1979: 225)

> 'You is more, Boya. More than what you show them. I is more than what I show you, not so?'
>
> (1979: 226)

This is one of the most self-asserting remarks made by Dolly in the novel. For a moment Pariag has no reply until he is forced to respond to her apologetic inquiry: ' " You not vex I say that?" He shook his head. "Everybody is more than what they show. That is why we have to live" ' (1979: 226). This moment represents his epiphany.

'We have to start to live, Dolly, you and me'.

'Me and you?' Dolly asked, her voice choking. 'Me and you?'

(1979: 226)

Pariag had come full circle: he acknowledges Dolly's personhood in the process of finding himself. For Pariag, in addition to his own struggle to define himself as an Indian man in a predominantly African Yard, this moment of reflection serves as a backdrop for the reconfiguring of his masculinity, mediated through race. This transformation is not as difficult for Pariag as for Fisheye and Aldrick. Unlike them, Pariag is not nearly as trapped by the conflation of masculinity and toughness, a quality which he shares at some level with Philo, the calypsonian.

Philo the Dan man

Philo is a minor character in the novel. His story is one in which social mobility leads to alienation from his erstwhile comrades in the Yard. Philo is a struggling calypsonian with an undistinguished career, whose relevance in the novel appears to be his friendship with Aldrick, and his obsession with Miss Cleothilda, the light-skinned prima donna who lives in the Yard. Philo is of much darker complexion: 'And Philo is not a bad-looking man. Black as he is, when he put on clothes and comb his hair he could get any reasonable woman; but it is she [Cleothilda] he want' (1979: 35). For some years Philo has pursued this woman without any encouragement on her part. Moreover Miss Cleothilda often insults him publicly but it does not seem to bother him.

Philo had been singing mostly social and political commentaries in his calypsoes. This message music was not bringing him the fame and adulation he craved. He wanted to do better than his father not as a demonstration of any lofty ambition on his part, since his father was a consummate low-achiever: 'His father lived his life, trying to offset a sense of defeat by being a comic' (1979: 237). Moreover his mother once told Philo: 'Your father didn't leave nutten excep' a cuatro without string and a rusty mout' organ . . . I can't even fine his tools' (1979: 237). Philo decides to sing a calypso about sexual bravado and prowess, 'The Axe Man', where the tree to be cut down is a metaphor for womanhood and female sexuality. Eventually, the Axe Man came upon a tree that 'blunted his axe and forced him to take it to hospital to have it repaired' (1979: 126). This song was hugely popular and catapulted him to fame and some fortune.

As Philo's popularity increases, so too did his ability to attract the formerly inaccessible Miss Cleothilda. Philo becomes the dandy, subscribing to 'wine, woman and song'. Lovelace provides a concept of masculinity filled with fantasy, sexual conquests and material gain. Here the author exposes

FEMINIST REVIEW NO 59, SUMMER 1998

a stereotypically male gaze in the character of Philo. Miss Cleothilda capitulates under the weight of Philo's success, much to the satisfaction of the folks in the Yard.

> This the Yard chose to view as their own personal victory. They saw it as the surrendering in Miss Cleothilda of a superiority that she could no longer claim, as a kind of coming down, a fall, that equalized all of them and that qualified her as a person in their eyes.
>
> (1979: 162)

The philosophy of the Yard is quite consistent here: in order to retain a community of the impoverished, vehicles of increased status must be immobilized to maintain the integrity of its members. In this case the woman is not responsible for the downfall of man, but she ends up losing status in the eyes of her contemporaries. However, as Philo's success as a calypsonian leads to increasing popularity with women, he loses the right to bond with his male friends. Like Boya's purchase of the bicycle, Philo's success is increasingly uncomfortable for the Yard, the Corner, Aldrick and Fisheye, even though he has made genuine efforts to retain his currency with the community. Like Boya also, he had violated the norms of being and nothingness.

His alienation leads Philo to reassess what it is to be a man. He begins to reflect on the bourgeois neighborhood to which he had moved (as a result of his social mobility): 'I is a' ole nigger, you know. I is a Calvary Hill man. I ain't no hifalutin Diego Martin jackass' (1979: 248). Philo comes to terms with his class background, and his need to reconnect with his community and its values. His new found affluence allowed him to employ the pose of the older man who dates younger women in an effort to validate his virility and desirability. His return to Cleothilda therefore seems to signal a more sensitive posture. As with Aldrick and Pariag, therefore, Philo's journey through the terrain of his interior, mediated by his improved material conditions, force him to reassess his own cultural and social practice, and ultimately leads to a revaluation of his masculinity.

Conclusion

As a writer, Lovelace has demonstrated considerable sensitivity to the issue of gender in his rendering of Trinidadian masculinity. From time to time lapses in his thinking about gender are apparent, for example in his treatment of the women in the novel. Their characters remain underdeveloped. These lapses should not however detract from the fairly sophisticated interpretation, analysis and formulation of masculinity that he provides in *The Dragon Can't Dance*.

This paper has attempted not merely to focus on the nuanced representation of masculinity in this novel but to suggest that these texts are some of the sites which Caribbean scholarship could explore in order to unearth some dimensions of gender at the popular level. Many scholars whose research concentrates on the Caribbean, have noted a dearth of information on masculinity in the region. This author is of the opinion that literary texts represent a fruitful area of research yet to be mined.

Social scientists might be wary of using texts rooted in creative imagination as the basis for reaching empirical conclusions. The point is that texts such as this novel or a calypso represent more than one experience. The writer herself or himself is a social being, facing similar foibles and frustrations in the struggle to survive. In short, the ideas of the writer have a material basis which should not be dismissed as fictive and therefore unreal. Social scientists therefore may find in these 'other' texts, an important supplement to their research. This is not to abandon the pursuit of social science investigation but perhaps to intimate the need to destabilize tradition in the interest of new visions and insights into traditional concerns.

The Dragon Can't Dance is a landmark text in the Caribbean, which, in its attempt to analyze certain dimensions of the construction of masculinity, demonstrates remarkable perspicacity on a topic which was not on the agenda at the time it was published. Today, as the issue of masculinity is debated in the Caribbean, there is much to learn from a close reading of Lovelace's work and of other texts, and much to reflect on about manhood in Trinidad and the wider Caribbean.

Figure 3 Left to right: Linden Lewis, Kirk Meighoo, Hilary McD Beckles.

FEMINIST REVIEW NO 59, SUMMER 1998

Notes

1 The author would like to thank Evelyn O'Callaghan for her comments and suggestions. While Evelyn was quite generous with her time and expertise, I am sure that she would not want her reputation to be based on what I have written here and hence she should be exonerated at least partially for her contribution to the paper.

2 The cool pose is a strategy and persona employed by some men to deal with their situation as it relates to their conditions of existence. Majors and Billison, writing in the North American context, describe the cool pose as masking behavior. It is according to this view, this concealing of the real self, which permits the appearance of 'coolness'. As the authors note, the behavior amounts to impression management. 'Playing it cool becomes a routinized, stylized method for expressing the aggressive masculinity that pervades black life' (Majors and Billison, 1992: 27).

3 Harassment in public places is defined as: 'that group of abuses, harryings, and annoyances characteristic of public places and uniquely facilitated by communication in public. Public harassment includes pinching, slapping, hitting, shouted remarks, vulgarity insults, sly innuendo, ogling, and stalking' (Gardner, 1995: 4).

4 It should be pointed out that Lovelace's concept of 'manness' could be read both as a gender-neutral aspect of humanity, as well as a particular quality of masculinity. My thanks to Evelyn O'Callaghan and Glyne Griffith for drawing this point to my attention. I am, however, persuaded by the logic of the text which suggests to me that Lovelace's use of the concept had a specific gendered intent.

5 The warrior is the quintessence of the construction of modern masculinity (see Mosse, 1996: 107). Warriorhood is a concept rooted in conquest, rivalry and competitiveness – all the stereotypical characteristics of manhood and virility. Lovelace uses the concept here to conjure ideas and ideals of hypermasculinity.

References

BADINTER, Elizabeth (1995) *XY On Masculine Identity*, New York: Columbia University Press.

CARTEY, Wilfred (1991) *Whispers From the Caribbean: I Going Away, I Going Home: A Critical Review of the Works of Caribbean Novelists*, Los Angeles: Center for Afro-American Studies, University of California.

CORNWALL, Andrea and LINDISFARNE, Nancy (1994) 'Dislocating masculinity: gender, power and anthropology' in A. Cornwall and N. Lindisfarne (eds) *Dislocating Masculinity*, London: Routledge.

GARDNER, Carol Brooks (1995) *Passing By: Gender and Public Harassment*, Berkeley, Los Angeles and London: University of California Press.

LOVELACE, Earl (1979) *The Dragon Can't Dance*, England: Longman.

MAJORS, Richard and BILLSON, Janet Mancini (1992) *Cool Pose: The Dilemmas of Black Manhood in America*, New York, London and Tokyo: Touchstone.

MOSSE, George (1996) *The Image of Man: The Creation of Modern Masculinity*, New York and Oxford: Oxford University Press.

RAMCHAND, Kenneth (1988) 'Why the Dragon can't dance: an examination of Indian-African relations in Lovelace's *The Dragon Can't Dance' Journal of West Indian Literature*, Vol. 2, No. 2: 1–14.

SAFA, Helen (1994) *The Myth of the Male Breadwinner: Women and Industrialization in the Caribbean*, Boulder: Westview Press.

Theorizing Gender Systems and the Project of Modernity in the Twentieth-Century Caribbean

Eudine Barriteau

FEMINIST REVIEW NO 59, SUMMER 1998, PP. 186–210

Abstract

A central thesis of this paper is that the philosophical contradictions of liberal ideologies predispose states to institute unjust gender systems. I argue that postcolonial Caribbean states have inherited a complexity of social relations and structures from the Enlightenment discourses of Liberalism, yet they seem unaware that the discourses which created colonialism and Western expansion were themselves part of the Enlightenment project of modernity. In this paper I apply this theoretical framework to a historical analysis of gender systems in the twentieth-century Caribbean. The paper examines three distinct periods: 1900–37, 1937–50s and 1950s–90s, the transition from colonial to postcolonial modernizing societies, and attempts to generate a gendered analytical model which can be widely applied both within and outside of the region.

Keywords

gender systems; postcolonial; Liberalism; Enlightenment; modernity; state; economy

Introduction

For women and men in the Caribbean[1] the twentieth century draws to a close in a manner radically different from the way (in which) it began. There have been some fundamental developments which distinguish twentieth-century social relations. There has also been a rupturing of traditional relations of gender inherited from the post-slavery, 'emancipated' nineteenth-century Caribbean.

Women's lives and feminist scholarship and practice have seriously challenged the inherited gender identity of 'woman' as a barren ontological and epistemological category. Through a combination of indigenous and external pressures the evolving Caribbean state has altered women's unequal access to its resources. It has removed, amended or reformed the legal inferiority or dependency assigned to women in constitutions and laws. By questioning the prevailing myths about Caribbean women and by prioritizing the multiple, complex realities of our lives, feminist scholars have destabilized the definition of masculinity as omniscient and omnipresent, even as it sought to escape any commonality with the concept of the feminine. Changes in the ideological and especially the material relations of gender have proven these constructions to be false and unacceptable. This work theorizes and examines these departures in Caribbean gender relations.

The paper is organized into two sections. In the first, I develop a theoretical framework around the concept of gender and gender systems to examine how they operate within the political, social, and cultural economy of states. In the second section, I apply this theoretical framework to an historical analysis of gender systems in the twentieth-century Caribbean. My specific aims are to create a typology of gender systems and to illustrate how the ideological and material dimensions reinforce each other through three distinct periods in the transition from colonial to postcolonial 'modernizing' societies. Ultimately I use this theoretical framework to interrogate the project of modernity in the Anglophone Caribbean. My larger goal, however, is to generate a gendered analytical model that can be applied to studying a wide range of social and economic phenomena inherent in Caribbean and other societies.

I argue that postcolonial Caribbean states inherited a complexity of social relations and structures from the Enlightenment discourses of Liberalism. This web of social relations and structures creates gender systems that pose critical challenges for women in the transition from colonial to postcolonial, modernizing state structures. A central theme of my work is that the philosophical contradictions of liberal ideologies predisposed states to institute unjust gender systems. Such liberal ideologies in turn formalized hierarchical and differential roles for women and men which were further embedded in new social relations when states actively pursue(d) the modernization project in the post-cold war, postcolonial phase of social and economic transformation.

Part of the difficulty for these states is that they seem unaware that the project of modernity began with the Enlightenment discourses that created colonialism and Western expansion, not with the pragmatic approach to development that they pursued in the post-Second World War period. The greater problem for women is that the inequalities and contradictions inherent in liberal ideology are replicated in gender systems.

FEMINIST REVIEW NO 59, SUMMER 1998

Section 1

Theorizing gender and gender systems in the Caribbean

In the Anglophone Caribbean the concept of gender is used in popular discussions, in the women in development literature, and in the media, yet there is confusion about the meaning of gender. As it relates to feminist analyses of women's experiences of domination, the concept is misused daily. At one level, gender has become a trendier but erroneous synonym for the word sex which implies biological differences and signifiers. Questionnaires and forms include the category 'gender' to which one is supposed to reply 'male' or 'female'. A popular radio competition in Barbados tells listeners to 'send your answers in with your name, age and gender'.[2] Errol Miller writes, 'Also there is justification for exposing all students to all areas of the curriculum without reference to the gender of the student' (Miller 1994: 127).

These simplistic interpretations are usually designed by those who want to ride the crest of popular awareness of gender issues without wanting to trouble themselves with the relevant extensive scholarship (Flax, 1989; Scott, 1988; Chodorow, 1995; Nicholson, 1994; Barriteau, 1992; Mohammed, 1994).

Gender also is used in the grammatical sense of masculine gender, feminine gender and neuter gender. At least there is a historical reason for this usage (Baron, 1986: 90). Rosi Braidotti reminds us that, 'Gender is not originally a feminist concept. It has a previous identity, derived from research in biology, linguistics and psychology' (Braidotti 1991: 8).

Feminist investigations and insights on the pervasiveness of gender reconceptualized the term to refer to a complex system of power differentials played out in the different experiences of women and men. Mary Hawkesworth notes that feminist scholars adopted the concept, 'To distinguish culturally specific characteristics associated with masculinity and femininity from biological features' (Hawkesworth, 1997: 650).

In interrogating the project of modernity I develop and use three inter-related aspects of the concept of gender. These are:

- The construct of relations of gender and gender systems;
- The methodologies of gender analysis; and
- The distinguishing features of gender systems.

I define gender to refer to complex systems of personal and social relations through which women and men are socially created and maintained and through which they gain access to, or are allocated, status, power and material resources within society (Barriteau, 1994). My definition recognizes that there is an important personal dimension to gender as well as the cultural and the political. I support Nancy Chodorow's arguments for the relevance of understanding the contributions of personal meanings to gendered subjectivity (Chodorow, 1995). However in this analysis I emphasize the interaction of political, economic and cultural dimensions of gender in the public domain since this is an area that is largely under-theorized.

I use postmodernist feminist insights to define a concept of gender that sees women as socially constructed beings subject to asymmetrical gender relations. Accordingly, women cannot be understood ontologically or epistemologically through androcentric perspectives, nor can women be defined as deficient men. The socially constructed relations of gender do not explain women-in-relation-to-men. From a postmodernist feminist perspective, both women and men experience relations of gender although they experience these from radically different positions of personal, social, economic, and political power.

Gender relations constitute the continuous social, political, economic, cultural, and psychological expressions of the material and ideological aspects of a gender system. Gender relations encode and often mask unequal power relations between women and men, and between women and the state. The extent to which the material and ideological dimensions of gender relations reinforce each other is frequently ignored. The extent to which prevailing ideologies affect women's access to status, power and material resources is rarely examined.

An unequal gender relation is a relation of *domination*. Its inequality is rooted in an asymmetry of power that has differential material and ideological outcomes. Though contemporary gender relations are relations of domination, those who experience that domination are not always victims. Caribbean women, like women elsewhere, experience conditions of inequality and asymmetric power relations that can and should be altered; nor are men automatically and intrinsically victims. The flipside of Errol Miller's 'Male marginalization thesis' and the backlash it has fuelled in the region, is that it recasts Caribbean men as the victims of a conspiracy among Caribbean feminists, élite male power brokers and international development institutions (Miller 1994).[3]

The asymmetry in contemporary social relations of gender places one socially constituted being at a disadvantage because of the absence of gender neutrality. Gender neutrality assumes an impartiality towards women and men in a social environment in relation to whatever issues are at stake.

Our understanding of gender relations is often limited to the level of interpersonal relations between women and men. We fail to view economic or political relations between women and the state, or men and the state as also relations of gender. Instead discussions of gender are often confined to the private sphere. This reflects a deep seated desire to view relations of gender as outside the scope of a state's relations with its citizens.

Most analyses of gender relations concentrate on the construct of gender ideologies and the processes of gender socialization. They focus primarily on the ideological dimensions of gender systems. What is missing is a focus on the material relations of gender. When, for instance, a state removes discriminatory wage differentials between male and female workers it alters the material aspects of gender. To modernize the postcolonial Caribbean governments may have opened up women's access to public resources, but they have done so without paying sufficient attention to the need for changes in the ideological dimensions of gender or without considering how changes in the material relations complicate ideological relations of gender.

For our epistemological project and to advance political agency, Caribbean feminist scholarship cannot afford to have the concept of gender reduced to a descriptive term. We should not attempt to do gender analysis without a commitment to investigating and explaining the many forms of domination that women experience. The relations of gender intersect with other oppressive relations such as those that arise from race, class, ethnicity, age or sexual preferences. Henrietta Moore correctly argues that the concept of gender cannot be understood outside of its interactions with other social relations (Moore, 1994: 15).

The methodologies of gender analysis

The second aspect of gender I prioritize refers to an analytical frame with its own conceptual tools and techniques, its own methodologies that allow us to investigate social conditions affecting the constituted beings 'women' and 'men'. As an analytical category, gender has been pivotal to feminist scholarship. Mary Hawkesworth notes that feminist scholars have used the concept analytically to: repudiate biological determinism; analyse the social organizations of relationships between men and women; investigate the reification of human differences; conceptualize the semiotics of the body, sex, and sexuality; explain the distribution of burdens and benefits in society; illustrate the microtechniques of power; illuminate the structure of the psyche; and account for individual identity and aspiration (Hawkesworth 1997: 650).[4]

The several components of the concept of gender cannot be understood in isolation from each other. Jane Flax (1989) and Joan Scott (1988) indicate how our understandings of particular social worlds and histories and the perceived differences between the sexes will change when gender is used as an analytical category.

Deploying gender as an analytical category changes what is asked in research. Nevertheless many aspects of that methodological shift need to be problematized and theorized if we are to minimize the confusion that now bedevils the use of the concept.

Abandoning the practice of explaining women's multiple, complex and continuously contested experiences through male-centred approaches opens up a fuller, richer focus on the heterogeneity of 'woman' the constructed being.

The distinguishing features of Caribbean gender systems

The postcolonial Caribbean state inherited a set of social relations influenced by the Enlightenment discourses of Liberalism. Gender systems constitute a significant aspect of that inheritance. A gender system comprises a network of power relations with two principal dimensions, one ideological and the other material. These dimensions map out the broad contours of gender systems. The material dimension exposes how women and men gain access to or are allocated power, status, and material and nonmaterial resources within a state and society. A feminist analysis of the material relations of gender makes visible the distribution of economic and political power and material resources (Folbre, 1995; Barriteau, 1996; Sparr, 1994).

The ideological dimension concerns the construct of masculinity and femininity. The ways in which masculinity and femininity are constructed reveal the gender ideologies operating in the state and society. The statements of public officials, the bureaucratic and social practices of institutions, and representations in popular culture, provide evidence of what is expected of, or appropriate for, the socially constituted beings, 'women' and 'men'.

Gender ideologies operating within a gender system expose how individuals create gender identities. The social expectations and the personal constructions of gender identities form the core of gender ideologies within a particular society. These ideologies establish the sexually-differentiated, socially-constructed boundaries for 'males' and 'females'.

These boundaries are complex and interact often in unexpected ways. They encode differing penalties, rewards, and outcomes for Caribbean women and men who transgress them. At times these boundaries are rigid and

FEMINIST REVIEW NO 59, SUMMER 1998

overt. Subverting societal boundaries that encode gendered relations of power invoke the greatest penalties for women in patriarchal societies. At other times the boundaries are more nuanced. At times Caribbean society may permit women to take on responsibilities essentially constructed as masculine, as long as these do not produce a corresponding shift in gendered relations of power.

The manoeuvres of the ideological and the material dimensions of a gender system disclose whether it is just or unjust. In a just gender system there would be no asymmetries of access to, or allocations of, status, power and resources. There would be no hierarchies of gender identities, no hierarchies implicit in the terms 'masculine' and 'feminine'. In an unjust gender system there is unequal distribution of, and access to, resources and power. Figure 1 illustrates the dimensions and interactions of a gender system.

The interactions and operations of gender systems are messy, contingent, continuously contested and negotiated, and are largely unjust to women in the Caribbean (Barriteau, forthcoming). Gender systems, none the less, like other social structures, change over time. Particular interest groups of the state and civil society will try to keep certain features constant, and try to guarantee outcomes. However, women's and men's personal and collective contestations, their challenges to existing relations of power, and attempts to change those relations will spawn unintended outcomes.

While states may seek to act in the best interests of all their citizens, state policies implemented by governments may reproduce existing gender asymmetries, they may intensify, decrease or subvert them, but policies are not gender neutral. To move towards gender neutrality the state must confront the hierarchies created with the construct of the masculine and the feminine. It is a construct that influences the distribution of resources and encodes relations of domination. States should recognize the nature of their gender systems in the same way they take stock of their political or economic systems and attempt to address imbalances. If states refuse to do this then state policies are gendered, and will involve gendered power relations.

In the postcolonial period, governments have introduced redistributive measures to facilitate their own goals which at the same time give women access to public resources. This indicates the extent to which structural and material aspects of gender systems can and do change.

Governments have concentrated on altering the material aspects of gender relations while de-emphasizing the ideological aspects and the interconnectedness of both. Researchers generally analyse gender systems through ideological constructs. The challenge is to forge an inclusive analysis.

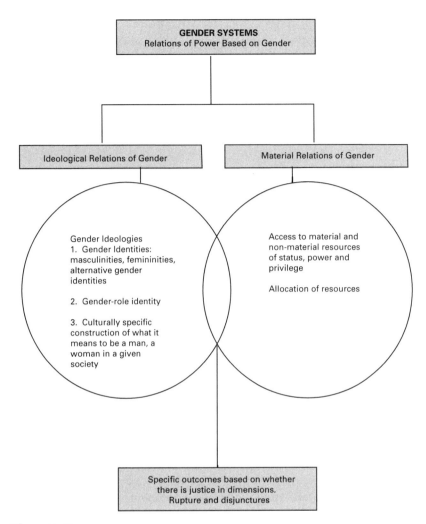

Figure 1

NB:1 Gender relations interact and are mediated and complicated by other social relations.

2 The separation is analytical. In social interactions they reinforce or negate each other. Interventions of the state are primarily aimed at material relations of gender, e.g. reform legislation, equality of access to education and health care. However, there are immediate consequences in ideological roles of gender from opening up the public domain to women.

Caribbean women persistently challenge prevailing gender ideologies. This is a serious and welcome source of rupture and change in our gender systems. One way we do this is by reconstructing new gender identities. A goal of feminism is to transform unjust gender systems.

FEMINIST REVIEW NO 59, SUMMER 1998

The Enlightenment legacy and the postcolonial Caribbean state

The ideological foundation of the Caribbean state is built on the Enlighten-ment discourse of liberalism with all its inherent contradictions for women. Contemporary state institutions and practices are stubbornly and proudly maintained according to the tenets of liberal political and economic theory (Lewis, 1968: 226–56). Some fundamental features of this discourse are:

1 The belief that rationality is the only means by which individuals achieve autonomy;
2 The notion that an individual and citizen is a male household head;
3 The separation of society into the private and the public: the world of dependence, the family, and the world of freedom, the state and work;
4 The gendering of that differentiation so that women are posed in oppo-sition to civil society, to civilization (Flax, 1990: 6).

These features became significant in the post-emancipation period. The notion that an individual and citizen is a male household head had no rel-evance for enslaved black women and men since they were equal in their inequality under slavery. However, European gender ideologies fed by the Enlightenment discourse of Liberalism promoted the notion of the male breadwinner and the dependent housewife. State policies now viewed women's labour as secondary or supplementary (Folbre, 1986; Marx, 1967: 372).

By the project of modernity I am also referring to the practices of inde-pendent Caribbean states to embrace a distinct praxis, a set of policies, and discourses dedicated to achieving the 'Enlightenment promise'. This promise of a greater understanding and mastery of nature, the progress of reason in human affairs, and steady, sustainable development in the quality of life (Hall *et al.*, 1992: 2) has lingered since the earliest colonial encounters. The idea of modernity embraces a linear view of progress. In the political economic expression of modernity, states are committed to pursuing modernization theories of development. A bourgeois liberal state structure expresses the socio-political dimension (Barker *et al.*, 1994: 15).

I theorize 'postcolonial' very differently from conventional interpretations. Rather than focus exclusively on the colonial legacy, I hold states and governments accountable for gendered features of civic and political life that continue and are sustained beyond the formal dismantling of the col-onial relationship. In other words, I see potentially transformative spaces between what is bequeathed and what continues to be practised. I want to make visible the new political agency of state systems that are overlooked, especially as these relate to transforming relations of gender.

As feminists, we are challenged to problematize and publicize these openings and insist that policy makers occupy them to subvert the legacy and transform existing practices. Therefore I avoid blaming colonial powers for the continuities in the modern constitution of asymmetric relations of gender. I argue that states have choices and they choose to maintain unjust gender systems because these satisfy specific, indigenously defined objectives of state interests.

British colonial policy formally introduced modernization strategies of development to the Caribbean in the 1940s. West Indian history of interaction with Europe is probably one of the best examples of the unfolding of the European project of modernity (Beckles, 1990). In the post-independent period, many of the policies governments introduced that benefited women were deliberate attempts to create a modern labour force for a rapidly restructuring, capitalist world economy. Nevertheless, these policies also generated ameliorative, remedial measures on the material dimensions of gender. Governments articulated these as part of the post-colonial project of modernity.

The introduction of these measures provokes paradoxical outcomes. The state intervenes to free women for expanded gender defined roles in a modernizing political economy. In the process women gain by becoming empowered in ways that enable them to further challenge oppressive gender relations and identities. Compounding these developments is the fact that the strategies the state employs destabilizes unequal gender relations through material means. One of the consequences is that women have further ammunition to contest unequal ideological relations inscribed in hierarchical gender identities and roles.

The material changes which the state oversees are generated by a combination of factors: changes in the international political economy, combined in some cases with pressure by donor governments, the activism of the Caribbean's women's movement (Wieringa, 1995), and a reluctant recognition by some governments that women are penalized in their public as well as private lives. A lesser known example of pressure from a donor government is the modification of the United States Foreign Assistance Act in 1974. The Percy amendment to this act tied aid to developing countries to their attempts to integrate women into development policy (United States Government, 1978).

Political scientists classify Caribbean states as liberal democratic, bourgeois democratic, authoritarian, popular statist, national democratic or socialist (Emmanuel, 1990: 7; Thomas, 1984; Stone, 1986). In their analyses these Caribbean scholars have not questioned whether the state is gendered, neither have they examined the differential impact of the state's activities on women and men. Their analyses pay no attention to the notion that the state is androcentric nor that policy formation contains gender biases.

Caribbean women do not experience the state as a monolithic, homogeneous, entity. We imagine the postcolonial state as an 'incoherent multifaceted ensemble of power relations. It is highly concrete and yet an elaborate fiction; powerful and intangible; rigid and protean; potent and boundary less; centralized and decentered' (Brown, 1992: 12). These relations are a potential vehicle for subordination and domination but they are not immutable or uncontested (Brown, 1992: 12). The Anglophone Caribbean state is a liberal, democratic, masculinist state whose activities and power relations affect the ways women's economic, political, social, and personal activities are perceived and constructed (Brown, 1992: 14).

Power within the Caribbean state is not centralized, fixed, nor immanent. It is continuously created and continuously shifts its sphere of operations between macro and micro institutional levels. For example, state power is exercised by a minister of health, and by sanitation workers cleaning the streets. The latter may daily extend the boundaries of state power in areas unknown both to the public and to ministers who may assume they alone define the scope of that power.

The Enlightenment legacy remained unchallenged when the political status of Caribbean countries changed from British colonies to independent nations (Howard, 1989; Thomas, 1988; Lewis, 1968). A dominant, recurring feature of liberal political ideology is the division of society into the private sphere of the household and kinship groups and the public sphere of the state and the economy. This division locates women in the private sphere and conceptualizes our activities, contributions and relevance to society within that sphere.

The core of women's problems occur in the hierarchies created in the dichotomies of Enlightenment thought. The private sphere is subordinate and inferior to the public. Rationality becomes the means by which individuals free themselves of the constraints of domestic life and prepare for a public life of service, civic duty, and freedom. As developed in Kant's work, the use of reason marks the beginning of autonomy and the preparation for public life. But Kant excludes women from the use of reason. He assumes we are too embedded in domestic life. Women represent the family and sexual life, not the cerebral qualities of public virtue. This establishes one of the enduring dilemmas which Enlightenment thought poses for women. As Flax argues, 'Although women may be "hostile" towards civilization both our exclusion from parts of it and our labor within its necessary "outside" continue to be an ironic necessity' (Flax, 1992a: 7).

Liberal ideology continues to shape the institutions of the postcolonial Caribbean state. It sets the contours of the politics of participation. It determines the development models and thus shapes the political, economic and social environment in which women exist. Liberalism maintains one set of rules for the market, the polity, and the arenas of public discourse and another set for the household. Women's lives are caught in the contradictions and disjunctures between the two.

Section 2

Historicizing gender systems in the twentieth-century Caribbean

Two outstanding features of Caribbean gender systems are continuous ruptures and contestations, and an absence of gender justice. When the material and ideological dimensions of gender systems advance opposing interests, major disjunctures and contestations occur.

The material and ideological dimensions may overtly pursue the same goals, yet the gender system may be unjust. Superficially, gender relations may appear to be in equilibrium because society's definition of what ends the material and ideological dimensions should serve, may correspond and reinforce each other. The constellation of power relations allow the state to enforce official ideologies governing access and representation. During these periods women's contestations and rejection of the unjust gender system will be diffuse and more covert. The appearance of equilibrium may mean that gender resistance is not at the level of organized groups or movements or organized groups may have been forced to be more circumspect in their quest to promote gender justice. It may mean challenging constructs at the personal level. But, from slavery and indentureship through to the contemporary Caribbean, women have always attempted to overcome violations of gender justice (Reddock, 1995; Mohammed, 1995; Brereton, 1995; French, 1995; Vassell, 1995).

Throughout the twentieth century gender systems have been unstable and unjust for women. Table 1 historicizes and summarizes some of the features of Caribbean gender systems. My analysis is clustered around three historical periods. Each period registers significant developments in the political economy of Caribbean states and the changing character of gender systems in the twentieth century.

1900s–1937

The twentieth century began with the region mired in deep poverty. The economic base was agricultural and depended on the export of primary

Table 1 *Historicizing gender systems in the Anglophone Caribbean*

Historical period	Features of political economy	Material relations of gender	Ideological relations of gender	State of gender relations	Gender justice
1900s–1937	labour unrest: riots; birth of nationalist movements	severely limited access/distribution of resources of women	inferior subordinate status of women	appearance of stability	unjust
1937–1950s The war years	universal adult suffrage; colonial welfare state; modernization approach to development	public sphere opening to women	subordinate status of women	evidence of instability	unjust
1950s–1990s Nationalist governments	postcolonial (independent) state; industrialization by invitation; economic and social mobility	legal equality of access/some biases in distribution	subordinate status of women; strong currents of misogyny	deep divisions between ideological and material dimensions	unjust

crops of sugar, cotton, and cocoa. Trinidad began an embryonic industrialization programme after pitch and petroleum were discovered (Drayton, 1997). The great depression of the 1920s, following on the heels of the First World War, exacerbated the now endemic poverty of the region. This level of economic deprivation had its roots in the inequities of slavery and the institutionalization of political and economic injustice for the vast majority of women and men in the post-emancipation period. The British Caribbean colonies were becoming more deeply integrated into the world economy and they experienced the traumas of widespread unemployment and political upheaval.

In this period the societal belief in the inferior, subordinate status of women was reinforced. At the level of the state and society, both the material and ideological dimensions of gender actively supported unjust gender systems. As a result, gender systems appear to be stable. Major social groups mounted no organized, widespread challenge to either ideological or material relations of gender. The material relation of gender foreclosed any notions of economic equality, civic relevance, or political participation for women. Ideologically women's gender-role identity was confined to that of homemaker, nurturer and reproducer of the labour force. The élite, propertied and educated could vote but the majority of women did not have this right and their social status was derived from the male heads of households: 'The West Indian family is certainly not matriarchal, since the status of women in society is undefined and weak. Although it is the woman who keeps the family together, it is the man who rules' (Simey 1946: 81).

In Trinidad, educated, middle-class women resisted this restrictive definition of womanhood. They organized conferences, lobbied for seats for women on the City Council, wrote letters to the press and held public debates (Reddock, 1995) but the colonial state was unresponsive.

Materially women enjoyed very limited access to state resources. Maxine Henry-Wilson observes that before 1942 in Jamaica married women were ineligible for any appointment in the civil service (Henry-Wilson, 1989: 250). Bridget Brereton records a similar situation in Trinidad. In 1919 legislation required that married teachers resign from their posts (Brereton, 1995, 89). And what about working-class women, who would not have access to such jobs in the first place? In Jamaica at the beginning of the twentieth century the majority of these women were in low-paying occupations:

> Men dominated the professional, industrial and commercial categories with women's access to the higher occupations [being] quite limited during these years (1891–1921). Women were primarily involved in own-account activities, such as dressmaking, hairdressing, higgerling. According to the 1921 census,

about 40 per cent of women were employed as domestics. Throughout the first half of the twentieth century, there were two significant characteristics of the Jamaican labour force participation. First, the sexual division of labour in industry relegated women to the routine, labour intensive monotonous and sedentary. Secondly, there were significant differences in the wage structure and working conditions of males and females.

(Henry-Wilson, 1989: 234)

For Indo-Caribbean women the rigidity of Asian cultural traditions compounded the inequalities in gender systems. Rawwida Baksh-Soodeen writes:

The predominantly Northern Indian culture which was brought to Trinidad and Tobago included such practices as the denial of education to girls, the segregation of men and women in public, the strict selection of a marriage partner from within the same caste; arranged marriages, the joint family system where young couples resided with the husband's parents, the subservience of the daughter-in-law to her mother-in-law and husband; and many others.

(Baksh-Soodeen, 1991)

The colonial state severely restricted educational opportunities in a context where education was the greatest means of social and economic mobility (Cole, 1982). Janice Mayers notes that: 'during the first half of the twentieth century there was discrimination against girls in access to public secondary education both in terms of the facilities provided, and in the means provided for taking advantage of the offering' (Mayers, 1995: 258).

Mayers' recount of an appeal by a female teacher to the Board of Education for an increase in salary in 1921 provides an excellent illustration of material and ideological relations of gender reinforcing each other to the detriment of women: 'The Board rejected her application on the basis of inadequate funds, the fact that the regulations would not permit it and the customary rationalization that male responsibility required that they be paid more' (Mayers, 1995: 271).

Young women from the middle class were educated to serve men as accomplished wives and homemakers. Those from the working class were trained to serve as domestics, seamstresses and labourers (Carty, 1988).

As the case of the teacher demonstrates, women did not receive comparable wages for comparable work. This applied to white collar occupations as well as labourers. Thus the ideological belief in the inferiority of the woman as citizen was supported by the economic realities of restricted access to or allocation of public and private resources:

The woman's position in the community is by no means equal to that of a man, who is generally accepted to have superior rights, and this apparent paradox underlies many of the social problems to be discussed later. It may well be that no general advance towards giving women their due place in society and, in particular, public life can be made until the value of their contribution as homemakers rather than as unskilled laborers is more clearly understood in the West Indies.

(Simey, 1946: 17–18)

1937–1950s

The second period began with great economic and political upheaval in the region. A wave of unrest swept through the Caribbean between 1935 and 1938 (French, 1995; Reddock, 1994; Howe, 1993: 90). Spontaneous protests over wages and labour conditions subsequently revealed fundamental political and economic dissatisfactions by Caribbean women and men. The various British commissions appointed to investigate the sources of West Indian discontent became acutely aware of the precarious conditions under which women lived. Still they dealt with questions of women's societal inequality only within in the context of family life and reproductive work.

The *ad hoc* policy of trusteeship yielded to more systematic statements of policy on colonial development and welfare (Simey, 1946). The Moyne Commission recommended a central planning committee to address the welfare of the colonies (Colonial Office, 1947: 4). The move towards planning also reflected the creation of the discipline of economic development.

This period witnessed several changes in the political economy of Caribbean states, changes which held specific implications for the material and ideological relations of gender. Pre-war nationalist movements gained impetus from the anti-imperialist movements set in train by the Second World War. The ethos of British colonial authority had weakened (Howe, 1993: 139) and by the mid-1950s colonial parliaments in the larger Caribbean countries had negotiated more direct control in their legislative, executive and administrative affairs. They instituted the Cabinet system of government.

During this period cardinal changes occurred in the way the colonial state interacted with women. This altered the material relations of gender and exposed deep upheavals in gender systems. Universal adult suffrage opened up the public sphere to women although full political participation would remain hemmed in by the ideological belief in women's second-class status as citizens.

Participation in the public domain was even more complex for Caribbean women of Asian or East Indian origin. Asian cultural legacy prescribed rigid gender-role identities as wife and mother (Seepaul, 1988: 90; Poynting, 1987: 235; Mohammed, 1988: 389). Indo-Caribbean families gave preference to educating boys since it was accepted that women were destined for a domestic role. In Trinidad in 1946 only 30 per cent of Indian women were literate. In the 1931 census only 4 per cent of Indian women were recorded as professionals while over 83 per cent were employed as domestic servants, general labourers, and agricultural labourers (Poynting, 1987: 235).

In 1948 the British government established the University of the West Indies and, while women comprised only a small percentage of the original student body, they now had access to tertiary and professional education within the region. The formation of a colonial welfare state further altered the material dimensions of gender by paying attention to health and nutrition; the state, however, continued to support women primarily in their reproductive roles.

Despite an expanded state sector, no official policy on women was articulated. However a deconstruction of development policy shows that differentiated economic roles were instituted around women's reproductive functions. Traditional gender roles were deliberately inscribed into this phase of development policy. Policies on issues of population, fertility, unemployment, health, and labour force participation all made reference to women (Barriteau, 1994).

1950s–1990s

By the beginning of this period, the larger countries of the Anglophone Caribbean were on the verge of achieving political independence, and gender systems remained unstable and unjust. Ideological relations of gender continued to reinforce the notion of a subordinate status of women even though Caribbean states reluctantly began to realize that (changes in the political economy to facilitate) modernization was beginning to challenge traditional gender roles.

Indo-Caribbean women were also reconstructing their gender identities, much to the concern of religious leaders and the Hindu and Islamic middle classes:

> In the current period, Indian girls and women from all classes are being educated at increasingly higher levels, and are actively competing on the job market. Segregation of the sexes presently still exists only at Hindu and Muslim religious services and functions. The death of the caste endogamy began during the indentureship period, and the institution of arranged marriages is now but a relic of the past, as both men and women have over many generations fought their

families for the right to choose their partners. The joint family system has been crumbling; as many newly married couples have the financial independence to live on their own. Daughters-in-law especially those who are educated and employed are refusing to play a subservient role to their mothers-in-law and husbands in personal, household and financial matters.

(Baksh-Soodeen, 1991)

Expanded educational and employment opportunities due to 'Industrialization by Invitation' (approach to development) deepened the divisions and contradictions of ideological and material relations of gender. Caribbean development planners drew extensively on the theorizing of Caribbean Nobel laureate, Sir Arthur Lewis, who advocated export oriented industrialization. This is a policy prescription for the creation of export enclaves requiring cheap labour, a euphemism in developing countries for women's labour (Deirdre Kelly, 1987; Kathryn Ward, 1990).

By the mid-1960s newly independent states replaced colonial welfare policy with formal development planning. The intent of such planning has been to control population, produce economic growth, improve living conditions, develop human resources, create higher levels of industrialization and enhance technological development. In other words to pursue the Enlightenment promise. Several states hinge the attainment of these objectives on regulating the fertility of women. Population control and economic development became inseparable.

Caribbean states introduced many changes in gender systems and continue to contribute to an ongoing reconstruction of gender roles. Three principal features stand out; the state's official recognition of women, retrenchment of the welfare state, expansion of private sector influence over economic policy and entrepreneurial development. These features generate, and at the same time obscure, new and complex economic and social relations for women. Many Caribbean states removed some of the entrenched legal discriminatory measures against women. In Barbados, between 1976 and 1985, the state introduced reform in twelve pieces of legislation ranging from The Marriage Act to The Accident Compensation (Reform) Act (Bureau of Women's Affairs, 1985).

Between 1974 and 1979 Jamaica, Antigua, Barbados and Grenada established government machinery to promote the advancement of women (Mondesire and Dunn, 1995: 35).

Reforms like these will not by themselves end relations of domination. However they capture instances of the state's willingness to examine and alter some aspects of its gender system. Additionally they illustrate the depth of inequality that exist for women both materially and ideologically. In keeping with its liberal foundations, the state sponsors mechanisms

203

FEMINIST REVIEW NO 59, SUMMER 1998

legislation to maintain legal equality but shies away from directly enhancing women's economic autonomy. The state does not examine the gender implications of economic relations. Caribbean states, 'Have also failed to connect widespread social, cultural and economic disruptions in women's lives to the shortcomings of existing development policy and practice. This has led to superficial analysis and irrelevant policies. The state ignores the contradictions between prioritizing the values of consumerism and mass consumption advocated by the modernization paradigm, and the increasing pauperization and subordination of many women:

> Caribbean women and men are expected to consume more to fuel the economy, but the welfare state is shrinking. Certain services of education, welfare, and health are returned to the private domain to be supplied by women's unpaid labor at great cost to their material and psychological well being.
>
> (Barriteau, 1995: 154)

Conclusion

Ideological relations of gender are at their worst for Caribbean women: women now exist in a climate of hostile gender relations. This hostility is fed by men and women who argue that the Caribbean feminist movement exists to emasculate and marginalize men. Newspaper articles and editorials speak of the damage done to boys by their being raised in female headed households, and taught primarily by female teachers (Barriteau, 1994: 283). This is a fairly pernicious charge since an average of 40 per cent of households in the Anglophone Caribbean are headed by women. There is increasing information on incidents of violence against women due to several factors. Women are now more likely to report these incidents and to seek help and protection. With the adverse economic climate of the last decade, some men have taken out their frustrations on women. Several men admit to feeling hostile to and threatened by women whom they perceive to be gaining material and psychological advantages over them.

Material relations of gender have improved significantly for Caribbean women since the beginning of this century. Caribbean states deserve some credit for guaranteeing equality of access to basic resources. However there is yet no gender justice. Forms of gender discrimination are many and nuanced. The basic belief in a subordinate role for women still exists and is often reflected in state policy as well as cultural expressions. Women's contradictory position in society is complicated by some negative developments for Caribbean men. The fact that the ratio of women to men at the

University of the West Indies is now 70:30 produces a range of interpretations, none concerned with how men construct their gender identities. The troubling statistics on men's involvement in crime and especially in a drug subculture, is simplistically blamed on women's new 'empowered' gender identities – the women 'who refuse to take their God-ordained role in societies'. Such responses never even glance at the rapid material affluence of drug running and money laundering *vis à vis* the slow accretion of gains in traditional 'male' jobs in agriculture and manufacturing.

Reactionaries and misogynists are unwilling or incapable of examining the pivotal changes in our gender systems and offer inane analyses in place of serious investigations.

Whatever inequities men experience, these are not grounded in nor supported by a societally held belief in the inferiority of men – nor should they be. Gender ideologies still construct men as superior to women and as citizens in the public and private domains. The legacy lingers. While prevailing gender ideologies construct men as superior for many there are negative economic and social consequences in the experiences of 'manhood'. We need to know more about what informs the concepts of masculinity. We need investigations informed by the methodologies of gender analysis to attempt to unravel what it means to be 'male', 'masculine' and 'man' in our societies.

In the meantime we have to recognize that in spite of the long overdue and necessary material gains for women Caribbean gender systems continue to be unstable and unjust. As we approach the twenty-first century we have a choice. We can abandon nostalgia and come to terms with the fact that gender systems have changed and will continue to do so in response to the interaction of societal and individual developments. Or we can bury our heads in the nineteenth century and persistently ignore the fundamental changes of twentieth-century gender systems. But we do so at a cost to our societies and our peoples. The past is never available. There is no second round.

Notes

1 I refer to the English-speaking countries of the Caribbean former, and in the case of a few still, British colonies. They share similar state and political infrastructures and practise Westminister style politics. The relative homogeneity of the state structures is important to my arguments. This definition of the Caribbean is not for the purpose of closure but rather to demarcate the countries with a similar historical, political and cultural legacy. However, I recognize there are internal variations and nuances within this grouping.

2 Voice of Barbados Call-in Competition, 790 Ways to Win, July 1996.

3 Miller makes a number of startling conclusions in his case study of Jamaica although he does so very cautiously by seeking to qualify each of these statements. A few include: primary school teaching and teacher education shifted from being male dominated to female dominated because 'those holding central positions in the society' wanted to restrict black men to agricultural and industrial labour occupations, they wanted to limit the upward mobility of black men in the society, they wanted to stifle the emergence of militant black educated men who could overthrow the power structure. He states, 'in a real sense the black woman was used against the black man' since a choice was made to allow black women to advance instead of black men through teacher education and elementary school teaching. Miller incredibly concludes that the experience of black Jamaican men in being marginalized will become the experiences of all males of subordinate groups in patriarchal societies and goes on to list seven different groups of men regionally and internationally who can expect to share the fate of Jamaican black men. He attributes the creation of the women's lobby to 'the process that marginalises the black male' rather than adverse conditions in women's lives forcing organization and articulation. Errol Miller's thesis seems to be that men have an a priori right to the resources of the state over and above women and attempts to correct for the explicit denial of women's political and economic relevance is designed to punish men. Miller's arguments are construed popularly to mean women are to blame for all the educational problems men, especially young men, are experiencing (See Miller, 1994 especially pp. 124–31).

4 Hawkesworth identifies the authors and texts that contribute the different types of gender analysis (see Hawkesworth, 1997: 650).

References

BAKSH-SOODEEN, Rawwida (1991) Letter to the *Trinidad Guardian*, May 17.
BARKER, Frances, HULME, Peter and IVERSEN, Margaret (1994) editors, *Postmodernism and the Re-reading of Modernity*, Manchester and New York: Manchester University Press.
BARON, Dennis (1986) *Grammar and Gender*, New Haven: Yale University Press.
BARRITEAU, Violet Eudine (1994) 'Gender and development planning in the postcolonial Caribbean: female entrepreneurs and the Barbadian State', PhD dissertation, Howard University.
—— (1995) 'Postmodernist feminist theorizing and development policy and practice in the Anglophone Caribbean,' in Marianne H. Marchand and Jane L. Parpart (1995) editors, *Feminism, Postmodernism, Development*, London: Routledge, pp. 142–58.
—— (1996) 'A feminist perspective on structural adjustment policies in the Caribbean' *National Women's Studies Association Journal*, Vol. 8, No. 1: 142–56.

BARRITEAU, Eudine (1992) 'The Construct of a Postmodernist Feminist Theory for Caribbean Social Science Research' *Social and Economic Studies*, Vol 35, No. 2: 1–43.

—— (forthcoming) 'Liberal ideologies and contradictions in Caribbean gender systems' in **Christine Barrow, Eudine Barriteau** and **Nan Peacocke** editors, *Gender Ideologies: A Reader*, Center For Gender and Development Studies.

BECKLES, Hilary Mc.D (1988) *Afro-Caribbean Women in Resistance to Slavery in Barbados*, London: Karnak House.

—— (1989) *Natural Rebels: A Social History of Enslaved Black Women in Barbados*, London: Zed Books.

—— (1990) *A History of Barbados: From Amerindian Settlement to Nation State*, Cambridge: Cambridge University Press.

BRAIDOTTI, Rosi (1991) 'Theories of gender, or: language is a virus' Faculteit der Letteren Rijksuniversiteit utrecht, Openings College.

BRERETON, Bridget (1995) 'Text, testimony and gender: an examination of some texts by women on the English-speaking Caribbean from the 1770's to the 1920s' in **Shepherd, Brereton** and **Bailey** (1995) pp. 63–93.

BROWN, Wendy (1992) 'Finding the man in the state' *Feminist Studies*, Vol. 18, No. 1: 1–34.

BUREAU OF WOMEN'S AFFAIRS n. d. [1985] *Where Are We Now? An Assessment of the Status of Women in Barbados*, Bridgetown: Government of Barbados.

BUSH, Barbara (1990) *Slave Women in Caribbean Society 1650–1838*, Kingston, Bloomington and Indianapolis: Heinemann and Indiana University Press.

CARRINGTON, Edwin (1971) 'Industrialization by invitation in Trinidad and Tobago since 1950' in **Norman Girvan** and **Owen Jefferson** (1971) editors, *Readings in the Political Economy of the Caribbean*, Kingston: New World Group Ltd.

CARTY, Linda (1988) 'The political economy of gender inequality at the University of the West Indies' PhD dissertation, University of Toronto.

CHODOROW, Nancy J (1995) 'Gender as a personal and cultural construction' *Signs: Journal of Women in Culture and Society*, Vol. 20, No. 3: 516–44.

COLE, Joyce (1982) 'Official ideology and the education of Women in the English speaking Caribbean, 1835–1950' in *Women and Education*, Barbados: Institute of Social and Economic Research.

COLONIAL OFFICE (1947) *Development and Welfare in the West Indies, 1945–1946*, Colonial Office no. 212, London: HMSO.

COX, Winston (1982) 'The manufacturing sector in the economy of Barbados' in **Delisle WORRELL**, editor, *The Economy of Barbados 1946–1980*, Bridgetown: The Central Bank of Barbados, pp. 47–80.

DRAYTON, Kathleen (1997) 'Women and organising in the English speaking Caribbean prior to 1975' in **Eudine Barriteau** and **Alan Cobley** (1997) editors, *Stronger, Surer, Bolder: Dame Nita Barrow and Regional and International Development*, Kingston: Ian Randle (forthcoming).

DUNCAN, Neville, DANN, Graham, COLE, Joyce and EMMANUEL, Patrick (1978) *Barbados 1976 General Elections: Public Opinion Survey*, Cave Hill: Institute of Social and Economic Research.

EMMANUEL, Patrick (1990) *The Role of the State in The Commonwealth Caribbean*, Working Paper no. 38, Kingston: Institute of Social and Economic Research.

FLAX, Jane (1989) 'Postmodernism and Gender Relations in Feminist Theory' in **Micheline Malson** *et al* editors, *Feminist Theory in Practice and Process*, Chicago: University of Chicago Press. pp. 51–73.

—— (1990) 'What is Enlightenment?: a feminist rereading' paper prepared for a conference of Postmodernism and the Rereading of Modernity, University of Essex, July 9–11.

—— (1992a) 'The end of innocence' in **Judith Butler** and **Joan W. Scott** (1992) editors, *Feminists Theorize the Political*, New York: Routledge.

—— (1992b) 'Is Enlightenment emancipatory?: a feminist reading of what is Enlightenment' in **Barker** *et al.* (1994) pp. 232–49.

FOLBRE, Nancy (1986) 'Hearts and spades: paradigms of household economics' *World Development*, Vol. 14 No. 2: 245–55.

—— (1995) *Who Pays For The Kids? Economics and the Structures of Constraints*, London and New York: Routledge.

FRENCH, Joan (1995) 'Women and colonial policy in Jamaica after the 1938 uprising' in **Wieringa** (1995) pp. 121–46.

HALL, Stuart, HELD, David and McGREW, Tony (1992) editors, *Modernity and its Futures: Understanding Modern Societies, an Introduction*, Cambridge: Polity Press.

HALL, Stuart, HELD, David and MCLENNAN, Gregor (1992) 'Introduction' in **Hall, Held** and **McGrew** (1992) pp. 1–11.

HAWKESWORTH, Mary (1997) 'Confounding gender' *Signs: Journal of Women in Culture and Society,* Vol. 22 No. 3: 649–86.

HELD, David (1992) 'Liberalism, Marxism and democracy,' in **Hall, Held** and **McGrew** (1992) pp. 13–61.

HENRY-WILSON, Maxine (1989) 'The status of the Jamaican woman, 1962 to the present' in **Rex Nettleford** (1989) editor, *Jamaica in Independence: Essays on the Early Years.*

HOWARD, Michael (1989) *Dependence and Development in Barbados 1945–1985*, Bridgetown: Carib Research and Publications Inc.

HOWE, Stephen (1993) *Anticolonialism in British Politics: The Left and the End of Empire, 1918–1964*, Oxford: Clarendon Press.

KELLY, Deirdre (1987) *Hard Work Hard Choices: A Survey of Women in St. Lucia's Export Oriented Electronics Factories*, Barbados: Institute of Social and Economic Research.

LEWIS, Gordon K. (1968) *The Growth Of The Modern West Indies*, New York: Monthly Review Press.

LEWIS, Vaughan A. (1983) 'Caribbean state systems and the contemporary world' in **Paget Henry and Carl Stone** (1983) editors, *The Newer Caribbean Decolonization, Democracy, and Development*, Philadelphia: Institute for the Study of Human Issues, pp. 123–39.

LEWIS, W. Arthur (1984) 'The state of development theory' *American Economic Review*, Vol. 74 No.1: 1–10.

—— (1978) *The Theory of Economic Growth*, London: George Allen & Unwin.

MCLENNAN, Gregor (1992) 'The Enlightenment period revisited' in **Hall, Held** and **McGrew** (1992) pp. 327–78.

MARX, Karl (1967) *Capital A Critique of Political Economy* Vol. I *The Process of Capitalist Formation*, ed. Frederick Engels, New York: International Publishers.

MAYERS, Janice (1995) 'Access to secondary education for girls in Barbados, 1907–43: a preliminary analysis' in **Shepherd, Brereton** and **Bailey** (1995) pp. 258–78.

MILLER, Errol (1991) *Men at Risk*, Jamaica Publishing House Limited.

—— (1994) *Marginalization of the Black Male Insights from the Development of the Teaching Profession*, Mona: Canoe Press.

MOHAMMED, Patricia (1994) 'Nuancing the feminist discourse in the Caribbean' *Social and Economic Studies,* Vol. 43 No. 3: 135–67.

—— (1995) 'Writing gender into history: the negotiations of gender relations among Indian men and women in post-indenture Trinidad society' in **Shepherd, Brereton** and **Bailey** (1995) pp. 28–48.

MONDESIRE, Alica and DUNN, Leith (1995) *Toward Equity in Development. A Report on the Status of Women in Sixteen Caribbean Countries*, Caribbean Community (CARICOM) Secretariat Georgetown, Guyana.

MOORE, Henrietta L. (1994) *A Passion For Difference*, Cambridge: Polity Press.

MUNROE, Trevor (1972) *The Politics of Constitutional Decolonization: Jamaica 1944–1962*, Kingston: Institute of Social and Economic Research.

NICHOLSON, Linda (1994) 'Interpreting gender' *Signs: Journal of Women In Culture and Society*, Vol. 20, No. 1: 79–105.

POYNTING, Jeremy (1987) 'East Indian women in the Caribbean: experience and voice' in **David Dabydeen and Brinsley Samaroo** (1987) editors, *India in the Caribbean*, London: Hansib Publishing Ltd, pp. 231–63.

REDDOCK, Rhoda E. (1994) *Women, Labor and Politics in Trinidad and Tobago: A History*, London: Zed Books.

—— (1995) 'The early women's movement in Trinidad and Tobago 1900–1937' in **Weiringa** (1995) pp. 101–20.

RIVIERE, Bill (1990) *State Systems in the Eastern Caribbean: Historical and Contemporary Features*, Kingston: Institute of Social and Economic Research.

SCOTT, Joan W. (1988) 'Gender: a useful category of historical analysis' *American Historical Review*, Vol. 91 No. 5: 1053–75.

SEEPAUL, Occah (1988) 'Hindu women in today's society: moving away from stereotypes of dolls and playthings' *Caribbean Affairs*, Vol.1, No. 3: 90–5.

SHEPHERD, Verene, BRERETON, Bridget and BAILEY, Barbara (1995) editors, *Engendering History: Caribbean Women in Historical Perspective*, Kingston and London: Ian Randle and James Currey.

SIMEY, T. S. (1946) *Welfare and Planning in the West Indies,* Oxford: Oxford University Press, pp. 232–49.

SPARR, Pamela (1994) *Mortgaging Women's Lives: Feminist Critiques of Structural Adjustment*, London: Zed Books.

STONE, Carl (1986) *Class, State and Democracy in Jamaica*, Kingston: Blackitt.

FEMINIST REVIEW NO 59, SUMMER 1998

THOMAS, Clive Y. (1984). *The Rise of the Authoritarian State in Peripheral Societies*, New York: Monthly Review Press.

—— (1988) *The Poor and the Powerless Economic Policy and Change in the Caribbean*, New York: Monthly Review Press.

UNITED STATES GOVERNMENT (1978) *Report on Women in Development*, submitted to the Committee on Foreign Relations, United States Senate and the Speaker of the House of Representatives, in fulfillment of Section 113(b) of the Foreign Assistance Act of 1961 as amended, August 3, 1977, Office in Development Agency for International Development.

VASSELL, Lynette (1995) 'Women of the masses: Daphne Campbell and "left" politics in Jamaica in the 1950's' in **Shepherd, Brereton** and **Bailey** (1995) pp. 318–36.

WARD, Kathryn (1990) *Women Workers and Global Restructuring*, New York: Cornell University Press.

WIERINGA, Saskia (1995) editors, *Subversive Women: Women's Movements in Africa, Asia, Latin America and the Caribbean*, Delhi: Kali for Women, London: Zed Books.

WILLIAMS, Fiona (1989) *Social Policy: A Critical Introduction Issues of Race, Gender and Class*, Cambridge: Polity Press.

Gender and International Relations:

A Global Perspective and Issues for the Caribbean

Jessica Byron and Diana Thorburn

FEMINIST REVIEW NO 59, SUMMER 1998, PP. 211–232

Abstract

In this paper we discuss the relatively recent integration of feminist thinking in the discipline of International Relations. We argue that the theoretical foundations of International Relations are still primarily based on traditional male–female dichotomies, particularly that of separate public and private spheres. By extension, women are largely excluded from state power and decision making. The state is itself gendered. The growing recognition of the links between the global economy and gender forces us to engage with International Relations in foreign and international policy. In this article we look at feminist interpretations of three main International Relations areas: international security, human rights, and international political economy and their implications for gender policies in the Caribbean. We also look at the contributions of Caribbean women to the international feminist agenda and suggest a research agenda for ongoing feminist theorizing in the discipline of International Relations.

Keywords

political economy; globalization; foreign policy; WID/GAD; human rights; security

Introduction

As feminist theory and gender studies continue to assert themselves throughout the academy, the discipline of International Relations (IR) has been one of the last bastions to succumb to feminist inquiry. This may seem surprising since International Relations as a discipline is itself new. Established in the 1940s in the US as a policy science in response to the First and Second World Wars, the discipline was developed during the Cold War period. Furthermore, International Relations theory comprises various aspects of social science theory which have been interrogated by feminist theorists. That International Relations has only been subject to feminist inquiry since the late 1980s attests to the extreme male dominance and bias in the field.

FEMINIST REVIEW NO 59, SUMMER 1998

Dating from the 1988 London School of Economics conference on Gender and International Relations, the theoretical walls of International Relations have become more permeable. With the growing recognition of the links between global economic forces and gender (Sen and Grown, 1987), and the momentum of nearly twenty years of feminist incursion in other social science fields, in the past ten years the field of Gender and International Relations, or feminist International Relations, has grown and gained legitimacy.

One might argue that international feminism is the predecessor of Feminist International Relations although the literature in this field has not so far acknowledged it. Prior to the first United Nations Conference on Women, held in Mexico City in 1975, international processes and women's lives were not linked at fundamental systemic levels. A number of UN resolutions were passed which pertained to women. These related to consent of marriage, equal remuneration for men and women, women's political rights, and women's education. Two main factors have since brought about the shift to a deeper understanding of women and gender in international relations processes. First, from 1975 onwards, feminist inquiry has gained legitimacy in the academy. Second, Ester Boserup's work on women and international development (1970) precipitated the field of Women in Development, a global movement which was largely concerned with the effects of international development interventions on women's lives.

Gradually 'Feminist International Relations' carved its own path and so far has sought to interrogate International Relations from a feminist or gender perspective, while international feminism has looked at women's and gender issues from a global perspective. These two fields are not separate and apart, but rather run parallel to and in tandem with each other, with regular 'cross-fertilization' from one field to the other.[1]

Two principal trends have been followed thus far in Feminist International Relations. The first brings to light gender issues as well as women's issues in foreign and international policy; the second exposes the gendered nature of mainstream International Relations theory and practice. Writers in both areas point to the absence of women's experiences in the consideration of issues such as security and peace. This process of inquiry has been conceptualized as a new feminist epistemology in which gender becomes a prime element in understanding International Relations theory and practice (Grant and Newland, 1991).

In deconstructing International Relations theory, feminist analysts argue that the theoretical foundations of International Relations are male-defined, and are constructed around male–female dichotomies which define female as 'other' and assign gender-specific roles which exclude women from the public sphere. J. Ann Tickner (1991), Rebecca Grant (1991) and Christine Sylvester (1994) argue that, although largely ignored, these issues shape and are shaped by international forces. Using a 'gender lens', these writers have broken down the discipline into its largely social science components, and have then reconstructed them with a feminist understanding of the discipline of International Relations. They have discovered that whether separate or consolidated, gender bias is entrenched in the components of this discipline in three interconnected ways.

First, International Relations theory depends on beliefs about how individuals behave in society and in the state. Following Hobbes' and Rousseau's approach, states are perceived to be anarchical and bellicose and concerned only with their own survival. Individual behaviour, according to realist theory, personifies state behaviour and is stereotypically masculine. The female gender is omitted, and the masculine gender, which is constructed on female subordination, is the standard and norm.

Second, the concept of the state, a fundamental tenet of International Relations theory, is also heavily gendered. The Greek or Athenian state is considered the model for the Western democratic state. Rebecca Grant (1991) reminds us that the formation of the ancient Grecian state was a patriarchal endeavour to subordinate women's labour within the family, which would then allow the state to concentrate resources on strengthening its economic power. Thus the foundations and persistence of the patriarchial state itself rest on a gendered sexual division of labour which devalues the domestic sphere, at the same time as it relegates women into these spheres.

Third, as Grant points out, the gendered concept of the state of nature – the state of nature being the model of the international arena – entirely excludes women, and, as Tickner maintains, is constructed in opposition to women. Yet it is this concept which is considered the basis of 'man's' behaviour in the international arena.

Consequently, feminist understandings of the state, of war and of security, differ widely from the androcentric assumptions which shape these three dominant mainstream International Relations themes. Cynthia Enloe (1989, 1993), Fred Halliday (1991), Rebecca Grant and Kathleen Newland (1991) and Sandra Whitworth (1994) have suggested new areas of inquiry. Halliday delineates three main areas: the gender-specific consequences of international processes, women as actors on the international scene, and gender components of foreign policy issues. Themes proposed by the others include issues of gender in migration and in the international sexual division of labour, the impact on gender roles and relations of the programmes of multilateral institutions, women and development, and women's rights as human rights.[2]

In this article we look at feminist interpretations of three main International Relations areas: international security, human rights, and international political economy. The areas were selected because of their centrality within the discourse and because of the growing body of work being generated on these themes. International political economy, moreover, has tremendous significance in the Caribbean, in a reality where economic processes, particularly those of global capital, dictate the nature of structures and institutions. We also examine the contributions of Caribbean women to the feminist international agenda. The conclusion suggests a research agenda for future feminist work in International Relations (IR) in the Caribbean context.

Engendering international security

The themes of conflict and security have attracted sustained scrutiny from feminist scholars because of their centrality to IR theory and practice, and because of their particularly strong masculine bias. Many, including Rebecca Grant, have identified national security structures and the attendant ways of thinking as the sources of much of the gender bias in international relations theory as a whole (Grant 1991). She argues that the initial gendered separation of the public and private spheres in the organization of state and society produced an exclusively male concept of citizenship. Men were given the military role of defenders of the state, thereby acquiring a privileged and active status in national life. Women were invisible, did not have access to the state machinery and did not participate in national decision making. Domestic concerns played little part in shaping 'the national interest'.

Marysia Zalewski (1995) and Cynthia Enloe (1993) point out the extent to which beliefs about gender differences have been deliberately constructed in the security sphere. The idea of the masculinity of war and the image of the macho soldier have reinforced the patriarchal order. The traditional exclusion of women from armed combat was a mechanism designed not primarily to protect them, but to protect male privileges (Zalewski, 1995). Beliefs and myths about masculinity and femininity act on their own, or are consciously manipulated by the authorities, in the process of escalating or terminating armed conflict.

The analytical lens of gender is a perspective which has attracted considerable interest during the last five years as a result of the gender dimensions of contemporary communal violence and of political, economic and social change in the post-Cold War world. Developments in Eastern Europe and elsewhere have underlined the need to uncover deep-seated beliefs about gender roles and identities, and to investigate their functions in conflict and immediate post-conflict situations. Recent research has focused on three important themes: (i) in many post-Cold War societies in transition, there has been a rise of conservative political forces and the reassertion of women's traditional roles within the family. State policies excluding women from political activity, employment and from access to legal abortion facilities are being justified on the basis of essentialist doctrines that reintroduce gender biases and inequalities in a new era (Molyneux, in Grant and Newland, 1991; Zalewski, 1995); (ii) in situations of ethnic conflict, women often find themselves caught between the defence of their individual reproductive rights and pro-natalist policies aimed at the ethnic and cultural survival of the community (Bracewell, 1996; Yuval Davis, 1996); (iii) rape and other forms of sexual violence against women have become integral parts of military strategy in the twentieth century. Particularly in communal conflicts, women's status as national and community icons causes them to be explicitly targeted for demoralization through such forms of torture (Seifert, 1996).

Feminist IR scholars generally agree on the need to provide more holistic definitions of security, applicable to all of humanity. Ann Tickner (1991, 1992), Spike Peterson (1992) and Christine Sylvester (1994) all point out the contradictions between state-centric projects of national security and global security. Human rights abuses and military threats are usually generated by the nation state itself. Effective environmental protection and management are beyond the capabilities of any one state. Finally, inequitable national and international economic systems are a fundamental source of human insecurity and suffering. However, the feminist critique goes beyond these observations to emphasize the structural violence that produces gender inequalities and point out that 'women's systemic insecurity is . . . an internal as well as external dimension of state systems' (Peterson, 1992: 32).

On an empirical level, these claims are supported by the work of feminist researchers who present a starkly contrasting picture of global security issues. They have thrown the spotlight on domestic violence, sexual crimes and female infanticide (NiCarthy, in Ashworth, 1995; Seifert, 1996; Zalewski, 1995). They have shown that 80 per cent of all refugees and displaced persons are women and children who are vulnerable not only to the insecurity as refugees, but also to sexual violence and forced prostitution (Longwe, 1995; Agarwal, 1996). Critics of this work have argued that feminist portrayals are skewed and ignore the damaging consequences of warfare for men. They claim that the methodology espoused by feminist thinkers does not adequately encompass the masculine gender and the human condition as a whole (Jones, 1996).

None the less, feminist scholarship in these areas has had a noticeable impact on international development and humanitarian policies and programmes. Since 1985, gender considerations have been increasingly integrated into the design of refugee relief programmes (Ager *et al.*, 1995; Walker, 1995). In the sphere of environmental security, women are now often cast in the role of environmental custodians and managers. Following upon the Bosnian conflict, rape during armed conflict has been categorized by the United Nations as a war crime. Finally, the influence is much evident in the United Nations Development Programme's concept of 'Human Security' which includes economic security, access to food and health services, personal security, political security and participation in community life (UNDP Human Development Reports, 1994, 1995).[3]

Feminist perspectives on security have made an impression also within the International Relations academy where one of the chief debates within feminist theory – the Essentialist/Constructivist debate – rears its head. Essentialists feel that women, for reasons of biology and socialization, are more inclined towards connection and co-operation. Many argue that the Realist security dilemma might disappear completely if gender roles were differently distributed. Women might interpret the national interest differently, be more sensitive to the social costs of conflict and use different approaches to conflict management (Tickner, 1992, 1995). Social constructivists, on the other hand, dismiss these claims, arguing that such stereotyping is invalid and may paradoxically reinforce traditional identities and roles (Forcey, 1995). One of the most penetrating critiques of essentialist claims comes from Jean Bethke Elshtain, who writes, 'women as leaders . . . mothers . . . and workers have sustained and supported the wars of their states in far greater numbers than women in any capacity have acted in opposition to wars and nationalistic excess' (Bethke Elshtain, 1995a: 345).

The fact is that on the eve of the twenty-first century women are no longer excluded from mainstream security establishments, neither are they entirely distanced from decision-making processes on security matters. An increasing number of women feature in the armed forces in many countries and a mixed picture emerges. To some extent their experiences have mirrored those of male soldiers (Grant, in Peterson, 1992). At the same time, women's presence in the armed forces in the United States, in particular, has led to growing consideration of the differential moral standards that are used to evaluate the conduct of men and women and to the examination of sexual discrimination in this field of employment. Rebecca

Grant argues that, rather than constituting a victory for feminism, the presence of women in the military poses difficult and contradictory questions for feminist epistemology. Now feminist perspectives on security are called upon 'to resolve the conflict of values between women's experiences in combat and feminist assumptions about security', in addition to exposing gender biases and researching aspects of human behaviour that are usually ignored in security studies (Grant, in Peterson, 1992: 95–6). Grant predicts that not one but several feminist epistemologies and various theories of international security may eventually emerge.

Little work has so far been done on the gender dimensions of conflict and security in the Caribbean. Save for the Spanish-speaking Caribbean, among these micro-states, the primary challenge has been to cope with the constraints on development and the vulnerabilities imposed by small size. From the early 1970s onwards, there was some preoccupation with Cold War ideological issues, the security dimensions of US–Caribbean relations, regime security and territorial integrity. More recently, there has been growing recognition of the non-military threats to security, notably narcotrafficking, environmental disasters and destabilizing shifts in the global market economy. In addition, Caribbean societies are increasingly aware of the pressures of their external environment on their internal security.

This is perhaps the best point of departure for developing feminist perspectives on security issues in the Caribbean. Here as elsewhere women's experiences indicate that the major sources of insecurity for them are internal – within the state and within the family. Feminist activist groups and researchers in the region have extensively documented the structural insecurity for many women that results from poverty, underdevelopment and the gendered division of labour. Nearly half of Caribbean households are headed by female single parents (Senior, 1991). Yet, there are lower rates of female participation in the labour force than male. In 1993 the rates ranged from 75 per cent male compared to 62 per cent female labour force participation in Jamaica, to 80 per cent male, 33 per cent female in Belize (Caricom/ILO 1995). While the Caribbean stands out among developing regions for having a significant proportion of educated professional women, at the same time women predominate in lower-paid, low status and insecure forms of employment. Economic insecurity increased sharply with structural adjustment programmes and with the Caribbean countries' shifting positions in the global division of labour in the 1980s and 1990s. Women's labour conditions were greatly affected, in the 1980s, by the proliferation of export processing zones that thrived on cheap female labour (Dunn, in Ashworth, 1995; Pearson, in Momsen, 1993), and then, in the 1990s, by the contraction of free zone employment with the establishment of the NAFTA and the changing strategies of North American multinationals.[4] In the Dominican Republic in the 1980s and Cuba in the 1990s, drastic structural adjustment processes led large numbers of women to resort to prostitution for economic survival (Elizalde, 1996).

Global market liberalization is causing crises in traditional export sectors across the region. The Caribbean has witnessed a concomitant growth in informal economic activity, and most notably, deepening involvement in the global narcotics trade (International Narcotics Reports, US Department of State, 1994, 1997). This has been accompanied by a sharp rise in criminality and breakdowns in law and order in many Caribbean societies (Harriott, 1996; Klaus Albuquerque, in Caribbean Week January–February 1996). With fewer employment opportunities, there is growing evidence of female involvement in drug trafficking and of women being used as couriers and market outlets by drug traffickers.[5]

The rising incidence of violent crime severely impinges on the personal security of all citizens, and especially on the lives of women and their families in depressed inner city areas, for instance in Jamaica and Haiti. Throughout the region and across social classes, sexual assaults and violation and domestic violence are major threats to women's security. The root causes identified range from tradition, culture, substance abuse and the media to economic structures, male marginalization and aggression and women's intensifying quest for economic survival. They combine to produce a pattern of deteriorating gender relations (Ffolkes, in Leo-Rhynie et al., 1997). In Trinidad and Tobago and Barbados, recent research shows that reported cases of domestic violence have risen in tandem with women's increasing economic independence (Gopaul and Morgan, 1997). In Jamaica, reported cases of domestic violence rose more than tenfold between 1985 and 1993 (UNICEF/Planning Institute of Jamaica, 1995). In the Eastern Caribbean, there have also been recent indications of an increase in reported rape, and of a growing social debate on measures to deal with the problem (remarks by Trinidad Attorney-General, Caribbean and Central American Regional Report December 1997). Statistics on the full extent of domestic violence and sexual assaults are still hard to come by throughout the Caribbean region. However, considerable progress has been made since the mid-1980s in documenting the issues and proposing policy solutions in the form of protective as well as punitive legislation, and appropriate training for the police and the judiciary (Ffolkes, in Leo-Rhynie et al., 1997).

There is sporadic evidence of women assuming conflict management roles in war-torn inner-city communities of Jamaica. Despite these 'real world' developments, there have been few attempts to integrate gender perspectives into explicitly International Relations analyses of Caribbean security issues.

There is no scarcity of themes or material – refugee movements, sexual violence, narcotrafficking, trafficking in women and children, women in the security forces, inner-city low intensity conflict, economic insecurity, the use of feminist epistemology to reinterpret Caribbean small state interaction with hegemonic powers – to name a few. The field is rich for those willing to take up the challenge of developing a Caribbean feminist International Relations.

Women's rights and human rights

Over the last fifteen years, human rights have assumed a greater prominence in international relations. There is growing consensus that the observance of human rights norms contributes to national and international peace and security. Women's rights activists have thus had greater possibilities since 1991 to integrate women's concerns into United Nations human rights and human development documentation.

None the less, writers argue that within the international human rights machinery insufficient attention has been paid to the need to *reconceptualize* human rights from the perspective of women's life experiences. Instead they have merely been accorded the conventional rights of man (Abeyesekera, 1995). Women's rights are still a sticking point in the arguments about the universality or cultural relativism of human rights. Debates about the role and status of women within their national societies have led to the 1979 UN Convention on the Elimination of All Forms of Discrimination Against Women (CEDAW) being subject to more reservations than any other major human rights instrument (Ashworth, 1993).

Other criticisms relate to the UN's limited powers of sanction or enforcement to protect human rights, and to the tendency of mainstream human rights organizations to give priority to the protection of civil and political rights. This has had a three-fold negative effect for women. Firstly, the private sphere of the home and family is only partially regulated by the state. Indeed state policies towards the family often reinforce the subordination and traditional roles of women. Yet the home is where much of the abuse and discrimination against women takes place (Rao, 1996). Secondly, a lower priority has been accorded implicitly to social and economic rights, with negative implications for women's attainment of equality through access to social goods and economic opportunities. Thirdly, for many years issues relating to women's sexuality and reproductive rights were not fully addressed either by mainstream human rights organizations, or in the work of UN human rights organs.

Considerable progress has been made internationally since the 1993 United Nations Conference on Human Rights. Women's rights activists were successful in including their concerns in the Vienna Human Rights Declaration and Programme of Action.[6] This was followed in December 1993 by the UN Declaration on the Elimination of Violence against Women, which breaks new ground by referring explicitly to any act of gender-based violence which occurs *in either the public or the private sphere*. In 1993, the UN Human Rights Commission also appointed the first ever Special Rapporteur on Violence against Women and its Causes. Finally, there is the work of the UN Human Rights bodies on various forms of sexual enslavement.

Since the International Decade for Women and the very basic stage of conceptualizing and gaining international acknowledgement of women's rights, the challenge has now shifted to the expansion and transformation of the definition of mainstream human rights (Bunch, 1992; Abeyesekera, 1995). The dividing line between the public and private spheres of human life has to be broken down and extensive changes still have to be effected in national legal systems. In political and practical terms this is a formidable goal. It underlines the importance of continuing to transform the international human rights concepts and norms which will function as permanent standards which states cannot easily erode.

Much of this international debate is highly relevant to the Caribbean even though the region is widely perceived as a region where women have advanced in many fields. All the countries in the region have become parties to the CEDAW. The Caribbean Community Secretariat has drafted model legislation aimed at eradicating discrimination in various areas of Family Law, Citizenship Law and Labour Law and at providing greater protection for women against violence (Caricom/ILO, 1995). There have been significant changes in some national legal systems pertaining to cohabitation rights, inheritance and nationality (UNICEF, 1996). Since the 1980s, there has been greater enforcement of paternal responsibilities through tougher child maintenance provisions. Legislation on maternity leave entitlements is in place across the region. In the 1980s, the laws on rape became more stringent, particularly where the rape of minors is concerned. Although many territories have established rape crisis centres, these are limited in number and cannot handle the scale of the problem. The Bahamas, Jamaica, Curacao, Trinidad and Tobago are examples of countries where Crisis Centres and Women's Bureaux offer training to the police and the judiciary on domestic violence and on the handling of victims of sexual assault. The establishment of Police Rape Units in Jamaica with specially trained officers is a successful policy response, which has resulted in increased reporting of rape cases (Ffolkes, in Leo-Rhynie *et al.*, 1997). In its legislation of 1990, Trinidad and Tobago was the first country to recognize the concept of rape within marriage.

There have also been policy responses to the problem of domestic violence. For instance, in the English-speaking Caribbean, Trinidad and Tobago, Barbados, and the Bahamas led the way in passing legislation against domestic violence. More recently Jamaica, Belize, Guyana and St Vincent have introduced legislation. These bills are preventive rather than punitive, and they concentrate on providing personal protection orders to the victims. The Barbados Domestic Violence (Protection Orders) Act 1992 is the most realist in its recognition of the possibility of the victims' financial dependence on the abuser. It may require the abuser to contribute to the household expenses although he/she may be banned from the premises (Ffolkes, in Leo-Rhynie *et al.*, 1997). In Jamaica, women's rights activists have been lobbying for amendments to their own bill that would also take into account financial dependence and domestic violence in the case of various types of visiting male/female relationships (Simms, 1998). Throughout the region, shelters for victims are few and enjoy limited assistance from the state (UNICEF, 1996). Finally, the issue of sexual harassment has received some public attention but little in the way of policy response. The Bahamas Sexual Offences and Domestic Violence Act of 1991 does specifically cover sexual harassment (Caricom/ILO, 1995).

In the area of employment, most Caricom countries have constitutional or legislative provisions that prohibit discrimination against women and about half have ratified the 1951 International Labour Organization Convention No. 100 on Equal Remuneration (Caricom/ILO, 1995). There is, however, a huge gap between formal legislative provisions and their enforcement. The reality is that women still account for the largest share of the unemployed in most countries. Most women are still clustered in the least remunerated jobs while bearing significant financial responsibility for the support household. Caribbean women also have more limited access to ownership of property and credit, than their male counterparts.

In a few countries, national debates on constitutional reform have provided platforms for feminist groups to present proposals on strengthening the safeguards against discrimination on the grounds of sex (*National Report on the Status of Women in Jamaica*, 1994). However, women's representatives attest to the formidable obstacles posed by 'negative attitudes towards gender equity' (Simms, quoted in the *Sunday Gleaner*, 27/07/97). Moreover, the growing regional discourse on the perceived marginalization of young men is likely to divert resources away from women's programmes, and is a fundamental and sensitive gender issue which Caribbean feminists are obliged to confront.

Much of the discussion on women's rights in the Caribbean has been confined to Gender and Development circles, to the reports compiled by national and regional women's activist groups and by the state women's bureaux. Few of these issues have surfaced in mainstream human rights literature in the region, which has tended to focus, predictably, on issues relating to civil and political rights. Once again, it underlines the need to integrate gender concerns into the area of International Relations.

Gender and Development: gender in the International Political Economy

The sub-discipline of International Political Economy (IPE) maintains a consistent critique of mainstream International Relations for its insufficient attention to the impact of international processes on people's lives. Ironically, while IPE identifies class, race and ethnicity as driving forces behind international relations, gender has not yet been included in a major way. Caribbean IPE scholars have recognized the unequal and inequitable international division of labour, but its gendered dimensions have largely escaped attention save by Cecilia Green on Caribbean women and global restructuring (1994).

So far it has been feminist theorists who have identified the capitalist system as based on and maintained by the subordination of women and their waged and unwaged labour. Maria Mies has given one of the first such analyses in *Patriarchy and Accumulation on a World Scale* (1986). Mies's thesis posits that the existing international division of labour is built on the exploitation of women and colonized peoples, towards the maintenance of the capitalist patriarchal system which constitutes the world economy (Mies, 1986). Thus, while there exists an *international* division of labour that relegates the peripheral groups in peripheral countries (as well as the peripheral groups in core countries) to subordinate positions, that division of labour is fundamentally gendered so that women are, so to speak, doubly oppressed in the historical and contemporary machinations of the global capitalist economy.

Into this framework Cecilia Green puts forward a detailed account and analysis of how these forces were played out in the Caribbean. Green traces women's relative independence during slavery, where women slaves were seen purely as labour, and subsequent parallel patterns of autonomy and dependence on male partners after abolition and emancipation, through to migration and farming patterns which are visible today in the lives of Caribbean women and the gender system presently at work. Green aptly explicates the gendered nature of the contemporary phase of global restructuring:

> As the globalization of high-technology production restructures technology, investment, employment, and labor, it shifts certain types of low-technology jobs in electronics and garment assembly activities to the Caribbean and elsewhere in the Third World. Women tend to be concentrated in these jobs because capital has defined them as women's work. This has been happening at the same time as traditional exports have contracted, thereby putting many men out of work, combined with the impact of structural adjustment programs on wages and employment, this process exacerbates problems for women in the Caribbean, especially heads of households who must now support their families and a growing number of unemployed males.
>
> (Green, 1994: 171)

The group Development Alternatives with Women for a New Era (DAWN) also recognizes and incorporates these concepts and analyses into its work. DAWN, a group of women's activists and scholars predominantly from and concerned about the developing world, links women's inequality with inequalities of class, race, ethnicity, religion, and a country's position in the world economy. DAWN links women's subordination to global economic inequalities, the Western bias of developmentalism, and the international and sexual division of labour (Sen and Grown, 1987). Unfortunately work such as this is rarely given consideration outside of the fields of women's or gender studies. Nevertheless, these analyses have entered the international arena – albeit in less radical language – under the banner, 'Gender and Development', or 'Women in Development' (WID).

The fields of Women in Development (WID) and Gender and Development (GAD), have been the primary influences in bringing gender to bear on development thinking. The mainstream International Relations approach in the Caribbean has not factored gender into the formulation or enactment of foreign policy. Nevertheless, foreign ministries and missions have been forced to deal with women's and gender issues such as migration, especially of domestic workers, international prostitution, female refugees, and the women inter-island traders (hucksters, higglers). At the multilateral level, national delegations from the Caribbean have attended and actively participated in international conferences, particularly the women's conferences since 1975 and the UN development-related conferences of the 1990s, at which gender issues have been a major focus.

The first World Conference on Women was held in Mexico City in 1975, and the UN Decade for Women (1975–85) was launched. Internationally, the WID movement became active at the same time as women's activists

FEMINIST REVIEW NO 59, SUMMER 1998

at national and regional levels in the Caribbean had been lobbying for official recognition of women's and gender issues (Gordon, 1984; Reddock, 1988). UN initiatives in the Caribbean were largely carried out by the women's organizations already in existence (Antrobus, 1988). WID theory and practice were concerned primarily with 'integrating women into development' through special projects for women. Early WID strategies did not problematize the neo-classical development economics paradigm, and the modernization process was seen as desirable and ultimately beneficial for women. There was little if any analysis of the historical processes of capital accumulation, or of patriarchal relations in and outside of the household.

By 1980, governments all over the world had established national machinery for women's advancement, as had many international organizations. By this time, however, those working in the field, particularly those in the Third World, began to question the more fundamental economic, political and social dynamics of the world-system and their implications for women (*Woman Speak!* 1981: 8). By the end of the Decade, according to Peggy Antrobus (1991: 311–17), the mood had changed:

> Women were not 'outside' development . . . women's contribution was central to 'development', but in a way that was deeply exploitative of their time, labour, both paid and unpaid, and their sexuality. [Development] policies are grounded in a set of assumptions which assign certain roles and characteristics to women [and are] dependent on assumptions about the roles into which most women have been socialized.

Along these lines, the 1985 Hastings Declaration, or Statement of Caribbean Women,[7] reads in part:

> Conventional growth-oriented models of development currently being pursued by some governments cannot lead to the achievement of the UN Decade of 'Equality, Development and Peace' . . . women's full and equal participation in all aspects of social, political and economic power can point a clear path towards people-oriented 'Development Alternatives with Women for a New Era' within the entire region.
>
> (*Hastings Declaration*, in Ellis, 1986: 18)

Since Nairobi, WID has 'developed' into the Gender and Development, or 'GAD', approach. The GAD approach claims to recognize the gendered dimensions inherent in societal, political and economic institutions, and how these are perpetuated by 'development' strategies. As such, GAD aims to be more transformative than remedial.

The GAD approach that has so far managed to best grasp the dimensions of IPE analysis is that articulated by DAWN. Andrée Michel (1995), citing DAWN, argues that Third World feminists have been the initial force in bringing feminism to international relations by making explicit the links between women's status and the international economic process. Michel's assertion supports the view stated earlier that international feminism paved the initial path for Feminist International Relations. But Third World women, including Caribbean women, have also played important roles in the international arena. Key Caribbean figures include: Lucille Mathurin Mair, Secretary General of the 1985 UN World Conference on Women; Dame Nita Barrow, who chaired the parallel NGO Forum in Nairobi; Dorienne Wilson-Smilie, the first Women's Affairs Officer at the Commonwealth Secretariat; Peggy Antrobus, a founding member of DAWN who took on its headship for some years; and, most recently, Angela King, the UN Secretary General's adviser on gender. This high level of representation was continued at the Fourth UN World Conference on Women where Caribbean women chaired three critical committees, and where the Caribbean positions were all reflected in the final conference document.

More recently, feminist work in international political economy has moved on to look at globalization and its gender dimensions[8] (Marchand, 1996). While the gender specific effects of global restructuring were revealed as early as 1987 in the landmark, *Adjustment With a Human Face* (Corneia *et al.*, 1987), and followed more in depth with *Engendering Adjustment* (Commonwealth Secretariat, 1991), these analyses have generally not been considered beyond WID/GAD arenas. Marianne Marchand (1996) in particular has taken an important step in identifying and bridging the gap between GAD work and IPE work, and examining GAD propositions on global restructuring. Marchand critiques GAD's emphasis on the adverse effects of globalization on women, and the focus on neoclassical economics as the paradigm within which all economic processes take place. She argues that these two tendencies maintain women's position as victim, and do not challenge the universalistic claims of liberalism. These tendencies in turn result in a void of propositions for the empowerment of women and for the development of strategies to counter ongoing processes of global restructuring (Marchand, 1996: 601).

Marchand does not problematize the state in these analyses. The feminist incursions in the context of globalization so far raise some disturbing questions regarding the role of the state and women's dependence on the state. The state had earlier on been identified as a primary institution in the underprivileging of women. Is it not then somewhat paradoxical to condemn globalization's impact on the reduction of the state and the expansion of market forces, and to issue a call, as Gita Sen does, 'to work to transform the state so that governments can begin to serve people and women in particular' (1997: 23)? Surely the feminist goal of empowerment and self-reliance cannot be served if analyses in this area do not conclude

FEMINIST REVIEW NO 59, SUMMER 1998

with some possibilities for gender equity in a globalized world economy, rather than attempting to stem the inevitable tide of global restructuring, and turning back to the state as provider. This is not to discount the recent signals from the World Bank, in particular, that the role of the state is being reassessed (World Bank 1997). One agrees with Sen that gender considerations must play a foremost role in the reform and restructuring of the state. However, the relationship between women and a transformed state needs to be more clearly conceptualized, as well as other avenues explored for the empowerment of women.

The challenges of gender in International Relations

While the fields of Feminist International Relations and feminist International Political Economy are growing exponentially, there remains little Caribbean contribution to the debate, despite the Caribbean's leading role in the fields of WID and GAD, and the high proportion of Caribbean diplomats who are women.

Feminist International Relations aims to interrogate the foundations of International Relations theory and practice, and provide feasible alternatives which would ultimately augur for a more gender equitable world. As with Caribbean 'versions' of mainstream International Relations, Caribbean feminist 'versions' of International Relations must take the analysis yet a step further so that they are representative of the realities of Caribbean gender patterns. As such, a specifically Caribbean feminist understanding of development, integration, diplomacy – the three main issues in Caribbean International Relations – would be a first step in defining the field from the Caribbean feminist perspective.

Specific International Relations issues abound and are ripe for feminist analysis, particularly as International Relations becomes more globalized. The greatest challenge to a Caribbean Feminist International Relations, however, is that which faces the field of Caribbean International Relations as a whole: not simply to develop, articulate and advocate a (Caribbean) Feminist International Relations agenda, but to effect the links between discourse and practice. There is little correlation between scholarship and practice in Caribbean International Relations (Watson, 1994), resulting in repetitions of misguided foreign policies which maintain underdevelopment and dependency (Stewart, 1994; Nurse, 1993). Whether the feminist project to humanize and engender International Relations succeeds will depend on the relevance which feminist writers can display in their work in the field. It will depend, equally, on the openness and progressiveness of international relations actors and foreign policy decision makers to the global feminist project of structural change.

Notes

1 Christine Sylvester's work, *Feminist Theory and International Relations in a Post-Modern Era* (1994) is a good example of this cross-fertilization. She concludes that a feminist International Relations has different understandings of co-operation and reciprocity than does mainstream/malestream International Relations. She suggests that a feminist International Relations is more aptly understood as 'relations international' – beyond interstate relations to 'inter-people' relations.

2 Foremost in US feminist work on foreign policy is Cynthia Enloe (1989, 1993). She attempts to 'make feminist sense of international politics' by answering the question, 'Where are the women?' She combines theoretical inquiry with examining actual issues. Enloe argues that gendered stereotypes of masculinity and femininity provide the basis upon which the international system is maintained and operated. She applies this theory by showing how diplomats' wives, prostitutes at overseas military bases, secretaries in UN missions, and migrants who work as domestic servants to middle-class North Americans all comprise the international system in fundamental ways, as they provide the means for the conduct of 'official' international relations.

Enloe's second work looks at the militarization processes of the Cold War. Here she continues her argument that militarization, security and war are based and dependent on gendered notions of 'man' and 'woman', and posits possible changes in gender roles in the post-Cold War era.

3 In 1995 the UNDP expressed its commitment to gender equity in the strongest possible terms, with the message on the first page of the *Human Development Report 1995* that 'Human development, if not engendered, is endangered'.

4 In Jamaica, for example, in 1996 the proportion of unemployed women increased to 66.5 per cent, with the rate of unemployment among young females under 25 years of age as high as 47 per cent. The unemployment rate for women was three times higher than that of men. The increase in female unemployment is attributed largely to the decline in employment opportunities in female dominated sectors like the community, social and personal services sector, garments and manufacturing (*Economic and Social Survey Jamaica* (PIOJ, 1996: 18.8)). Figures further in 1997 although final statistics are not yet available.

5 Harriott (1996: 27) mentions that in 1994 women accounted for 23 per cent of those arrested for Breaches of the Dangerous Drugs Law, and for 34 per cent of arrestees for cocaine trafficking.

6 See articles 18, 36–44 of *The Vienna Declaration and Programme of Action adopted at the World Conference on Human Rights*, A/CONF.157/24, 25 June 1993, reprinted as Document 85 in *The United Nations and Human Rights 1945–1995*, United Nations, New York, 1995, pp. 448–64.

7 Party to this declaration were ECLAC, CARICOM, WAND, CARIWA, national machineries for women from throughout the Caribbean, and other Caribbean regional and national governmental and non-governmental organizations.

8 See, for example, Safa, 1995; Dunn, 1995; Robinson, 1997; Sen, 1997.

References

ABEYESEKERA, S. (1995) 'Women's human rights: questions of equality and difference', ISS Working Paper No. 186, The Hague: Institute of Social Studies.

AGARWAL, B. (1996) 'From Mexico 1975 to Beijing 1995' *Indian Journal of Gender Studies*, Vol. 3, No. 1: pp. 87–92.

AGER, A., AGER, W and LONG, L. (1995) 'The differential experiences of Mozambican refugee women and men' *Journal of Refugee Studies*, Vol. 8, No. 3.

ANDERSON, P. and DAVIES, O. (1987) 'Impact of recession and adjustment policies on poor urban women in Jamaica', University of the West Indies ISER/Dept. of Economics Report prepared for UNICEF, Mona, Jamaica.

ANSINE, J. (1997) 'Gender plans falling behind' *The Sunday Gleaner*, July 27, p. 1A.

ANTROBUS, P. (1987) 'The gender implications of the debt crisis in the Commonwealth Caribbean: the case of Jamaica' paper presented at Conference of Caribbean Economists, Jamaica, July 5–7.

—— (1988) 'Women in development programmes: the Caribbean experience (1975–1985)' in P. Mohammed and C. Shepherd (1988) editors, *Gender in Caribbean Development*, University of the West Indies, Women and Development Studies Project, Cavehill, Barbados, pp. 36–53.

—— (1991) 'Women in Development' in T. Wallace with C. March editors, *Changing Perceptions: Writings on Gender and Development*, Oxford: Oxfam, pp. 311–17.

ASHWORTH, G. (1993) *Changing the Discourse: A Guide to Women and Human Rights*, London: CHANGE.

—— (1995) *A Diplomacy of the Oppressed: New Directions in International Feminism*, London: Zed Books.

BENERIA, L. and SEN, G. (1986) 'Accumulation, reproduction and women's role in economic development: Boserup revisited' in E. and H. Safa (1985) editors, *Women's Work: Development and the Division of Labour by Gender*, Massachusetts: Bergin and Garvey.

BOSERUP, E. (1970) *Women's Role in Economic Development*, London: Allen & Unwin.

BRACEWELL, W. (1996) 'Women, motherhood and contemporary Serbian nationalism' *Women's Studies International Forum*, Vol. 19, Nos. 1 and 2: 25–33.

BRAIDOTTI, R., CHARKIEWICZ, E., HAUSIER, S. and WIERINGA, S. (1994) *Women, the Environment and Sustainable Development: Towards a Theoretical Synthesis*, London: Zed Books/INSTRAW.

BUNCH, Charlotte (1992) 'Women's Rights as Human Rights' in *Women, Violence and Human Rights*, the 1991 Women's Leadership Institute Report, Centre for Women's Global Leadership, Douglass College, Rutgers, USA.

CARIBBEAN AND CENTRAL AMERICAN REGIONAL REPORT (1997) 2 December, p.3.

CARICOM/ILO (International Labour Organization) (1995) *Women, Labour and the Law: A Caribbean Perspective*, Georgetown: Caricom Secretariat.

CHEN, M. A. (1996) 'Engendering world conferences: the international women's movement and the UN' in L. Gordenker and T. Weiss (1996) editors, *NGOs, the UN and Global Governance*, Boulder, Col.: Lynne Rienner.

COMMONWEALTH SECRETARIAT (1991) *Engendering Adjustment*, London: Commonwealth Secretariat.

CORNEIA, G., JOLLY, R. and STEWART, F. (1987) *Adjustment with a Human Face*, New York: Oxford University Press.

ELIZALDE, R. M. (1996) *Flores Desechables: Prostitucion en Cuba?*, Ciudad de la Habana: Ediciones Abril.

ELSHTAIN, J. Bethke (1995a) 'Feminist themes and international relations' in J. Der Derian (1995) editor, *International Theory: Critical Investigations*, London: Macmillan, pp. 340–62.

—— (1995b) 'Exporting feminism' *Journal of International Affairs*, Vol. 48, No. 2: 541–58.

ENLOE, C. (1989) *Bananas, Beaches and Bases: Making Feminist Sense of International Politics*, Berkeley: University of California Press.

—— (1993) *The Morning After: Sexual Politics at the end of the Cold War*, Berkeley: University of California Press.

FORCEY, Linda Rennie (1995) 'Integrating women's studies with peace studies: challenges for feminist theory' *Indian Journal of Gender Studies*, Vol. 2, No. 2: 211–26.

GOPAUL, Roanna and MORGAN, Paula (1997) *Spousal Violence: Spiralling Patterns in Trinidad and Tobago*, St. Augustine: University of the West Indies, Mimeo.

GORDON, Shirley (1984) editor, *Ladies in Limbo: The Fate of Women's Bureaux. Six case studies from the Caribbean*, London: Commonwealth Secretariat Women and Development Programme.

GRANT, Rebecca (1991) 'The sources of gender bias in International Relations theory' in R. Grant and K. Newland editors, *Gender and International Relations*, Bloomington: Indiana University Press, pp. 27–40.

GRANT, R. and NEWLAND, K. (1991) editors, *Gender and International Relations*, London: Oxford University Press.

GREEN, Cecilia (1994) 'Historical and Contemporary Restructuring and Women in Production in the Caribbean' in H.A. Watson editor, *The Caribbean in the Global Political Economy*, Kingston: Ian Randle Publishers, pp. 149–72.

HALLIDAY, F. (1994) *Rethinking International Relations*, London: Macmillan.

HARRIOTT, A. (1996) 'The changing social organization of crime and criminals in Jamaica' unpublished mimeo, University of the West Indies, Mona, Kingston, Jamaica.

HASTINGS DECLARATION OF CARIBBEAN WOMEN (1985) Hastings, Barbados, March 18 in P. Ellis (1986) editor, *Women of the Caribbean*, Kingston Publications, Jamaica, p. 18.

JAMAICA BUREAU OF WOMEN'S AFFAIRS (1997) *Report on Justice System Workshops on Violence against Women*, Kingston, Jamaica, 29 July 1997.

JAMAICA NATIONAL PREPARATORY COMMISSION FOR THE BEIJING CONFERENCE ON WOMEN (1994) *National Report on the Status of Women in Jamaica*, Jamaica National Preparatory Commission, Kingston, Jamaica.

JONES, A. (1996) 'Does "gender" make the world go round? Feminist critiques of International Relations' *Review of International Studies*, Vol. 22: 405–29.

LEO-RHYNIE, E., BAILEY, B., and BARROW, C. (1997) editors, *Gender: A Caribbean Multi-Disciplinary Perspective*, Kingston: Ian Randle.

LONGWE, S. (1995) 'A gender analysis of war' *African Women*, March–September: 6–12.

LYCKLAMA A NIJEHOLT, G. (1987) 'The fallacy of integration: the UN strategy of integrating women into development revisited' *Netherlands Review of Development Studies*, Vol. 1: 23–7.

MARCHAND, M. (1996) 'Reconceptualizing 'Gender and development' in an era of globalization' *Millennium Journal of International Studies*, Vol. 25, No. 3: pp. 577–603.

MICHEL, Andrée (1995) 'Militarisation of Contemporary Societies and Feminism in the North' in G. Ashworth editor, *A Diplomacy of the Opressed, New Directions in International Feminism*, London: Zed Books, pp. 33–51.

MIES, M. (1986) *Patriarchy and Accumulation on a World Scale*, London: Zed Books.

MOMSEN, J.(1993) editor, *Women and Change in the Caribbean*, Kingston: Ian Randle.

NURSE, K. (1993) 'The developmental role of export-oriented industrialization in the new international division of labour: the case of Caricom countries', PhD thesis, University of the West Indies, St Augustine, Trinidad.

SHIV PARSAD, B. (1988) 'Domestic violence: a study of wife abuse among East Indians of Guyana' paper presented at Caribbean Studies Association Conference, Guadeloupe, May 25–27.

PETERSON, V. S. (1992) editor, *Gendered States: Feminist Revisions of International Relations Theory*, Boulder, Col.: Lynne Rienner.

PIOJ (Planning Institute of Jamaica) (1992) 'Refrain in a minor key: reflections on women's socio-economic place in Jamaican development approaches', PIOJ Background Paper for Caricom Economic Summit, 1992.

—— (1997) *Economic and Social Survey Jamaica 1996*, Kingston: PIOJ.

RAO, A. (1996) 'Home-word bound: women's place in the family of international human rights' *Global Governance*, Vol. 2, No. 2: 241–60.

REDDOCK, Rhoda (1988) 'Feminism and Feminist Thought: An Historical Overview' in P. Mohammed and C. Shepherd editors, *Gender and Caribbean Development*, University of the West Indies: Women and Development Studies Project, pp. 55–77.

ROSS-FRANKSON, J. (1987) 'The economic crisis and prostitution in Jamaica: a preliminary study' paper presented at Friedrich Ebert Stiftung/UWI Symposium *Issues Concerning Women*, Department of Economics, UWI, Mona, Kingston, Jamaica, March 7.

SAFA, H. (1995) *The Myth of the Male Breadwinner*, Boulder, Col.: Westview Press.

SEIFERT, R. (1996) 'The second front: the logic of sexual violence in wars' *Women's Studies International Forum*, Vol. 19, Nos. 1–2: 35–43.

SEN, G. (1997) 'Globalization, justice and equity: a gender perspective' *Development*, Vol. 40, No. 2: 21–6.

SEN, G. and GROWN, C. (1987) *Development, Crises and Alternative Visions: Third World Women's Perspectives*, New York: Monthly Review Press.

SENIOR, O. (1991) *Working Miracles: Women's Lives in the English-Speaking Caribbean*, Institute of Social and Economic Research, University of the West Indies, Cave Hill, Barbados.

SIMMS, G. (1998) Interview on *Straight Talk* Programme, Power FM, Kingston, Jamaica, January 7.

STEWART, T. (1993) 'Debt crises in the periphery as manifestations of the continuity of imperialism thesis', PhD thesis, University of the West Indies, St Augustine, Trinidad.

SYLVESTER, C. (1994) *Feminist Theory and International Relations in a Post-Modern Era*, Cambridge: Cambridge University Press.

THORBURN, D. (1997) 'Gender, regionalism and Caribbean development: an examination of Caricom policy', MSc thesis, University of the West Indies, St Augustine, Trinidad.

—— (1997) 'Engendering Caribbean security: national security reconsidered from a feminist perspective' *Caribbean Quarterly*, Vol. 43, No. 3: 74–89.

TICKNER, J. A. (1992) *Gender in International Relations: Feminist Perspectives on Achieving Global Security*, New York: Columbia University Press.

—— (1995) 'Hans Morgenthau's principles of political realism' in Der Derian J. (1995) editor, *International Theory: Critical Investigations*, London: Macmillan, pp. 53–74.

—— (1991) 'Hans Morgenthau's principles of political realism: a feminist reformulation' in R. Grant and K. Newland editors, *Gender and International Relations*, Bloomington: Indiana University Press, pp. 8–26.

TOMASEVSKI, K. (1993) *Women and Human Rights*, London: Zed Books.

UNITED NATIONS (1995) *The United Nations and Human Rights 1948–1995*, New York: United Nations Blue Book Series.

UNITED NATIONS DEVELOPMENT PROGRAMME (1994) *Human Development Report 1994*, Oxford/New York: Oxford University Press.

—— (1995) *Human Development Report 1995*, Oxford/New York: Oxford University Press.

UNICEF (1996) *Country Summaries of Girls and Women in Latin America and the Caribbean*, Bogota, Colombia: UNICEF Regional Office for Latin America and the Caribbean.

—— (1996) *Developing Profiles of Girls and Women in Latin America and the Caribbean*, Bogota, Colombia: UNICEF Regional Office for Latin America and the Caribbean.

UNICEF/PLANNING INSTITUTE OF JAMAICA (1995) *Situation Analysis of Children and Women in Jamaica*, Kingston: UNICEF.

US DEPARTMENT OF STATE (1994) *International Narcotics Control Strategy Report*, US State Department Bureau for International Narcotics and Law Enforcement Affairs, Washington DC, April 1994.

—— (1997) *International Narcotics Control Strategy Report*, US State Department Bureau for International Narcotics and Law Enforcement Affairs, Washington DC, March 1997.

WALKER, B. (1995) 'The question of gender' *Refugee Participation Network*, Issue 20: 8–11.

WATSON, H. A. (1994) editor, *The Caribbean in the Global Political Economy*, Kingston, Jamaica: Ian Randle .

—— (1993) 'Globalization, liberalism and the Caribbean: deciphering the limits of nation, nation-state and sovereignty under global capitalism' *Caribbean Studies*, Vol. 26, Nos. 3–4: 213–408.

WHITWORTH, S. (1994) *Feminism and International Relations*, New York: St. Martin's Press.

—— (1994) 'Theory as exclusion: gender and international political economy' in **R. Stubbs** and **G. Underhill** (1996) editors, *Political Economy and the Changing World Order*, London: Macmillan, pp. 116–29.

WOMAN INC., JAMAICA (1997) *Crisis Centre Statistics 1985–1996*, Kingston: Woman Inc.

WOMENSPEAK! (1981) Newsletter published by the Women and Development Unit, Cave Hill, Barbados.

YUVAL-DAVIS, N. (1996) 'Women and the biological reproduction of "The Nation"' *Women's Studies International Forum*, Vol. 19, Nos. 1-2: 17–24.

ZALEWSKI, M. (1995) 'Well, what is the feminist perspective on Bosnia?' *International Affairs*, Vol. 71, No. 2: 339–56.

Reviews

Women and the Sexual Division of Labour in the Caribbean

Keith Hart (ed.)

Canoe Press: University of the West Indies, Barbados, Jamaica and Trinidad, Kingston and Consortium Graduate School of Social Sciences, University of the West Indies, Mona, first published 1989, this edition 1996

ISBN 976-8125-18-7 (Canoe Press) ISBN 976-41-0075-9 (CGS)

FEMINIST REVIEW NO 59, SUMMER 1998, PP. 233–242

The seven essays in this volume come from a series of seminars sponsored by the Consortium Graduate School of Social Studies and the Women and Development Studies Project of the University of the West Indies, Mona, Jamaica in early 1987. Following an introduction by the editor, the volume contains an essay on evolutionary anthropology, a review of labour market theories, a theoretical and empirical piece on Trinidad, and four Jamaican case studies. Most of the authors are highly respected scholars in the region, and the book is an excellent source of information on regional thinking on gender issues; the four case studies in particular should be required reading for those doing research on gender and employment in Jamaica.

Keith Hart begins by observing that the West Indian family form, consisting of fluid and unstable conjugal unions and female headed households, and described as 'deviant' by Western scholars, is in fact appearing in other more developed western societies. Thus he states that the region 'is one of the major crucibles of the social forms that are evolving in the face of modern conditions'. Unfortunately this exciting idea is not pursued in the essays which follow, and even now, nearly ten years later, it is a line of inquiry that deserves more analysis.

Following the introduction, the first essay by Keith Hart is an anthropological review of the evolution of the sexual division of labour. The thesis is that industrialization undermines the 'natural' sexual division of labour, that markets interfere in the complementary interdependence of productive and reproductive activities. Illustrative examples are given from western Europe, the Caribbean and West Africa.

The second essay, by Roslyn Lynch, reviews six different labour market theories on the sexual division of labour, and concludes that the segmented labour market hypotheses are more appropriate than neo-classical ones in explaining sex segregation in the region, although this assertion is not substantiated. This essay will be useful (though outdated) to students in gender studies.

Rhoda Reddock's chapter starts out by arguing that mainstream social science, including Marxist variants, explain the sexual division of labour as fundamentally biologically determined. The author's own view is that such a division is caused by the social and economic interests of ruling groups. Her empirical analysis shows that unemployment and labour force participation have declined over time among women in Trinidad and Tobago. She attributes this result to the fact that unemployed women are placed in the 'housewife' category while unemployed men are not. From her more detailed analysis of gender-based occupational segregation she contends that not only are women underrepresented in white collar occupations, but that occupational segregation does not follow a systematic pattern of skill differential or comparative advantage. This leads her to conclude that the sexual division of labour is based on hierarchical relationships that appropriate women's labour at little or no cost.

Leo-Rhynie's chapter looks at gender segregation in the educational system. Leo-Rhynie notes that although girls outperform boys in the national Common Entrance and CXC examinations, so that more girls than boys attend secondary school, students' subject choice is still highly segregated along gender lines in very traditional ways. This segregation, she argues, leads to the occupational segregation observed by Gordon in the labour force.

The essay on petty trading by Le Franc provides some fascinating details on the business of 'higglering', an occupation which is traditionally dominated by females. Although her sample is very small and unlikely to be representative, the data provide some surprising insights into the attitudes and work arrangements of higglers. Foremost among these is the fact that most higglers do not view their job as a profession or career, but rather as a necessary measure to make ends meet. Consequently very little time is spent in recruiting clients or finding the cheapest sources, and very little of the proceeds are invested back into the business. According to Le Franc, this lack of dynamism and innovation is the reason why higglering tends not to lead to social mobility.

Dorian Powell completes the volume with a short essay on women's domestic work, and some of the issues raised by the feminist movement and women's groups regarding the status and definition of unpaid domestic labour. Her data, based on a sample of lower-class women, indicate that most women feel housework is work, but do not support the 'wages for housework' concept.

Except for Gordon and Hart, the authors in this volume approach their subject from a strong institutional and often Marxist perspective, focusing on power and class to explain and understand the subject at hand – as Keith Hart states at the end of the introduction, 'The women's struggle, here as elsewhere, is also a class struggle.' This perspective was representative of the prevailing ideology among scholars in this field at the time, and I (for one) would be curious to know whether the same ideological view exists among these scholars (most of whom are still active in the field) in today's neo-liberal world. Given the importance of the issues, the drastic economic adjustments of the 1980s and 1990s and the availability of most of the original authors and seminar participants, it would be extremely useful to organize another series of seminars to assess the status of Caribbean women in the labour market as we approach the millennium.

Sudhanshu Handa

Gender in Caribbean Development

Patricia Mohammed and Catherine Shepherd (eds)
The University of the West Indies, Women and Development Studies Project: Jamaica, Trinidad and Barbados, 1988
ISBN 976 8057 00 9

Exactly ten years after the publication of this book, the reprint under review can still be considered relevant for serious scholars of gender. It is not surprising that Lucille Mathurin-Mair in the foreword to the first edition, written during the United Nations Decade for Women (1975–85), expressed the hope that a gender-focused critique of development would penetrate academia and inform processes of national and regional planning within the Caribbean. This dream is slowly becoming a reality, ten years later and post-United Nations Conference on Women, held in Beijing in 1995. The University of the West Indies has established on each campus Centres for Gender and Development Studies which offer courses at both undergraduate and postgraduate level. We have found that this text provides an excellent interdisciplinary introduction to the field of gender and development from a Caribbean perspective.

The book is divided into eight sections and contains twenty-three papers. It opens with some general considerations of Women's Studies and then moves onto papers that deal with theoretical modes of gender and development, and feminism viewed from a Caribbean historical and conceptual frame of reference. This is of particular import for most theory on feminism has its roots in non-Caribbean, European thought. Chhachhi, a contributor in this section puts it succinctly 'I do not believe in an obverse ethnocentricism . . . but do believe that the experiential situation for Third World women can lead to a further development in crucial areas'. The papers in this section also call for a need for a multidisciplinary and inter-disciplinary collaboration.

The next section contains six papers that explore some disciplines which pay attention to gender: history, sociology, anthropology (with particular emphasis on the family), development studies and labour studies. An analysis of these papers again brings to the forefront the necessity for a holistic and decompartmentalized study of gender particularly in the Caribbean, where it is impossible to separate the influence of class, caste, race, ethnicity and gender from any model of society. All writers in this section argue for a reinvestigation of the existing social science disciplines from the perspective of gender, echoing the views expressed by Mathurin-Mair.

The next two sections reinforce the multidisciplinary nature of gender studies and comprise four papers dealing with cultural ideology and women's writing. In any reprint, I would have preferred to see these two sections merged as all the papers deal with the images of and perceived by men and women in the Caribbean.

The next two papers jump in a different direction and explore an alternative methodology for the teaching of women's health issues – the participatory workshop methodology of the Sistren Theatre Collection. The final section contains three papers on the experiences of women activists in Trinidad, and the problems that they encountered when bold enough to challenge the status quo.

Ten years later I can with confidence echo the words of Editor, Patricia Mohammed in her original introduction to the book the aim is to – 'provide a source-book which can be used to introduce both students and novices to the complexity which is Women's Studies, and to the richness, variety and relevance of the work being undertaken under the rubic of feminism' – for these words are indeed as relevant in 1998.

I have only one reservation about the text. Rather than reproducing the text as initially presented in 1988, where the text followed the exact order of the conference proceedings, I would prefer to see a merging of some sections and a concluding section on alternative methodologies. I would also like to see a postscript written by the editors on the position of gender studies in the Caribbean at the end of the millennium.

Despite this, the book is still valid and provides reliable and interesting food for thought for those interested in gender. Another bonus is that the book is written with minimum technical jargon, in a reader-friendly style suitable for both the serious student and the interested non-academic. For those outside the region it provides valuable insights into the situation of Caribbean women; such insights can only benefit their analysis of gender in their own countries, and must direct them to ponder the other broad issues of race and class in issues of inequity. For women of the 'two thirds world' (as referred to by Nettleford (1992) *Inward Stretch Outward Reach*, London: Longman) the book will in all likelihood provide parallels for them in their own pursuit of knowledge. For women of the Caribbean, on whom the research for this book was based, it gives reassurance of our untapped potential, our resilience, and also provides the very necessary road map to show us not only where we have come from, but also where we would like to go.

Veronica Salter

Women and Change in the Caribbean: A Pan Caribbean Perspective

Janet Henshall Momsen

Ian Randle: Kingston/Indiana University Press: Bloomington and Indianapolis/James Currey: London, 1993
ISBN 0-85255-403-6 £12.95 (Pbk) ISBN 0-85255-404-4 £35 (Hbk)

Janet Momsen makes an insightful observation in her introduction to this book:

> Within the Caribbean regional diversity of ethnicity, class, language and religion there is an ideological unity of patriarchy, of female subordination and dependence. Yet there is also a vibrant living tradition of female economic autonomy, of female-headed households and of a family structure in which men are often marginal. **So Caribbean gender relations are a double paradox**: of patriarchy within a system of matrifocal and matrilocal families; and of domestic ideology coexisting with the economic independence of women. The roots of this contemporary paradoxical situation lie in colonialism. (p. 1)

The eighteen essays included all contemplate some aspect of this double paradox in the lives of women in the Caribbean, focusing particularly on elements of change in the historical shift from past colonialism to present day imperialism and structural adjustment policies.

Momsen presents one of the best collection of essays to date on women in the Caribbean. The book brings together the wide range of language, ethnic and class divisions which coexist in the region. Not only are the English, French, Dutch and Spanish speaking territories represented, but the issue of size is also deliberately addressed. Smaller groups and societies such as Curacao, Nevis and Grenada are examined alongside those which are more traditionally selected as representing the totality of the 'Caribbean experience', such as Jamaica, Cuba or Puerto Rico.

The subject matter of gender in relation to women's lives is approached from different perspectives in the territories visited in the text. Jean Besson, for instance, reconsiders an idea which preoccupied anthropologists in the 1960s. She questions whether Caribbean peoples opted for the colonial metropolitan-oriented value system of 'respectability', in which legal marriage was posited as the most desired state for a woman, or for the indigenous counter culture of 'reputation' which men achieved by their sexual conquests and social skills. Besson argues that Afro-Caribbean women are not passive recipients of Eurocentric values of respectability and are as resistant as men in defining their own cultural values.

The significance of this text is that it has made room for other ethnic groups in these societies. Eva Abraham-Van der Mark writes on 'Marriage and Concubinage among the Sephardic merchant elite of Curacao', a 'minority' ethnic group in the Caribbean setting which has been generally overlooked in the study of the region. Abraham-Van der Mark's research and conclusions are relevant for comparisons with all other migrant groups of the region such as the Europeans, Chinese and Indians, particularly during the periods of their settlement into a new society. She notes for instance that the Sephardic women of Curacao were expected to 'preserve the purity of blood lines and the values of the patriarchal society. The continuously low sex ratio, however, weakened women's position, especially in the case of daughters of the less affluent' (p. 41). This negotiated relationship between gender and ethnicity provides us with valuable empirical data to understand the implications of migration for the shaping of both gender and ethnic identity.

The editors also refer to Keith Hart's (1989) critical comment that the Caribbean 'region is the site of a precocious experiment in social engineering and a major crucible from which modern social organizations have evolved'. In this respect Kevin Yelvington's ethnographic research in a Trinidadian factory provides, as it were, the subcutaneous layer of gender and ethnic factors at work on the factory floor. In such ways, research on the Caribbean represents a microcosm of the reality faced by many other societies at present, certainly in Britain and the Netherlands, which have attracted large numbers of colonial or ex-colonial populations.

Among others who highlight the predicament of migration in the lives of Caribbean people is the essay by Karen Fog Olwig on Nevisian women at home and abroad. Fog Olwig writes that

> The impermanence of sexual relationships, the difficulties of obtaining support from children's fathers and the dependence on economic assistance from one's offspring, are all accentuated in the migration situation. Many of the women interviewed on Nevis had lost touch with their children's fathers through emigration, or found it difficult to put pressure on men living abroad to send them money. . . . It instilled into children from an early age that if they have any 'mind' and ambition they will emigrate so that they can help the family left behind. (p. 155)

These phenomena of absent fathers or mothers, and of the need to migrate for better opportunities and to 'improve theyself' are deeply ingrained in Caribbean life. The consequent impact on family life, where many men are led to migrate, and on the paradoxical position of women in particular, has accentuated the popular notions of the Caribbean male and female – as matrifocal or marginal in the society.

The findings of the different essays provide a rich source of material for elucidating the double paradox as coined by Momsen. Huguette Dagenais, for example, concludes her investigation on the 'paradoxes of reality in the lives of Guadeloupean women' with the comment that their situation

> is a far cry from the mythical 'super woman' ideal and Guadeloupe is a far cry from being a 'matriarchal' society. Guadeloupean women do not participate in the social power structure and do not have the wherewithal to control or even influence decisions which directly affect them (such as abortion and contraception.(p. 103)

The continuing process of both male and female migration, the importance of women's roles in rural development (Barrow, p. 181; Brierley, p. 194; Harry, p. 205; Stubbs, p. 219; Momsen, p. 232), their co-optation as 'unskilled' labour in new technology (Pearson, p. 294) with the continued dependence on female attention to the domestic sphere, have not challenged the paradox of women's lives. If anything, these have reinforced a Caribbean, and perhaps universal, myth – the resilience and adaptability of the female gender, whose goal it seems is that of ever greater autonomy for women. But this is precisely what has led to the double paradox. If autonomy has already been part of their ongoing history, then what changes do Caribbean women ultimately want? In collating this volume, in her introduction to the text, and by the title of the book, Momsen

FEMINIST REVIEW NO 59, SUMMER 1998

challenges us, the readers and scholars, to reshape the feminist discourse in the Caribbean Region from new and critical perspectives.

Patricia Mohammed

References

HART, Keith (1989) *Women and the Sexual Division of Labour*, Kingston, Jamaica, University of the West Indies: Consortium Graduate School of Social Sciences.

Women, Labour and Politics in Trinidad and Tobago: A History

Rhoda Reddock

Ian Randle: Kingston, Jamaica, 1994

ISBN 976 8100 47 8 £10 (Pbk)

Rhoda Reddock's *Women, Labour and Politics in Trinidad and Tobago: A History*, is a pioneering attempt to address a few simple yet incisive questions: 'What has been the nature of women's work in the Caribbean region?' and 'What has been the relationship of paid work to unpaid work in women's lives, and how has this varied in relation to class, ethnicity and colour?'

Reddock's work is a pioneering study of Caribbean history from a feminist perspective. It encourages us to examine the concept of work and women's work activity as features which differentiate Northern and Caribbean feminist discourses.

In addition, the work forces a recognition of women's involvement in the political process of state creation and transformation. This is itself an important theme in a very political text. The achievement of democracy is assessed by the way democracy is experienced in reality by the masses, rather than as an elitist response to the granting of independence in the region. Reddock, therefore, examines democratic state creation as a process of activism and struggle in which spaces for transformatory action and personal autonomy were seized by the population.

More important to this thematic exploration is Reddock's rich historical documentation of the ways in which Trinidadian women contributed and, in many instances, initiated this process of activism both within the labour movement and in the formal electoral processes. The politics of the text is located in the challenge which it presents to the Western epistemological construction of women as other, passive, and apolitical.

This being the point of departure, the development of feminist movements and a feminist consciousness become integrally linked to the nationalist struggles of the late nineteenth and early twentieth century. These struggles are seen both in terms of women's nationalist activism, as well as the space they created for avowedly feminist groupings and movements in the early twentieth century. Trinidadian feminism is born out of struggle for individual and collective recognition of self-worth and identity within a post-colonial state.

The tone of the text, one of confrontation and challenge, also extends to the theoretical framework, located as it is in a Marxist frame of historical material dialectics. Despite the many criticisms being directed at present towards the applicability of Marxist dialectics, this approach is still a very useful one. It facilitates an indepth analysis of the impact of shifts in capital on women's participation in the labour force and the gradual process of 'housewifization' and feminization of certain tasks. This analysis is further enriched by the various racial/ethnic and gender sub-groupings which are integrated into the analysis.

However, this theoretical framework causes the text to falter into a sense of economic determinism, as is often the case with Marxist analysis. Reddock's attempts to overcome this by examining the colonial, patriarchal ideology which informed gender (scripts) in the late nineteenth/early twentieth century. There is room for expanding the theoretical framework to examine the multiple factors which may have had an impact on Trinidadian women's involvement in the labour movement and in the broader political processes. This expansion will require, however, the incorporation of women's subjective experiences.

The methodological strength of the text is found in its historical probing of both primary and secondary historical databases, as well as its integrated use of both qualitative and quantitative data. Reddock interrogates these conventional databases to provide a challenge to traditional historiography. In so doing, she provides a rich re-interpretation of Trinidadian women's activities, rendering by example Joan Scott's dictum that 'the articulation of gender (or sexual difference) as a category of historical analysis, the incorporation of gender into the historian's analytical toolbox . . . makes possible a genuine re-writing of history' (Scott 1983: 147). The periodization of the text 1898–1960, is a craftily chosen one. It stands as a watershed period in the history of the society in which there was a series of confrontations between local groupings competing, albeit unequally, against the colonial interests of the day.

FEMINIST REVIEW NO 59, SUMMER 1998

Above all else, the factor which makes Reddock's work recommended and essential reading is its contemporary relevance to any serious exercise of forging and exploring a Caribbean feminist epistemology. Reddock's work expands the parameters of existing knowledge by legitimizing the political nature of the (activities and) involvement of Trinidadian women in the labour movement. In this regard Reddock writes:

> Deep down, many of us suspected that there had to be such history, it seemed inconceivable that there was any group of women who over time did not make some overt or covert effort to transform their exploited and subordinated social situation. But this had not been of the collective knowledge or history which had been passed down to us. (p. 1)

Transformation is an on-going process which requires one to look steadfastly forward, while constantly conceptualizing and re-negotiating the boundaries and nature of the journey. *Women Labour and Politics in Trinidad and Tobago: A History* stands as a welcome contribution to this process.

Michelle Rowley

References

SCOTT, Joan (1983) 'Survey Articles – Women in History', *Past and Present*, Vol. 101: 141–57.

Book Notes

Family in the Caribbean: Themes and Perspectives

Christine Barrow

Ian Randle: Kingston and James Currey: Oxford, 1997
ISBN 976-8100-75-3   472 pp.

The book provides a comprehensive review of the extensive literature on family, household and conjugal unions in the Caribbean. The work is constructed around six themes prominent in Caribbean family studies, namely, definitions of family, plural and creole society, social structure, gender roles and relationships, methodology, history and social change.

The book is organized into two sections. Part I critically assesses theoretical trends and interpretations from the perspectives of African heritage, colonial social welfare, responses to poverty and patterns of kinship. Key concepts are examined, such as matrifocality, male marginality and female headed households. Part II reviews family structure under slavery, the East Indian family, child rearing patterns, and social policy.

The author aims to show how studies of the family have arrived at present theoretical interpretations and methodological approaches, and to point the way for future inquiry to move beyond the ethnocentric images of past research.

Engendering History: Caribbean Women in Historical Perspective

Verene Shepherd, Bridget Brereton and Barbara Bailey (eds)

Ian Randle: Kingston and James Currey: London, 1995
ISBN 085255-726-4 (Pbk) ISBN 085255-727-2 (Hbk)

As an outcome of an international symposium held at the University of the West Indies, Mona Campus, in 1995, the book broadens the base of empirical knowledge on Caribbean women's history. The twenty chapters

FEMINIST REVIEW NO 59, SUMMER 1998, PP. 243–244

FEMINIST REVIEW NO 59, SUMMER 1998

are organized under several topics: theoretical perspectives; text and testimony as sources and methods for 'engendering' history; women and women's work under slavery; migration, settlement, education in the post-slavery period; women, protest and political movement. A strong theme which threads its way through this volume is women's survival strategies and women's resistance.

The book provides a synthesis and re-evaluation of the body of work that already exists in the area. Though a pan-Caribbean approach is taken, most articles are on the English-speaking Caribbean. Above all the book contributes to development of an intellectual tradition which moves women towards the centre of historical discourse on the Caribbean.

Gender: A Caribbean Multi-Disciplinary Perspective

Elsa Leo-Rhynie, Barbara Bailey and Christine Barrow (eds)
Ian Randle: Kingston, in association with the Centre for Gender and Development
Studies of the University of the West Indies and the Commonwealth of Learning 1997
ISBN 085255-250-5

This book brings together a wide range of research findings, theoretical perspectives and policy prescriptions provided by over twenty contributors, highlighting the key issues in the study of gender in the Caribbean region.

The book opens with a section which provides a theoretical and methodological framework to guide the reader through the five sections which follow. The second section on engendering justice examines the legal position of women in the home and in the workplace. Next is a section on gender in education, followed by several chapters which explore the relationship between gender and theory and practice of the arts and humanities. Section Five looks at gender issues in health and the reform required in health-care for women, and seeks to identify a health research agenda. In the final section the contributors provide an historical overview of women's role in Caribbean agriculture and provide prescriptions for policy change, research and strategic alliances.

Hilary Nicholson

FEMINIST REVIEW NO 58, SPRING 1998, PP. 246-254

1 Women and Revolution in South Yemen, **Molyneux**. Feminist Art Practice, **Davis & Goodal**. Equal Pay and Sex Discrimination, **Snell**. Female Sexuality in Fascist Ideology, **Macciocchi**. Charlotte Brontë's *Shirley*, **Taylor**. Christine Delphy, **Barrett & McIntosh**. OUT OF PRINT.

2 Summer Reading, **O'Rourke**. Disaggregation, **Campaign for Legal & Financial Independence** and **Rights of Women**. The Hayward Annual 1978, **Pollock**. Women and the Cuban Revolution, **Murray**. Matriarchy Study Group Papers, **Lee**. Nurseries in the Second World War, **Riley**.

3 English as a Second Language, **Naish**. Women as a Reserve Army of Labour, **Bruegel**. Chantal Akerman's films, **Martin**. Femininity in the 1950s, **Birmingham Feminist History Group**. On Patriarchy, **Beechey**. Board School Reading Books, **Davin**.

4 Protective Legislation, **Coyle**. Legislation in Israel, **Yuval-Davis**. On 'Beyond the Fragments', **Wilson**. Queen Elizabeth I, **Heisch**. Abortion Politics: **a dossier**. Materialist Feminism, **Delphy**.

5 Feminist Sexual Politics, **Campbell**. Iranian Women, **Tabari**. Women and Power, **Stacey & Price**. Women's Novels, **Coward**. Abortion, **Himmelweit**. Gender and Education, **Nava**. Sybilla Aleramo, **Caesar**. On 'Beyond the Fragments', **Margolis**.

6 'The Tidy House', **Steedman**. Writings on Housework, **Kaluzynska**. The Family Wage, **Land**. Sex and Skill, **Phillips & Taylor**. Fresh Horizons, **Lovell**. Cartoons, **Hay**.

7 Protective Legislation, **Humphries**. Feminists Must Face the Future, **Coultas**. Abortion in Italy, **Caldwell**. Women's Trade Union Conferences, **Breitenbach**. Women's Employment in the Third World, **Elson & Pearson**.

8 Socialist Societies Old and New, **Molyneux**. Feminism and the Italian Trade Unions, **Froggett & Torchi**. Feminist Approach to Housing in Britain, **Austerberry & Watson**. Psychoanalysis, **Wilson**. Women in the Soviet Union, **Buckley**. The Struggle within the Struggle, **Kimble**.

FEMINIST REVIEW NO 59, SUMMER 1998

9 Position of Women in Family Law, **Brophy & Smart**. Slags or Drags, **Cowie & Lees**. The Ripper and Male Sexuality, **Hollway**. The Material of Male Power, **Cockburn**. Freud's *Dora*, **Moi**. Women in an Iranian Village, **Afshar**. New Office Technology and Women, **Morgall**.

10 Towards a Wages Strategy for Women, **Weir & McIntosh**. Irish Suffrage Movement, **Ward**. A Girls' Project and Some Responses to Lesbianism, **Nava**. The Case for Women's Studies, **Evans**. Equal Pay and Sex Discrimination, **Gregory**. Psychoanalysis and Personal Politics, **Sayers**.

11 Sexuality issue
Sexual Violence and Sexuality, **Coward**. Interview with Andrea Dworkin, **Wilson**. The Dyke, the Feminist and the Devil, **Clark**. Talking Sex, **English, Hollibaugh & Rubin**. Jealousy and Sexual Difference, **Moi**. Ideological Politics 1969–72, **O'Sullivan**. Womanslaughter in the Criminal Law, **Radford**. OUT OF PRINT.

12 ANC Women's Struggles, **Kimble & Unterhalter**. Women's Strike in Holland 1981, **de Bruijn & Henkes**. Politics of Feminist Research, **McRobbie**. Khomeini's Teachings on Women, **Afshar**. Women in the Labour Party 1906–1920, **Rowan**. Documents from the Indian Women's Movement, **Gothoskar & Patel**.

13 Feminist Perspectives on Sport, **Graydon**. Patriarchal Criticism and Henry James, **Kappeler**. The Barnard Conference on Sexuality, **Wilson**. Danger and Pleasure in Nineteenth Century Feminist Sexual Thought, **Gordon & Du Bois**. Anti-Porn: Soft Issue, Hard World, **Rich**. Feminist Identity and Poetic Tradition, **Montefiore**.

14 Femininity and its Discontents, **Rose**. Inside and Outside Marriage, **Gittins**. The Pro-family Left in the United States, **Epstein & Ellis**. Women's Language and Literature, **McKluskie**. The Inevitability of Theory, **Fildes**. The 150 Hours in Italy, **Caldwell**. Teaching Film, **Clayton**.

15 Women's Employment, **Beechey**. Women and Trade Unions, **Charles**. Lesbianism and Women's Studies, **Adamson**. Teaching Women's Studies at Secondary School, **Kirton**. Gender, Ethnic and Class Divisions, **Anthias & Yuval-Davis**. Women Studying or Studying Women, **Kelly & Pearson**. Girls, Jobs and Glamour, **Sherratt**. Contradictions in Teaching Women's Studies, **Phillips & Hurstfield**.

16 Romance Fiction, Female Sexuality and Class, **Light**. The White Brothel, **Kappeler**. Sadomasochism and Feminism, **France**. Trade Unions and Socialist Feminism, **Cockburn**. Women's Movement and the Labour Party, **Interview with Labour Party Feminists**. Feminism and 'The Family', **Caldwell**.

17 Many voices, one chant: black feminist perspectives

Challenging Imperial Feminism, **Amos & Parmar**. Black Women, the Economic Crisis and the British State, **Mama**. Asian Women in the Making of History, **Trivedi**. Black Lesbian Discussions, **Carmen, Gail, Shaila & Pratibha**. Poetry. Black women Organizing Autonomously: a collection.

18 Cultural politics

Writing with Women. A Metaphorical Journey, **Lomax**. Karen Alexander: Video Worker, **Nava**. Poetry, by **Riley, Whiteson** and **Davies**. Women's Films, **Montgomery**. 'Correct Distance' a photo-text, **Tabrizian**. Julia Kristeva on Femininity, **Jones**. Feminism and the Theatre, **Wandor**. Alexis Hunter, **Osborne**. Format Photographers, Dear Linda, **Kuhn**.

19

The Female Nude in the work of Suzanne Valadon, **Betterton**. Refuges for Battered Women, **Pahl**. Thin is the Feminist Issue, **Diamond**. New Portraits for Old, **Martin & Spence**.

20

Prisonhouses, **Steedman**. Ethnocentrism and Socialist Feminism, **Barrett & McIntosh**. What Do Women Want? **Rowbotham**. Women's Equality and the European Community, **Hoskyns**. Feminism and the Popular Novel of the 1890s, **Clarke**.

21

Going Private: The Implications of Privatization for Women's Work, **Coyle**. A Girl Needs to Get Street-wise: Magazines for the 1980s, **Winship**. Family Reform in Socialist States: The Hidden Agenda, **Molyneux**. Sexual Segregation in the Pottery Industry, **Sarsby**.

22

Interior Portraits: Women, Physiology and the Male Artist, **Pointon**. The Control of Women's Labour: The Case of Homeworking, **Allen & Wolkowitz**. Homeworking: Time for Change, **Cockpit Gallery & Londonwide Homeworking Group**. Feminism and Ideology: The Terms of Women's Stereotypes, **Seiter**. Feedback: Feminism and Racism, **Ramazanoglu, Kazi, Lees, Safia Mirza**.

23 Socialist-feminism: out of the blue

Feminism and Class Politics: A Round-Table Discussion, **Barrett, Campbell, Philips, Weir & Wilson**. Upsetting an Applecart: Difference, Desire and Lesbian Sadomasochism, **Ardill & O'Sullivan**. Armagh and Feminist Strategy, **Loughran**. Transforming Socialist-Feminism: The Challenge of Racism, **Bhavnani & Coulson**. Socialist-Feminists and Greenham, **Finch & Hackney Greenham Groups**. Socialist-Feminism and the Labour Party: Some Experiences from Leeds, **Perrigo**. Some Political Implications of Women's Involvement in the Miners' Strike 1984–85, **Rowbotham & McCrindle**. Sisterhood: Political Solidarity Between Women, **Hooks**. European Forum of Socialist-Feminists, **Lees & McIntosh**. Report from Nairobi, **Hendessi**.

24

Women Workers in New Industries in Britain, **Glucksmann**. The Relationship of Women to Pornography, **Bower**. The Sex Discrimination Act 1975, **Atkins**. The Star Persona of Katharine Hepburn, **Thumim**.

FEMINIST REVIEW NO 59, SUMMER 1998

25 Difference: A Special Third World Women Issue, **Minh-ha**. Melanie Klein, Psychoanalysis and Feminism, **Sayers**. Rethinking Feminist Attitudes Towards Mothering, **Gieve**. EEOC v. Sears, Roebuck and Company: A Personal Account, **Kessler-Harris**. Poems, **Wood**. Academic Feminism and the Process of De-radicalization, **Currie & Kazi**. A Lover's Distance: A Photoessay, **Boffin**.

26 Resisting Amnesia: Feminism, Painting and Post-Modernism, **Lee**. The Concept of Difference, **Barrett**. The Weary Sons of Freud, **Clément**. Short Story, **Cole**. Taking the Lid Off: Socialist Feminism in Oxford, **Collette**. For and Against the European Left: Socialist Feminists Get Organized, **Benn**. Women and the State: A Conference of Feminist Activists, **Weir**.

27 Women, feminism and the third term
Women and Income Maintenance, **Lister**. Women in the Public Sector, **Phillips**. Can Feminism Survive a Third Term?, **Loach**. Sex in Schools, **Wolpe**. Carers and the Careless, **Doyal**. Interview with Diane Abbott, **Segal**. The Problem With No Name: Re-reading Friedan, **Bowlby**. Second Thoughts on the Second Wave, **Rosenfelt & Stacey**. Nazi Feminists?, **Gordon**.

28 Family secrets: child sexual abuse
Introduction to an Issue: Family Secrets as Public Drama, **McIntosh**. Challenging the Orthodoxy: Towards a Feminist Theory and Practice, **MacLeod & Saraga**. The Politics of Child Sexual Abuse: Notes from American History, **Gordon**. What's in a Name?: Defining Child Sexual Abuse, **Kelly**. A Case, **Anon**. Defending Innocence: Ideologies of Childhood, **Kitzinger**. Feminism and the Seductiveness of the 'Real Event', **Scott**. Cleveland and the Press: Outrage and Anxiety in the Reporting of Child Sexual Abuse, **Nava**. Child Sexual Abuse and the Law, **Woodcraft**. Poem, **Betcher**. Brixton Black Women's Centre: Organizing on Child Sexual Abuse, **Bogle**. Bridging the Gap: Glasgow Women's Support Project, **Bell & Macleod**. Claiming Our Status as Experts: Community Organizing, **Norwich Consultants on Sexual Violence**. Islington Social Services: Developing a Policy on Child Sexual Abuse, **Boushel & Noakes**. Developing a Feminist School Policy on Child Sexual Abuse, **O'Hara**. 'Putting Ideas into their Heads': Advising the Young, **Mills**. Child Sexual Abuse Crisis Lines: Advice for Our British Readers.

29 Abortion: the international agenda
Whatever Happened to 'A Woman's Right to Choose'?, **Berer**. More than 'A Woman's Right to Choose'?, **Himmelweit**. Abortion in the Republic of Ireland, **Barry**. Across the Water, **Irish Women's Abortion Support Group**. Spanish Women and the Alton Bill, **Spanish Women's Abortion Support Group**. The Politics of Abortion in Australia: Freedom, Church and State, **Coleman**. Abortion in Hungary, **Szalai**. Women and Population Control in China: Issues of Sexuality, Power and Control, **Hillier**. The Politics of Abortion in Nicaragua: Revolutionary Pragmatism – or Feminism in the Realm of Necessity?, **Molyneux**. Who Will Sing for Theresa?, **Bernstein**. She's Gotta Have It: The Representation of Black Female Sexuality on Film, **Simmonds**. Poems, **Gallagher**. Dyketactics for Difficult Times: A Review of the 'Homosexuality, Which Homosexuality?' Conference, **Franklin & Stacey**.

30
Capital, gender and skill
Women Homeworkers in Rural Spain, **Lever**. Fact and Fiction: George Egerton and Nellie Shaw, **Butler**. Feminist Political Organization in Iceland: Some Reflections on the Experience of Kwenna Frambothid, **Dominelli & Jonsdottir**. Under Western Eyes: Feminist Scholarship and Colonial Discourses, **Talpade Mohanty**. Bedroom Horror: The Fatal Attraction of *Intercourse*, **Merck**. AIDS: Lessons from the Gay Community, **Patton**. Poems, **Agbabi**.

31
The past before us: 20 years of feminism
Slow Change or No Change?: Feminism, Socialism and the Problem of Men, **Segal**. There's No Place Like Home: On the Place of Identity in Feminist Politics, **Adams**. New Alliances: Socialist-Feminism in the Eighties, **Harriss**. Other Kinds of Dreams, **Parmar**. Complexity, Activism, Optimism: Interview with **Angela Y. Davis**. To Be or Not To Be: The Dilemmas of Mothering, **Rowbotham**. Seizing Time and Making New: Feminist Criticism, Politics and Contemporary Feminist Fiction, **Lauret**. Lessons from the Women's Movement in Europe, **Haug**. Women in Management, **Coyle**. Sex in the Summer of '88, **Ardill & O'Sullivan**. Younger Women and Feminism, **Hobsbawm & Macpherson**. Older Women and Feminism, **Stacey; Curtis; Summerskill**.

32
'Those Who Die for Life Cannot Be Called Dead': Women and Human Rights Protest in Latin America, **Schirmer**. Violence Against Black Women: Gender, Race and State Responses, **Mama**. Sex and Race in the Labour Market, **Breugel**. The 'Dark Continent': Africa as Female Body in Haggard's Adventure Fiction, **Stott**. Gender, Class and the Welfare State: The Case of Income Security in Australia, **Shaver**. Ethnic Feminism: Beyond the Pseudo-Pluralists, **Gorelick**.

33
Restructuring the Woman Question: *Perestroika* and Prostitution, **Waters**. Contemporary Indian Feminism, **Kumar**. 'A Bit On the Side'?: Gender Struggles in South Africa, **Beall, Hassim and Todes**. 'Young Bess': Historical Novels and Growing Up, **Light**. Madeline Pelletier (1874–1939): The Politics of Sexual Oppression, **Mitchell**.

34
Perverse politics: lesbian issues
Pat Parker: A tribute, **Brimstone**. International Lesbianism: Letter from São Paulo, **Rodrigues**; Israel, **Pittsburgh**, Italy, **Fiocchetto**. The De-eroticization of Women's Liberation: Social Purity Movements and the Revolutionary Feminism of Sheila Jeffreys, **Hunt**. Talking About It: Homophobia in the Black Community, **Gomez & Smith**. Lesbianism and the Labour Party, **Tobin**. Skirting the Issue: Lesbian Fashion for the 1990s, **Blackman & Perry**. Butch/Femme Obsessions, **Ardill & O'Sullivan**. Archives: The Will to Remember, **Nestle**; International Archives, **Read**. Audre Lorde: Vignettes and Mental Conversations, **Lewis**. Lesbian Tradition, **Field**. Mapping: Lesbians, AIDS and Sexuality: An interview with Cindy Patton, **O'Sullivan**. Significant Others: Lesbians and Psychoanalytic Theory, **Hamer**. The Pleasure Threshold: Looking at Lesbian Pornography on Film, **Smyth**. Cartoon, **Charlesworth**. Voyages of the Valkyries: Recent Lesbian Pornographic Writing, **Dunn**.

35 Campaign Against Pornography, **Norden**. The Mothers' Manifesto and Disputes over 'Mutterlichkeit', **Chamberlayne**. Multiple Mediations: Feminist Scholarship in the Age of Multi-National Reception, **Mani**. Cagney and Lacey Revisited, **Alcock & Robson**. Cutting a Dash: The Dress of Radclyffe Hall and Una Troubridge, **Rolley**. Deviant Dress, **Wilson**. The House that Jill Built: Lesbian Feminist Organizing in Toronto, 1976–1980, **Ross**. Women in Professional Engineering: the Interaction of Gendered Structures and Values, **Carter & Kirkup**. Identity Politics and the Hierarchy of Oppression, **Briskin**. Poetry: **Bufkin, Zumwalt**.

36 'The Trouble Is It's Ahistorical': The Problem of the Unconscious in Modern Feminist Theory, **Minsky**. Feminism and Pornography, **Ellis, O'Dair Tallmer**. Who Watches the Watchwomen? Feminists Against Censorship, **Rodgerson & Semple**. Pornography and Violence: What the 'Experts' Really Say, **Segal**. The Woman In My Life: Photography of Women, **Nava**. Splintered Sisterhood: Antiracism in a Young Women's Project, **Connolly**. Woman, Native, Other, **Parmar** interviews **Trinh T. Minh-ha**. Out But Not Down: Lesbians' Experience of Housing, **Edgerton**. Poems: **Evans Davies, Toth, Weinbaum**. Oxford Twenty Years On: Where Are We Now?, **Gamman & O'Neill**. The Embodiment of Ugliness and the Logic of Love: The Danish Redstockings Movement, **Walter**.

37 Theme issue: Women, religion and dissent
Black Women, Sexism and Racism: Black or Antiracist Feminism?, **Tang Nain**. Nursing Histories: Reviving Life in Abandoned Selves, **McMahon**. The Quest for National Identity: Women, Islam and the State in Bangladesh, **Kabeer**. Born Again Moon: Fundamentalism in Christianity and the Feminist Spirituality Movement, **McCrickard**. Washing our Linen: One Year of Women Against Fundamentalism, **Connolly**. **Siddiqui** on *Letter to Christendom*, **Bard** on *Generations of Memories*, **Patel** on *Women Living Under Muslim Laws Dossiers 1–6*, Poem, **Kay**. More Cagney and Lacey, **Gamman**.

38 The Modernist Style of Susan Sontag, **McRobbie**. Tantalizing Glimpses of Stolen Glances: Lesbians Take Photographs, **Fraser and Boffin**. Reflections on the Women's Movement in Trinidad, **Mohammed**. Fashion, Representation and Femininity, **Evans & Thornton**. The European Women's Lobby, **Hoskyns**. Hendessi on *Law of Desire: Temporary Marriage in Iran*, **Kaveney** on *Mercy*.

39 Shifting territories: feminism & Europe
Between Hope and Helplessness: Women in the GDR, **Dölling**. Where Have All the Women Gone? Women and the Women's Movement in East Central Europe, **Einhorn**. The End of Socialism in Europe – A New Challenge For Socialist Feminism? **Haug**. The Second 'No': Women in Hungary, **Kiss**. The Citizenship Debate: Women, the State and Ethnic Processes, **Yuval-Davis**. Fortress Europe and Migrant Women, **Morokvasíc**. Racial Equality and 1992, **Dummett**. Questioning *Perestroika*: A Socialist Feminist Interrogation, **Pearson**. Postmodernism and its Discontents, **Soper**. Feminists and Socialism: After the Cold War, **Kaldor**. Socialism Out of the Common Pots, **Mitter**. 1989 and All That, **Campbell**. In Listening

Mode, **Cockburn. Women in Action: Country by Country:** The Soviet Union; Yugoslavia; Czechoslovakia; Hungary; Poland. **Reports:** International Gay and Lesbian Association: Black Women and Europe 1992.

40 Fleurs du Mal or Second-Hand Roses?: Nathalie Barney, Romaine Brooks, and the 'Originality of the Avant-Garde', **Elliott & Wallace.** Poem, **Tyler-Bennett.** Feminism and Motherhood: An American 'Reading' **Snitow.** Qualitative Research, Appropriation of the 'Other' and Empowerment, **Opie.** Disabled Women and the Feminist Agenda, **Begum.** Postcard From the Edge: Thoughts on the 'Feminist Theory: An International Debate' Conference at Glasgow University, July 1991, **Radstone.** Review Essay, **Munt.**

41 Editorial. The Selling of HRT: Playing on the Fear Factor, **Worcester & Whatley.** The Cancer Drawings of Catherine Arthur, **Sebastyen.** Ten years of Women's Health 1982–92, **James.** AIDS Activism: Women and AIDS activism in Victoria, Australia, **Mitchell.** A Woman's Subject, **Friedli.** HIV and the Invisibility of Women: Is there a Need to Redefine AIDS?, **Scharf & Toole.** Lesbians Evolving Health Care: Cancer and AIDS, **Winnow.** Now is the Time for Feminist Criticism: A Review of *Asinimali!*, **Steinberg.** Ibu or the Beast?: Gender Interests in Two Indonesian Women's Organizations, **Wieringa.** Reports on Motherlands: Symposium on African, Carribean and Asian Women's Writing, **Smart.** The European Forum of Socialist Feminists, **Bruegel.** Review Essay, **Gamman.**

42 **Feminist fictions**
Editorial. Angela Carter's *The Bloody Chamber* and the Decolonization of Feminine Sexuality, **Makinen.** Feminist Writing: Working with Women's Experience, **Haug.** Three Aspects of Sex in Marge Piercy's *Fly Away Home*, **Hauser.** Are They Reading Us? Feminist Teenage Fiction, **Bard.** Sexuality in Lesbian Romance Fiction, **Hermes.** A Psychoanalytic Account for Lesbianism, **Castendyk.** Mary Wollstonecraft and the Problematic of Slavery, **Ferguson.** Reviews.

43 **Issues for feminism**
Family, Motherhood and Zulu Nationalism: The Politics of the Inkatha Women's Brigade, **Hassim.** Postcolonial Feminism and the Veil: Thinking the Difference, **Abu Odeh.** Feminism, the Menopause and Hormone Replacement Therapy, **Lewis.** Feminism and Disability, **Morris.** 'What is Pornography?': An Analysis of the Policy Statement of the Campaign Against Pornography and Censorship, **Smith.** Reviews.

44 **Nationalisms and national identities**
Women, Nationalism and Islam in Contemporary Political Discourse in Iran, **Yeganeh.** Feminism, Citizenship and National Identity, **Curthoys.** Remapping and Renaming: New Cartographies of Identity, Gender and Landscape in Ireland, **Nash.** Rap Poem: Easter 1991, **Medbh.** Family Feuds: Gender, Nationalism and the Family, **McClintock.** Women as Activists; Women as Symbols: A Study of the Indian Nationalist Movement, **Thapar.** Gender, Nationalisms and National Identities: Bellagio Symposium Report, **Hall.** Culture or Citizenship? Notes from the Gender and Colonialism Conference, Galway, Ireland, May 1992, **Connolly.** Reviews.

FEMINIST REVIEW NO 59, SUMMER 1998

45 Thinking through ethnicities

Audre Lorde: Reflections. Re-framing Europe: Engendered Racisms, Ethnicities and Nationalisms in Contemporary Western Europe, **Brah**. Towards a Multicultural Europe? 'Race' Nation and Identity in 1992 and Beyond, **Bhavnani**. Another View: Photo Essay, **Pollard**. Growing Up White: Feminism, Racism and the Social Geography of Childhood, **Frankenberg**. Poem, **Kay**. Looking Beyond the Violent Break-up of Yugoslavia, **Coulson**. Personal Reactions of a Bosnian Woman to the War in Bosnia, **Harper**. Serbian Nationalism: Nationalism of My Own People, **Korac**. Belgrade Feminists 1992: Separation, Guilt and Identity Crisis, **Mladjenovic** and **Litricin**. Report on a Council of Europe Minority Youth Committee Seminar on Sexism and Racism in Western Europe, **Walker**. Reviews.

46 Sexualities: challenge and change

Chips, Coke and Rock-'n-Roll: Children's Mediation of an Invitation to a First Dance Party, **Rossiter**. Power and Desire: The Embodiment of Female Sexuality, **Holland, Ramazanoglu, Sharpe, Thomson**. Two Poems, **Janzen**. A Girton Girl on the Throne: Queen Christina and Versions of Lesbianism 1906–1933. Changing Interpretations of the Sexuality of Queen Christina of Sweden, **Waters**. The Pervert's Progress: An Analysis of 'The Story of O' and The Beauty Trilogy, **Ziv**. Dis-Graceful Images: Della Grace and Lesbian Sadomasochism, **Lewis**. Reviews.

47

Virgin Territories and Motherlands: Colonial and Nationalist Representations of Africa, **Innes**. The Impact of the Islamic Movement in Egypt, **Shukrallah**. Mothering on the Lam: Politics, Gender Fantasies and Maternal Thinking in Women Associated with Armed, Clandestine Organizations in the US, **Zwerman**. Treading the Traces of Discarded History: Photo-Essay, **Marchant**. The Feminist Production of Knowledge: Is Deconstruction a Practice for Women?, **Nash**. 'Divided We Stand': Sex, Gender and Sexual Difference, **Moore**. Reviews.

48 Sex and the state

Editorial. Legislating Sexuality in the Post-Colonial State **Alexander**. State, Family and Personal Responsibility: The Changing Balance for Lone Mothers in the United Kingdom, **Millar**. Moral Rhetoric and Public Health Pragmatism: The Recent Politics of Sex Education, **Thomson**. Through the Parliamentary Looking Glass: 'Real' and 'Pretend' Families in Contemporary British Politics, **Reinhold**. In Search of Gender Justice: Sexual Assault and the Criminal Justice System, **Gregory and Lees**. God's Bullies: Attacks on Abortion, **Hadley**. Sex, Work, HIV and the State: an interview with Nel Druce, **Overs**. Reviews.

49 Feminist politics – Colonial/postcolonial worlds

Women on the March: Right-Wing Mobilization in Contemporary India, **Mazumdar**. Colonial Encounters in Late-Victorian England: Pandita Ramabai at Cheltenham and Wantage, **Burton**. Subversive Intent: A Social Theory of Gender, **Maharaj**. My Discourse/My Self: Therapy as Possibility (for women who eat compulsively), **Hopwood**. Poems, **Donohue**. Review Essays. Reviews.

50 The Irish issue: the British question

Editorial. Deconstructing Whiteness: Irish Women in Britain, **Hickman and Walter**. Poem, **Smyth**. States of Change: Reflections of Ireland in Several Uncertain Parts, **Smyth**. Silences: Irish Women and Abortion, **Fletcher**. Poem, **Higgins**. Irish Women Poets and the Iconic Feminine, **Mills**. Irish/Woman/Artwork: Selective Readings, **Robinson**. Self-Determination: The Republican Feminist Agenda, **Hackett**. Ourselves Alone? Clár na mBan Conference Report, **Connolly**. Conflicting Interests: The British and Irish Suffrage Movements, **Ward**. Women Disarmed: The Militarization of Politics in Ireland 1913–23, **Benton**. 'The Crying Game', **Edge**.

51 In Love with Inspector Morse

Beleagured but Determined: Irish Women Writers in Irish, **Harris**. In Love with Inspector Morse: Feminist Subculture and Quality Television, **Thomas**. Great Expectations: Rehabilitating the Recalcitrant War Poets, **Plain**. Creating a Space for Absent Voices: Disabled Women's Experience of Receiving Assistance with their Daily Living Activities, **Morris**. Imagining (the) Difference: Gender Ethnicity and Metaphors of Nation, **Molloy**. Poems, **Sharp**.

52 The world upside down: feminisms in the Antipodes

Feminism and Institutionalized Racism, **Wilson**. At the Back of the Class. At the Front of the Class, **Behrendt**. The Curse of the Smile, **Ang**. Mururoa, **Brownlee**. Of Mail-Order Brides and 'Boys' Own' Tales, **Robinson**. Warmth and Unity with all Women? **Murdolo**. The Republic is a Feminist Issue, **Irving**. Negotiating the Politics of Inclusion, **Johnson**. Gender, Metaphor and State, **Sawer**. Unravelling Identities, **Genovese**. Feminism and Sexual Abuse, **Guy**. Woman Ikat Raet Long Human Raet O No? **Jolly**.

53 Speaking out: researching and representing women

Who's Who and Where's Where: Constructing Feminist Literary Studies, **Eagleton**. Situated Voices, **Lewis**. Insider Perspectives or Stealing Words out of Women's Mouths: Interpretation in the Research Process, **Reay**. Revolutionary Spaces: Photographs of Working-Class Women by Esther Bubley 1940–43, **Ellis**. The Ambivalence of Identification: Locating Desire in *Rebecca*, **Harbord**. Poem, **Nicol**.

54 Contesting feminist orthodoxies

Queer Black Feminism, **Harris**. A straight Playing Field or Queering the Pitch? Centring Sexuality in Social Policy, **Carabine**. Island Racism: Gender, Place and White Power, **Ware**. Poem, **Cargan**. All Het up! Rescuing Heterosexuality on *The Oprah Winfrey Show*, **Epstein & Steinberg**.

55 Consuming cultures

Editorial. Troubled Teens: Managing Disorders of Transition and Consumption, **Griffin**. The Virtual Speculum in the New World Order, **Haraway**. Bridging the Gap: Feminism, Fashion and Consumption, **McRobbie**. Desperately Seeking, **Gregory**. Looking Good: The Lesbian Gaze and Fashion Imagery, **Lewis**, Gender, 'Race', Ethnicity in Art Practice in Post-Apartheid South Africa: Annie Coombes and Penny Siopis in Conversation, **Coombes**. After the Ivory Tower: Gender, Commodification and the 'Academic', **de Groot**.

FEMINIST REVIEW NO 59, SUMMER 1998

New from Princeton

Worlds of Women

The Making of an International Women's Movement

Leila J. Rupp

Worlds of Women is a groundbreaking exploration of the "first wave" of the international women's movement, from its late nineteenth-century origins through the Second World War. Making extensive use of archives in five countries, Leila Rupp examines the histories and accomplishments of three major transnational women's organizations to tell the story of women's struggle to construct a feminist international collective identity.

"Comprehensive, judicious, and compassionate . . . a milestone in comparative and cross-national women's history . . . I couldn't put *Worlds of Women* down!" —Karen Offen, Institute for Research on Women & Gender, Stanford University

Paper £13.95 ISBN 0-691-01675-5
Cloth £39.50 ISBN 0-691-01676-3

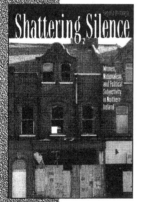

Shattering Silence

Women, Nationalism, and Political Subjectivity in Northern Ireland

Begoña Aretxaga

This book is the first feminist ethnography of the violence in Northern Ireland. Begoña Aretxaga argues that the political tactics of nationalist women were an integral part of the social dynamic of the conflict and had important implications for the broader organization of nationalist forms of resistance and gender relationships.

"This work captures a moment in the recorded history that has escaped [all] but a passing reference from other scholars. There is an integrity and passion in Aretxaga's analysis."—Joan Vincent, Barnard College

Paper £10.95 ISBN 0-691-03754-X
Cloth £33.50 ISBN 0-691-03755-8

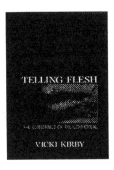

Routledge PROSPECTS

Women, Work and the Family in Europe

Edited by **Eileen Drew, Evelyn Mahon**, both at Trinity College, Dublin, Eire and **Ruth Emerek,** Aalborg University, Denmark

With a foreword by **Sylvia Walby**, Leeds University, UK

A new and timely analysis of major changes in society within the extended European Union. Addresses the consequences of altered family forms, the restructuring of the labour markets and the conflicting demands of family and working life.

June 1998: 234x156: 256pp
Hb: 0-415-15350-6: **£50.00**
Pb: 0-415-15351-4: **£14.99**

Part-Time Prospects

An International Comparison
Edited by **Jacqueline O'Reilly**, WZB, Berlin, Germany and **Colette Fagan**, University of Liverpool, UK

'This excellent book is essential reading for social scientists and policy makers seeking a deeper and broader understanding of part-time employment and the debates and issues surrounding it, in a global context.' - *Sue Lewis, Manchester Metropolitan University*

Presents for the first time a systematically comparative analysis of the common and divergent patterns in the use of part-time work in Europe, America and the Pacific Rim.

April 1998:234x156: 304pp
Hb: 0-415-15669-6: **£55.00**
Pb: 0-415-15670-X: **£17.99**

Citizenship and the Ethics of Care

Feminist Considerations on Justice, Morality and Politics

Selma Sevenhuijsen, University of Utrecht, The Netherlands

'Everyone interested in doing justice in a context of care should read this book. *Citizenship and the Ethics of Care* is engaging and stimulating. Most importantly, it demonstrates how care can be integrated into concepts and practices of social justice and democratic citizenship. Agency and judgement, morality and politics are cast afresh.' - *Dr Elisabeth Porter, University of Ulster*

This book marks a new and significant contribution to the debates surrounding the whole nature of care and citizenship. It proposes a new political concept of an ethics of care that will integrate themes from feminist ethics and gender theories.

March 1998: 234x156: 208pp
Hb: 0-415-17081-8: **£45.00**
Pb: 0-415-17082-6: **£14.99**

Routledge books are available from all good bookshops or order direct on
Tel: 01264 342 2939
*For more information or for a **Free** Sociology catalogue please contact:*
Geraldine Joyce,
11 New Fetter Lane, London EC4P 4EE
E-mail: info.sociology@routledge.co.uk
Internet:www.routledge.com

Feminist Review was founded in 1979. Since that time it has established itself as one of the UK's leading feminist journals.

• Why not subscribe?
Make sure of your copy

All subscriptions run in calendar years. The issues for 1998 are Nos. 58, 59 and 60.

• Subscription rates, 1998 (3 issues)

Individual Subscriptions

UK/EEC	£25
Overseas	£25
North America	£40

A number of reduced cost (£20 per year: UK only) subscriptions are available for readers experiencing financial hardship, e.g. unemployed, student, low-paid. If you'd like to be considered for a reduced subscription, please write to the Collective, c/o the Feminist Review office, 52 Featherstone Street, London EC1Y 8RT.

Institutional Subscriptions

UK	£96	**Single Issues**	£9.99
Overseas	£96		
North America	$150		

☐ Please send me one year's subscription to **Feminist Review**
☐ Please send me _____ copies of back issue no. _____

METHOD OF PAYMENT

☐ I enclose a cheque/international money order to the value of _____
    made payable to Routledge Journals
☐ Please charge my Access/Visa/American Express/Diners Club account

Account no. ☐☐☐☐☐☐☐☐☐☐☐☐☐☐☐☐☐☐☐

Expiry date _____ Signature _____

If the address below is different from the registered address of your credit card, please give your registered address separately.
PLEASE USE BLOCK CAPITALS
Name _____
Address _____
_____
_____
_____
_____ Postcode_____
☐ Please send me a Routledge Journals Catalogue
☐ Please send me a Routledge Gender and Women's Studies Catalogue

Please return this form with payment to:
Routledge Subscriptions Department, Cheriton House, North Way, Andover, Hants SP10 5BE